T0246041

THE TOUGHEST GUN CONTROL LAW IN THE NATION

The Toughest Gun Control Law in the Nation

The Unfulfilled Promise of New York's SAFE Act

James B. Jacobs and Zoe Fuhr

NEW YORK UNIVERSITY PRESS

New York

NEW YORK UNIVERSITY PRESS
New York
www.nyupress.org

References to Internet websites (URLs) were accurate at the time of writing. Neither the author nor New York University Press is responsible for URLs that may have expired or changed since the manuscript was prepared.

Library of Congress Cataloging-in-Publication Data
Names: Jacobs, James B., author. | Fuhr, Zoe.
Title: The toughest gun control law in the nation : the unfulfilled promise of New York's SAFE Act / James B. Jacobs and Zoe Fuhr.
Description: New York : New York University Press, 2019. |
Includes bibliographical references and index.
Identifiers: LCCN 2018055366 | ISBN 9781479835614 (cl : alk. paper)
Subjects: LCSH: New York (State). SAFE Act of 2013. | Assault weapons—
Law and legislation—New York (State)
Classification: LCC KFN5640.5.A352013 J33 2019 | DDC 344.74705/33—dc23
LC record available at https://lccn.loc.gov/2018055366

New York University Press books are printed on acid-free paper, and their binding materials are chosen for strength and durability. We strive to use environmentally responsible suppliers and materials to the greatest extent possible in publishing our books.

Manufactured in the United States of America

10 9 8 7 6 5 4 3 2 1

Also available as an ebook

From James B. Jacobs to Rowan, Anna, Aurora, and Alma

From Zoe Fuhr to Rosemary, Clive, Adam, and Louis

CONTENTS

FOREWORD

Mass Shootings and the Paradoxical Politics
of State-Level Gun Control

FRANKLIN E. ZIMRING

What does this detailed study of politics and legislation in New York
after Sandy Hook have to teach the citizens of the other forty-nine
states? Important lessons about the impact of symbolic agendas on
firearms regulation in the age of mass shootings. Sandy Hook was a
national tragedy and also an important case study in the symbolic
politics of firearms control in the United States. Firearms control laws
have both operational and symbolic significance in American life. They
influence whether, at what cost, and under what circumstances people
can own and use guns. They also make important symbolic statements
of significance to citizens about violence.

The Sandy Hook killings put intense pressure on citizens and on political institutions to respond with symbolic statements about both firearms and violence. The result at the national level of government was a
stalemate in the legislative branch and executive action that made much
less impact than the symbolic politics of the mass killings of small children probably required. At the state level of government, the symbolic
needs of Sandy Hook produced legal changes in just about every state in
the federal union.

But the kind of statement that these new state laws made differed significantly between red states and blue states. States with strong pro–gun
control sentiment in public opinion polls passed laws aiming to increase
restrictions on firearms ownership and use. States with strong anti–gun
control sentiment in public opinion polls passed legislation affirming
gun owners' privileges and rights.

The paradox, however, is that the very political sentiments that made gun laws in these states easy to pass often made them operationally redundant or marginal. The blue states that were anxious to pass new restrictions already had passed numerous state-level restrictions prior to Sandy Hook. Their strong pro-control orientations had produced substantial levels of regulation. The remaining options for future laws were either marginal or extreme. And the states with a symbolic need to reaffirm gun rights in the face of Sandy Hook already had pro-gun-rights orientations that had removed restrictions and affirmed individual rights to own and bear arms. The remaining options for these states were also either marginal or extreme, as when proposals were made to allow guns in colleges, churches, or taverns.

This book is a case study of the occupational hazards of symbolic legislation in states that already have extensive restrictions on firearms ownership and commerce. The City of New York probably has the most extensive restrictions on handgun ownership and commerce to be found in the United States. And the city's investment in handgun restrictions seems to have contributed to its spectacular success in the reduction of life-threatening violence (on this topic, see my book *The City That Became Safe*). The marginal impacts that additional layers of control might promise will probably be the most modest where the existing system of controls is the thickest. This means that the statewide effects of new controls will probably be lower in New York than in places with fewer gun controls in their current laws. Within New York State new controls will have a greater potential impact in those parts of the state with more guns and fewer controls.

But that potential encounters a second irony that this book documents in rich detail. The geographic areas and units of government where the new controls make the most demands on local officials and citizens are also the places where both citizens and law enforcement officials are the least supportive of firearms control and its attendant paperwork. Making programs such as recertification and mental health reporting requirements work well in upstate counties and cities is a challenge that demands careful administrative planning and diplomatic skills in the care and feeding of local enforcement.

The requirements for effective administration of new gun controls in upstate counties and cities do not fit well with the priorities of symbolic legislation. In New York, the political priority was passing the SAFE Act rather than administering it. *The Toughest Gun Control Law in the Nation* documents the fiscal and administrative consequences of the lack of commitment to implementation of the SAFE Act's many parts.

The manifold ambitions of the SAFE Act are a worst-case legislative structure for inattention to the details of how laws get implemented. There are no fewer than ten different regulatory areas of firearms controls. There was no explicit emphasis on which areas of control should be prioritized, coupled with a failure to provide human and financial resources to administer the regulatory changes. Doing everything under such circumstances is often a prescription for doing nothing.

New York is among the bluest of the fifty states, and its reaction to Sandy Hook was a classic case study in the paradoxical politics of gun control in state government. It is also a preview of coming attractions for gun politics and governance in the federal system.

Introduction

For US gun violence, the year 2012 was the best of times and the worst of times. Gun crime had declined dramatically over two decades, but rampage shootings, while difficult to define, appeared to have significantly increased. These massacres typically attracted intense national and international attention, none more so than the December 14, 2012, massacre at Sandy Hook Elementary School in Newtown, Connecticut. Adam Lanza, a reclusive twenty-year-old who had exhibited serious psychological problems since childhood, killed his mother with a rifle she kept in their shared home.[1] Then armed with her AR-15 assault weapon, a semiautomatic pistol, and more than two hundred rounds of ammunition (all purchased legally by his mother), he drove to Sandy Hook Elementary School, where he gunned down twenty first graders and six teachers and staff before committing suicide. Given the children's tender ages and the appalling number of fatalities (the most in any primary or secondary school shooting in US history), this massacre prompted outpourings of sympathy and explosions of national outrage. Since Democrats controlled the White House and the US Senate, the Sandy Hook massacre spurred the strongest push in a generation for stronger federal gun controls.

Within days of the massacre, President Obama vowed to use the full authority of his office to prevent future school shootings. He instructed an interagency taskforce, headed by Vice President Joe Biden, to develop "a multifaceted approach to preventing mass shootings like the one in Newtown, Conn. and the many other gun deaths that occur each year."[2] On January 20, 2013, after consulting scores of advocacy groups and lawmakers, the taskforce urged Congress to restore the federal assault weapons ban, impose a ten-round capacity limit on ammunition-feeding devices, pass a universal background-checking law on purchasers, and enhance punishments for straw purchasers. The administration mustered only forty Senate votes in favor of a

1

ban on assault weapons and large-capacity magazines. The Manchin-Toomey bill to establish universal background checking on gun purchasers garnered fifty-four votes, six short of the number needed to overcome a filibuster.[3] (The president immediately issued two dozen modest executive orders recommended by the taskforce.)[4]

The Sandy Hook massacre had a more significant legislative impact at the state level. In the year following the shootings, a majority of states passed gun laws, although more states weakened their gun controls than strengthened them.[5] Among pro-gun-control laws, New York State's Secure Ammunition and Firearms Enforcement Act (the SAFE Act) stands out as the first and most comprehensive.

New York had long been a strong gun control state and New York City even stronger; the state had significantly strengthened its gun control regime with a comprehensive package of initiatives in 2000. However, immediately after Sandy Hook, Governor Andrew Cuomo committed the state to enacting a new omnibus gun control law. Drafted in mere weeks by a team of the governor's close advisers, the thirty-nine-single-spaced-page bill contained at least ten separate gun control initiatives, including strengthened bans on assault weapons and large-capacity ammunition-loading devices; universal background checking for firearms purchasers; ammunition seller licensing and sales reporting; ammunition purchaser background checking; mandatory reporting by mental health professionals on patients believed to be mentally ill and dangerous; disarmament of persons reported as mentally ill and dangerous; disarmament of persons subject to domestic violence protection orders; quinquennial recertification of handgun licenses; and numerous new gun offenses and sentence enhancements. The SAFE Act breezed through the state legislature in under twenty-four hours, practically without debate. The governor signed it into law on January 13, 2013, a few days before President Obama's interagency taskforce was scheduled to deliver its recommendations. Governor Cuomo boasted that the SAFE Act was "the toughest gun control law in the nation" and a model for the rest of the country.

Politically, New York is a "true blue" state. Fiscally, it is a high tax and spend state. It has a long history of gun control and a relatively low level of gun ownership and gun violence. It is practically an ideal jurisdiction for gun control experimentation and, in turn, for assessing the potential and limitations of politically feasible maximal state-level gun control.

Therefore, when we launched our case study, we did not anticipate the depth and breadth of anti–SAFE Act opposition, especially from county officials and sheriffs outside the New York City metropolitan area. Nor did we anticipate the fiscal and technological obstacles that made it impossible for the state to implement several SAFE Act strategies.

This case study aims to move the gun control debate beyond the desirability of proposed laws. Historically, advocacy groups, politicians, and commentators have shown little, if any, interest in how existing federal and state gun control laws are implemented and enforced, nor concern for the implementability and enforceability of proposed new laws. Gun control proposals are discussed as if they are self-executing and self-enforcing. In fact, much gun control regulation is poorly implemented and enforced, sometimes not implemented or enforced at all. This should direct attention to the administrative, fiscal, and legal obstacles that blunt the effects of various on-the-books gun controls.

Consider that the Brady Campaign to Prevent Gun Violence and the Giffords Law Center to Prevent Gun Violence publish annual "scorecards" that grade and rank each state on gun control.[6] A state's score is based on its laws on the book —no matter how effectively the laws are implemented and enforced and no matter how easily they can be circumvented. For example, a state gets credit for banning large-capacity magazines manufactured after a specified date, although it is *practically impossible to tell* when a particular magazine was manufactured. This means there is no way to enforce the law against someone who possesses a large-capacity magazine, since a possessor can always claim to have thought that the magazine was manufactured before the cutoff date. Similarly, laws requiring guns to be safely stored at home are almost completely unenforceable; police agencies lack the willingness, resources, and authority to enter homes to check on storage.

We recognize that laws on hot-button social issues have huge symbolic importance for their partisans. They publicly acknowledge a problem and, more importantly, promise a solution. Passing laws affirms proponents' values and energizes their cause. If, subsequently, a law is shown not to have achieved its aim, because the problem at which it is directed persists, politicians can double down, proposing more laws. Passing laws is also part of the business model for advocacy groups, which raise money by announcing a legislative agenda and take credit for its realization. This is why gun control is a central issue in the "culture wars."

Politicians take credit for passing laws, not for overseeing their implementation and enforcement. It is easy to rally public opinion in favor of "taking back our streets," "preventing the slaughter of schoolchildren," and "defeating special interests." Calling for more and better implementation and enforcement triggers yawns. Indeed, as this book attests, it is very difficult to even determine the extent to which a law has been implemented and enforced. Finding out how state, county, and local agencies are carrying out their SAFE Act responsibilities required patience, persistence, and good luck over several years. Some agencies, the State Police in particular, seem to regard the execution of their gun control responsibilities as a secret.

When gun control laws are evaluated, it is almost always by trying to attribute changes in gun violence to changes in gun laws. These studies try to control for independent variables other than the law being tested. The point is that a law was enacted and firearm harms decreased at some point(s) after a law was passed, or at least did not increase as much as in a matched jurisdiction or jurisdictions without the law being tested. These studies do not require data on how, or even whether, the law in question was implemented and enforced.

Even when no reduction of firearm harms is found, many gun proponents insist on a gun control law's efficacy. A good example is banning assault weapons, which still ranks at the top of the gun control agenda despite the best study of the 1994 federal assault weapons ban having found no measurable effect on gun casualties (not surprisingly, since 90 percent of gun casualties are inflicted by handguns).

This book is *not* a critique of longitudinal and cross-sectional research methods and other before-and-after gun control law evaluations. This research is valuable, although it is difficult to sort through findings pointing in different directions. We aim to supplement that research corpus via a different empirical strategy: an in-depth case study of how, after five years, New York's omnibus SAFE Act has been, and has not been, implemented, enforced, and circumvented. We argue that if one or more SAFE Act provisions was not implemented (for example, ammunition background checking) or, if implemented, not enforced (for example, prohibition of large-capacity magazines), it is unlikely to have reduced gun fatalities and injuries. This is especially true of regulatory requirements that can easily be evaded.

Admittedly, "unlikely" does not mean impossible. A law could have real-world effects even if it is not implemented or enforced at all. Perhaps just the announcement of a new law causes some people to change their behavior because they fear apprehension and punishment, the law changes their opinion about the safety or morality of the conduct that the law seeks to change, or they are habitually law-abiding. If gun control laws produce effects without being implemented or enforced, we will have learned something important about how law works. If unimplemented and unenforced gun control laws do not "work," we will have learned something important about what a successful gun control regime requires.

This case study of the SAFE Act demonstrates that the efficacy of gun control laws is also undermined by the ease with which they can be circumvented. An earlier book by Jacobs, *Can Gun Control Work?*, critiqued the 1993 federal Handgun Violence Prevention Act ("Brady Law"), which required federally licensed firearms dealers (FFLs) to submit a prospective gun purchaser's name and other identifying information to the FBI for background checking. If FBI personnel find the prospective purchaser's name in a database of firearms-disqualified persons, they instruct the FFL not to complete the sale. Proponents claim that the law has prevented several million dangerous persons from obtaining a gun. Jacobs pointed out that persons whose gun purchases are blocked by the FBI, or persons deterred from attempting to purchase a gun from an FFL because they anticipate being rejected, can easily acquire a gun on the secondary market (or on the black market). They can respond to a "gun for sale" ad or place their own "gun wanted" ad in a newspaper or on a convenient bulletin board. These days, they can make contact with a private seller on a website devoted to putting prospective private sellers and purchasers in touch with one another. The Brady Law left private sales completely unregulated—no background checks, no forms to fill out, no reports to government authorities. Some pundits refer to this Brady Law lacunae as "the gun show loophole," but it is more like a black hole, because it exempts from background checking gun acquisition from anyone other than an FFL. (It is estimated that 40 percent of gun transfers involve non-FFLs.) That the Brady Law could be circumvented by simply placing an ad in the paper, posting a gun-wanted message on a bulletin board, or recruiting a "straw purchaser" casts serious doubt on its efficacy. This skeptical conclusion is supported by Duke economist Phil Cook, the nation's preeminent empirical gun control researcher who, using multiple regression analysis, found that the Brady Law had no effect on gun homicides.[7] Still, it took more than a quarter century for gun control proponents to begin campaigning for universal gun purchaser background checking. This book cautions that it is one thing to pass a universal-background-checking law and another thing to implement and enforce it. The SAFE Act's universal-background-checking law has only been partially implemented, has hardly been enforced, and is easily circumvented.

Although this book illuminates on-the-ground obstacles to implementing and enforcing a wish list of enacted gun controls in a strongly pro-gun-control state, it is not an "anti-gun-control" book. Rather, it is realistic and tough-minded. Even where there is strong political support for keeping guns out of the hands of dangerous persons, as there is in New York, implementing and enforcing a regulatory regime that can achieve that goal, even partially, is an enormous political and administrative challenge. This book is for readers who want to understand the challenges and complexities of controlling access to weapons in a nation where more than three hundred million guns *are already* in private hands, whose Constitution guarantees the right to keep and bear arms, and whose leading gun owners' advocacy organization is consistently rated the nation's most effective single-issue lobbyist. (Given ubiquitous and justified concern about conflicts of interest in the gun control debate, the reader should know that this book's authors have never been members of, nor have they ever received grants, financial support, or remuneration from, any gun owners' rights or gun control advocacy organization; nor are we gun owners.)

Effective gun control is often equated with passing "sensible" laws. While it would be absurd to argue that no gun control law can diminish gun crime, suicides, accidents, rampage shootings, or the number of casualties when rampage shootings occur, enacting laws is, at best, only a first step toward effective gun control. If gun control laws are to be more than political theater, there must be effective implementation and enforcement. Consequently, there is much that other states' policy makers, executive branch regulators, and law enforcement officials can learn from New York's difficulties in implementing and enforcing "the toughest gun controls in the nation." The SAFE Act's first five years highlight the critical importance of sustained political commitment to implementing and enforcing gun controls, coupled with sufficient resources, regulatory competence, state and local government cooperation, and law enforcement capacity.

1

The Politics of the SAFE Act

When people understand what the law is really about, and
it's not about taking their gun or a government intrusion
on the Second Amendment, they'll feel better about it. . . .
There's no novelty to the controversy about gun control.
—Governor Andrew Cuomo, March 1, 2013[1]

Albany's customary top-down and largely undemocratic legislative methods were inappropriate for such a complex bill.
—*New York Times* editorial, January 16, 2013[2]

After the December 14, 2012, Sandy Hook massacre, the media, politicians, pundits of all stripes, and, of course, gun control advocates
clamored for "something to be done" to prevent future mass shootings. Governor Andrew Cuomo said, "We as a society must unify and
once and for all crack down on the guns that have cost the lives of far
too many innocent Americans. Let this terrible tragedy finally be the
wake-up call for aggressive action and I pledge my full support in that
effort."[3] The governor's team drafted a bill during the Christmas and
New Year's period. While the governor was surely assuming that public
opinion was with him, this bill was entirely his project. No gun control
advocacy groups were needed to push the governor or the legislators.
Cuomo signed the bill on January 14, 2013, just eighteen hours after it
was introduced into the legislature.

Governor Andrew Cuomo

The son of three-time New York State Governor Mario Cuomo and a
seasoned politician in his own right, Andrew Cuomo was no stranger
to gun control politics. As President Bill Clinton's Secretary of the US
Department of Housing and Urban Development (HUD), in March

2000 he settled the federal government's lawsuit against Smith & Wesson (America's oldest and largest handgun manufacturer). Fifteen cities had brought suit against Smith & Wesson seeking monetary damages and injunctive relief, charging the manufacturer with failing to properly monitor its distribution chain. The Clinton administration joined the plaintiffs, and Cuomo negotiated a settlement that was praised by gun control groups and excoriated by other gun manufacturers and the National Rifle Association (NRA). Smith & Wesson agreed to install on new firearms internal locking mechanisms, hidden serial numbers, and child-safety devices and to allocate 2 percent of annual revenue to developing smart gun technology (also known as "personalized guns," referring to a firearm with safety features that allow it to fire only when activated by an authorized user). Cuomo called the settlement "a framework for a new enlightened gun policy for this nation."[4]

When Clinton left office, Cuomo returned to New York to run for governor. He failed but was elected New York State Attorney General in 2006. Then, in 2010, he won the gubernatorial election with more than 60 percent of the vote. Despite the April 2009 massacre at Binghamton, New York's American Civic Association Immigration Center, gun control was not a key campaign issue in that election; nor did Governor Cuomo identify gun control as a legislative priority in his 2011 or 2012 State of the State addresses.

The Sandy Hook massacre presented a significant political opportunity. According to Cuomo's biographer Michael Schnaverson, "[Cuomo's] true Next Big Thing came in the form of a horrible tragedy. . . . He wanted the toughest gun control bill in the land, and he wanted it now. . . . A bill to be proud of. And, perhaps, to run [for president] in 2016."[5] Rapid passage of a high-profile gun control package would attract nationwide attention, furthering Cuomo's presidential ambitions. Moreover, if President Obama was unable to obtain congressional approval for a federal gun control bill, Cuomo's decisiveness would be all the more salient. For Cuomo, it was essential that New York produce a law before January 16, the deadline for President Obama's interagency taskforce, headed by Vice President Joe Biden, to report its recommendations.

Cuomo's drafting team incorporated a number of bills on diverse gun control issues that Democratic state lawmakers had introduced over the previous decade. On December 21, just seven days after Sandy Hook, a coalition of New York State Legislators Against Illegal Guns (SLAG), composed of twenty senators and forty-three assemblymen, issued "Stronger Gun Laws: A Plan to Protect New Yorkers." The plan proposed universal background checking for all firearms purchasers, strengthening the bans on assault weapons and large-capacity magazines, requiring that gun licenses be renewed every five years, and regulating ammunition sales.

The governor's team worked "secretly" in order to prevent mobilization of opposition that might slow things down. The governor called the confidential drafting process necessary to prevent a surge in assault weapon sales if gun owners anticipated an imminent ban.[6] (Assault weapon sales skyrocketed, in any event, because of gun enthusiasts' concern about the passage of a post–Sandy Hook federal assault weapons ban.) Thus, the SAFE Act was drafted without input from gun owners and Second Amendment advocates, although the Senate's Republican leadership was regularly briefed and some of its objections were taken into account. (Republicans, though a minority in the Senate, exercised control of that chamber because a few independent Democrats and one unaffiliated senator caucused with them.)

The *New York Daily News* reported that Governor Cuomo threatened an "all out-assault" on the GOP if Republicans tried to block passage of the soon-to-be-introduced gun control bill.[7] No doubt Senate Majority Leader Dean Skelos was wary of being excoriated for blocking legislation aimed at preventing future school shootings. Moreover, he represented a suburban Long Island constituency for whom gun owners' rights are not a high priority, unlike in upstate Republican-dominated counties. The Senate's other Long Island Republican senators followed Skelos's lead.

Skelos publicly proposed several tough law-and-order measures: "increased mandatory prison time for possession and sale of illegal weapons; stiffer penalties for criminals who use guns to commit felonies; life in prison without parole for individuals who kill emergency responders; enhanced sentences for gun possession on school grounds and school buses; . . . stronger criminal penalties for selling or possessing guns in children's homes and the use of guns in gang violence."[8] The governor accepted most of these proposals in exchange for Skelos's support for the rest of the package.

On January 9, 2013, five days before submitting the SAFE Act bill to the legislature, Governor Cuomo set out his gun control agenda in his State of the State address:

> In the area of public safety—gun violence—has been on a rampage as we know firsthand and we know painfully. We must stop the madness, my friends. And in one word it is just enough. It has been enough. We need a gun policy in this state that is reasonable, that is balanced, that is measured. We respect hunters and sportsmen. This is not taking away people's guns. I own a gun. I own a Remington shotgun. I've hunted, I've shot. That's not what this is about. It is about ending the unnecessary risk of high-capacity assault rifles. That's what this is about. We have a seven point agenda.
>
> Number 1: Enact the toughest assault weapon ban in the nation period.
> Number 2: Close the private sale loophole by requiring federal background checks.
> Number 3: Ban high-capacity magazines.
> Number 4: Enact tougher penalties for illegal gun use, guns on school grounds and violent gangs.
> Number 5: Keep guns from people who are mentally ill.
> Number 6: Ban direct internet sales of ammunition in New York.
> Number 7: Create a State NICS check on all ammunition purchases.[9]

Perhaps because these gun control proposals were mentioned in a wide-ranging speech that touched on dozens of important issues, they did not attract much attention. Perhaps Second Amendment advocates assumed that there would be plenty of time to mount opposition after an actual bill was introduced. Maybe there simply was not enough time between January 9 and January 14 for Second Amendment advocacy groups to rally opposition. Whatever the reasons, there was no public debate over the SAFE Act bill.

Enacting the SAFE Act

At an early-evening press conference on January 14, 2013, Governor Cuomo announced that he was about to introduce, under "a message of necessity," major gun control legislation. The message of necessity procedure allows the legislature to pass a bill without adhering to the otherwise constitutionally required three-day period between a bill's introduction and a final vote. When invoking this procedure, the governor must certify facts that necessitate an immediate vote.[10] Interestingly, Governor Cuomo's message accompanying the SAFE Act bill specifically mentioned only the need to ban assault weapons and large-capacity magazines:

> If there is an issue that fits the definition of "necessity" in the State of New York today, I believe it's reducing gun violence. . . . Some weapons are so dangerous, and some ammunition devices so lethal, that New York State must act without delay to prohibit their continued sale and possession in the state in order to protect its children, first responders and citizens as soon as possible. This bill, if enacted, would do so by immediately banning the ownership, purchase and sale of assault weapons and large capacity ammunition feeding devices, and eliminate them from commerce in New York State. For this reason, in addition to enacting a comprehensive package of measures that further protects the public, immediate action by the Legislature is imperative. Because the bill has not been on your desks in final form for three calendar legislative days, the Leaders of your Honorable bodies have requested this message to permit immediate consideration of this bill.[11]

Governor Cuomo was probably hoping to attract the attention of a nationwide audience as well as energize his liberal base in New York. Contrary to his rhetoric, there was no "rampage of gun violence" in New York; instead, gun crime and violent crime generally had been steadily declining for two decades. Moreover, since 2000, New York State had an assault weapons ban in force, which prohibited semiautomatics with two or more military-like features, as well as a ban on large-capacity magazines (with more than ten-round capacity).

Assembly Speaker Sheldon Silver and Senate Majority Leader Dean Skelos scheduled an extraordinary six p.m. legislative session for the very evening the bill was announced (January 14). However, the thirty-nine-single-spaced-page SAFE Act bill was not distributed to the legislators until ten p.m.[12] In the Assembly, the bill's nominal sponsors were Assembly Speaker Silver, along with Brooklyn Assemblyman Joseph Lentol, who was responsible for explaining and defending the bill on the floor. Instead of Skelos, who presumably did not want to be closely associated with the bill, the Senate's formal sponsors were the independent Democrats Jeffrey D. Klein (Bronx/Westchester) and Malcolm A. Smith (Queens), who caucused with the Republicans. The bill was distributed to the lawmakers without a staff summary. Legislators would themselves have to read and absorb a lengthy and complex bill that amended ten New York codes: Penal Law, Criminal Procedure Law, Correction Law, Family Court Act, Domestic Relations Law, Executive Law, General Business Law, Judiciary Law, Mental Hygiene Law, and Surrogate's Court Procedure Act. (Digesting "raw" legislation such as this is a monumental effort even for lawyers who specialize in this area.)

The Senate Rules Committee, of which Skelos and six other Long Island Republicans were members, immediately recommended the bill's passage. That same night, the full Senate, without discussion, moved directly to a final roll-call vote. Party discipline being extremely strong in Albany, upstate Republican senators, who represented anti-gun-control constituencies, did not stage an anti-Skelos revolt. Skelos, for his part, having no wish for eighteen upstate Republican senators to commit political suicide, acquiesced to their voting no on the bill. All thirty-two Democrat senators plus eleven Republican senators (the Long Island senators plus a few others) voted in favor of it.

The Assembly, controlled by Democrats, adjourned after midnight and reconvened the next morning. Republican assemblymen and assemblywomen complained about not having had time to digest the bill. Some, who were gun owners, queried Assemblyman Lentol about a number of ambiguities including (1) How could magazines with greater than seven-round capacity be prohibited when standard magazines hold ten rounds? (2) What did the bill mean by "folding stock" and "second pistol grip" (features said to define a prohibited assault weapon)? (3) What kind of "permanent modification" renders a high-capacity magazine lawful? (4) Are shooting ranges required to initiate background checks for on-premises ammunition purchasers? (5) What is the scope of a mental health care professional's obligation to report to county officials patients who, on account of mental illness, might pose a risk if armed?[13]

Lentol, who played no role in drafting the bill, replied to the Republicans' questions by restating the bill's provisions. "Debate" was closed after just five hours. The bill passed 104 to 43 (with 3 excused); 96 (of 106) Democrats voted yes, along with 7 of 43 Republicans and 1 independent. Governor Cuomo signed the bill into law on the afternoon of January 15 in West Webster, a town outside Rochester where two first responders had been assassinated on December 24. At the signing ceremony, Cuomo predicted that "this new law will limit gun violence through common sense, reasonable reforms that will make New York a safer place to live. When society confronts serious issues, it is the function of government to do something, and *the NY SAFE Act will now give New York State the toughest, strongest protections against gun violence in the nation.*"[14] This was exactly the claim that Governor Pataki had made in respect of the omnibus gun control law he signed in 2000. Governor Cuomo did not explain why the Act was urgently needed, nor did he specify its goals, except to say that "it will limit gun violence" and make New Yorkers "safer." Curiously, he did not mention the Sandy Hook school massacre or mass shootings in general. Perhaps by "gun violence" he was referring to gun crime, although such crime in New York was practically at a historic low. He did not mention gun suicides or gun accidents at all, although several SAFE Act provisions seemed aimed at those categories of firearms harm.

Praise for the SAFE Act

The SAFE Act received immediate praise from many quarters. Leah Barrett, executive director of New Yorkers Against Gun Violence, said, "The Act really meets the test of good gun policy. It keeps guns out of the wrong hands, and I think it does that quite effectively."[15] The *New York Times* editorial board (on January 17) opined, "State gun laws matter. . . . That's why it's good to see several states step up to their responsibilities to prevent violence instead of following the southern and western states that appear to be encouraging it. New York was out front this week in passing a ban on assault weapons and large-capacity magazines, among other measures."[16] According to the *Journal News* (serving suburbs north of New York City), "New York on Tuesday became the first state since the Newtown slaughter to declare that enough was enough, passing a range of new gun and ammunition control laws, along with new mental health measures. Now it is Washington's turn."[17]

New York City Mayor Michael Bloomberg, himself a nationally prominent gun control activist, praised the governor "for demonstrating that it's possible to act quickly . . . to enact gun laws that will make our communities safer. The bi-partisan cooperation that produced these bills sets an example for Washington to follow, and it makes clear that the Senate's new majority coalition is capable of working with the Assembly and delivering results for New York State."[18] New York State Comptroller Thomas DiNapoli said, "New York took a bold step to curb gun violence and make sure that our communities are safer. The Governor and Legislature were right to take swift action and pass sensible legislation to expand the state's ban on assault weapons and pass tougher measures to ensure that guns are kept out of the wrong hands. As a state and a nation, we must find common sense ways to end the tragedies caused by gun violence. States across the nation should follow New York's lead."[19] Rochester Police Chief James Sheppard praised the legislation: "Law enforcement will now have the tools we need to crack down on gun violence, allowing us to track weapon ownership, regulate ammunition sales and keep our communities safer." He said that the new law made "New York a national model for sensible gun control."[20]

Criticism of the SAFE Act

The SAFE Act drew sharp criticism for its substance and for the process of its passage. The New York State Rifle and Pistol Association (NYS-RPA), the NRA's New York State affiliate, said that gun owners "should be ashamed and afraid."[21] Harold Schroeder, chairman of the Shooters Committee on Political Education (SCOPE), a Second Amendment advocacy organization with twelve New York chapters, argued that "to have Cuomo dictate to the honest gun owners of New York because of the few criminals is criminal in itself."[22] The NRA called the "draconian gun control bill" an "outrage" and accused Governor Cuomo and the legislature of a "secretive end-run around the legislative and democratic process." "While lawmakers could have taken a step toward strengthening mental health reporting and focusing on criminals, they opted for trampling the rights of law-abiding gun owners in New York, and they did it under a veil of secrecy in the dark of the night. The legislature caved to the political demands of a Governor and helped fuel his personal political aspirations."[23]

Upstate Republican Assemblyman Chris Friend denounced Albany's "rushed backroom, late night deals and lack of transparency." "In honor of all victims of violence, we must approach this problem with patience and good faith. Disregarding the 72 hour aging requirement for legislation and working in secret late at night does not help anyone."[24] Rensselaer County Republican Assemblyman Steve McLaughlin posted to his Assembly website, "Moscow would be proud of our State Legislature and Executive Chamber, but every New Yorker should be outraged."[25] The *New York Post* columnist Fred Dicker, a longtime Cuomo supporter, called the SAFE Act unusually "divisive" and challenged the governor to a radio debate. According to Dicker, "This bill takes people's rights away. Now, it may be a minority, but it is a substantial minority. And a great many people are upset about that, as you know."[26]

The day after the SAFE Act was signed, Senator Kathleen Marchione (R-Saratoga County), supported by Tom Libous (R-Binghamton) and George Maziarz (R-Niagara County), posted online a petition to repeal it.[27] By early April 2013, 127,000 individuals had signed it.[28] A similar petition by Senator William Larkin (R-Orange County), accompanied by a draft repeal bill, attracted nearly ten thousand signatures.[29] These expressions of opposition were meant to mobilize gun owners.

Popular Opposition Mobilizes

Governor Cuomo did not anticipate much opposition to the SAFE Act. After all, New York has been a strong gun control state since the early twentieth century. It is one of the nation's bluest states. It gave President Obama his fifth-largest margin in 2008 and 2012. In 2016, its voters overwhelmingly preferred Hilary Clinton to Donald Trump, 59 percent to 36.52 percent. However, as will be discussed in chapter 2, despite being solidly Democratic, New York State contains a significant minority of gun owners and a surprisingly robust gun culture.

At the end of February, the Gun NY2A Grassroots Coalition of gun rights groups that was formed in opposition to the SAFE Act, sent busloads of gun owners and Second Amendment supporters from all over the state to an anti–SAFE Act rally at the state capitol building. The event drew more than five thousand demonstrators, making it one of Albany's largest rallies in thirty years. Several upstate Republican legislators and NRA president David Keene urged resistance to the SAFE Act. The crowd chanted, "We will not comply." "Repeal the SAFE Act" signs sprang up on home lawns in upstate counties.

With the SAFE Act's deadline (April 15, 2014) for assault weapon registration looming, NY2A sponsored events at which assault weapon owners symbolically burned registration forms.[30] NY2A cofounder Lisa Donovan told media that the coalition's "goal is to keep the registration numbers as low as possible."[31] (As we shall see in chapter 3, compliance with the assault weapon registration law was very low.)

County and Local Government Opposition

Opposition to the Act also came from county and local officials. In part, this reflected their constituents' unhappiness with the SAFE Act. However, it also reflected the officials' own grievance about not having been consulted about their roles in implementing and enforcing the Act. They criticized the Act as an unfunded mandate that would strain their resources and increase their workloads. Forty counties and 271 municipalities passed resolutions urging that the Act be repealed.[32] Dutchess County's March 2013 resolution is representative:

> The [SAFE Act] fails to offer any meaningful solution to the gun violence that it was intended to address and places increased burdens where they do not belong, upon law abiding citizens. . . . Therefore, be it RE-SOLVED, that the Dutchess County Legislature on behalf of all the people of Dutchess County strongly encourages members of the New York State Legislature to hold public hearings to address the impact of this new law and the issue of gun violence in a way that will produce meaningful results; and be it further RESOLVED, that the Dutchess County Legislature calls upon the New York State Legislature and Governor Andrew M. Cuomo to work with counties to repeal and revise the NY SAFE Act in order to address concerns expressed herein.[33]

Figure 1.1. New York State counties that passed resolutions opposing the SAFE Act. (New York SAFE Resolutions, www.nysaferesolutions.com)

On January 24, 2013, just ten days after the SAFE Act's enactment, the New York State Sheriffs' Association, via a public letter addressed to Governor Cuomo, expressed disapproval of several SAFE Act provisions, saying:[34]

1. The assault weapons ban is too broad;
2. There is no need to have shifted responsibility for reviewing school safety plans to state agencies when county sheriffs are well positioned to carry out this role with proper funding;
3. The limit on magazine capacity limits the ability of law-abiding citizens to buy firearms and will not reduce gun violence;
4. All records related to recertification of handgun permits and registration by current assault weapon owners should be maintained at the local, not the state, level; and pistol permit and registration information should be protected from Freedom of Information Law disclosure;
5. Use of the internet as a vehicle for ammunition sales needs clarification;
6. Current and retired police should be explicitly exempted from several provisions.

The Sheriffs' Association also criticized the way the SAFE Act was passed: "Unfortunately the process used in adoption of this Act did not permit the mature development of the arguments on either side of the debate, and thus many of the stakeholders in this important issue are left feeling ignored by their government. Even those thrilled with the passage of this legislation should be concerned about the process used to secure its passage, for the next time they may find themselves the victim of that same process."[35] In 2014 and again in 2015, Senators Kathleen Marchione and Patty Ritchie (both former county clerks) sponsored legislation prohibiting state agencies from using county seals on any SAFE Act communications without the express permission of the county.[36] The bill passed the Senate in 2015 but failed to get out of committee in the Assembly.

Opposition from Mental Health Clinicians

Complaining that the SAFE Act stigmatized persons suffering from mental illness, a number of organizations that advocate for the rights of the mentally ill or that represent those who treat mental illness opposed the mandatory obligation for mental health care professionals to report patients who might be dangerous and the practically automatic addition of the reported patients' names to a state government database. Additionally, county mental health officials objected to being saddled with responsibility for reviewing reports submitted under the mandatory reporting provision, calling it an "unfunded mandate of an unknown and potentially disastrous magnitude, for which localities are neither equipped nor funded to implement."[37]

The 2014 Gubernatorial Election

Anti–SAFE Act protests continued into 2014, a gubernatorial election year. In a radio interview in January 2014, Governor Cuomo denounced his SAFE Act critics:

> Is the Republican Party in this state a moderate party or is it an extreme conservative party? That's what they're trying to figure out. It's a mirror of what's going on in Washington. The gridlock in Washington is less about

Democrats and Republicans. It's more about extreme Republicans versus moderate Republicans. . . . You're seeing that play out in New York. . . . The Republican Party candidates are running against the SAFE Act—it was voted for by moderate Republicans who run the Senate! Their problem is not me and the Democrats; their problem is themselves. Who are they? Are they these extreme conservatives who are right-to-life, pro-assault-weapon, anti-gay? Is that who they are? Because if that's who they are and they're the extreme conservatives, they have no place in the State of New York, because that's not who New Yorkers are.[38]

These remarks, which gun owners criticized for demonizing them, fueled further protest and civil disobedience.

On April 1, 2014, several thousand anti–SAFE Act protesters demonstrated outside the state capitol building. Cuomo's Republican opponent, Westchester County Executive Rob Astorino, berated Cuomo's sponsorship of the SAFE Act: "He took away your rights. You should take away his job." Donald Trump, his own political ambitions percolating, blasted Cuomo: "On top of everything, they give you the SAFE Act. . . . I'm a big Second Amendment person; I'm a strong believer in it. You have the constitutional right to keep and bear arms and you have that right and they are taking it away, slowly, but surely, they're taking it away. And they're not taking it away from the bad guys."[39] On the campaign trail, Astorino hammered away at the SAFE Act:

It was a disaster and it was done for all the wrong reasons. Here the governor had the opportunity to do something thoughtful that could make a difference in many lives and hit hard on the real issues. Instead what he choose to [sic] in contrast to what we did in Westchester, the governor in the middle of the night because he wanted to be first, he wanted to have a big political headline, rammed through with no transparency a law that was struck down partially as unconstitutional by a federal judge, which put every police officer in violation of that law, and really will do nothing to make us safer.[40]

The November 2014 election was much closer than the election four years earlier. Cuomo received 54 percent of the vote, down from his 63 percent in 2010. Astorino defeated Cuomo in forty-six of New York's sixty-two counties. Republicans won the Senate outright (32–31). Two senators and one assemblyman who had voted in favor of the SAFE Act lost their seats to anti–SAFE Act opponents. Nevertheless, a 2015 Sienna College poll found that, while 51 percent of upstate voters opposed the SAFE Act, all told, 62 percent of all voters supported it.[41] (In November 2018, riding a huge New York City anti-Trump vote in the midterm congressional election, Cuomo won his third gubernatorial term with 59 percent of the vote. He piled up huge majorities in New York City and its surrounding suburbs, while carrying just ten of fifty-seven counties outside New York City. Democrats won a majority in the Senate.)

In May 2015, Senate Majority Leader Dean Skelos resigned his position after being indicted for corruption.[42] (He was later convicted and sentenced to prison.) After a contentious battle, Senator John Flanagan (also a Long Island Republican) became the new Senate majority leader, despite having voted for the SAFE Act. Flanagan promised to seek changes in the Act: "because my colleagues have been so outspoken on the issue." The NYSRPA was not mollified. In a statement that, in retrospect, harbingered Trump's victories in the 2016 Republican presidential primaries, it excoriated the mainstream Republican Party: "What this says is that the Republican Party cares nothing about the hardworking God-fearing and 2nd Amendment loving residents of New York State. While paying lip service to the concerns of their core constituencies, they elect a leader who will continue the status quo. The Senators who cast their vote for Senator Flanagan must pay for this breach of trust in the next election."[43]

The SAFE Act remains highly contentious. Republican senators and assemblymen have repeatedly introduced legislation to repeal it. Of course, repeal is politically impossible as long as Democrats control the Assembly and the governorship. In 2016 and again in 2017, Republicans introduced into both chambers a bill that would repeal the SAFE Act for counties other than New York City. Like its predecessors, the bill died in the Assembly. In 2017, once the State Police finally set the wheels in motion to begin implementing the SAFE Act's recertification requirement for handgun permits, forty-four counties, with the support of the New York Association of County Clerks, passed resolutions purporting to prohibit state agencies from using county seals on communications with gun owners regarding SAFE Act compliance.[44] The county clerks did not want gun owners mistakenly concluding that they were in any way responsible for the SAFE Act's initiatives.[45]

Legal Attacks on the SAFE Act

SAFE Act opponents have been active in the courts as well as on the streets and in the legislature. The first tranche of litigation challenged the manner in which the SAFE Act had been passed. In late February 2013, Robert Schulz, a gun rights attorney and libertarian activist, filed a class-action lawsuit in New York Supreme Court (the lowest state-level court) seeking to enjoin enforcement of the SAFE Act on the ground that the message of necessity procedure used to pass it violated the state constitution.[46] He insisted that there had been no real necessity that warranted bypassing the state constitution's three-day waiting period between a bill's introduction and a final vote: "There was no need for speed. The legislature was not scheduled to adjourn for the year, we were not under attack and there was no natural or man-made disaster."[47]

The trial court dismissed Schulz's motion for a preliminary injunction, holding that the state constitution requires no more than the governor's assertion of facts alleging a necessity.[48] Governor Cuomo claimed that extraordinary legislative speed was necessary in this case in order to prevent a surge in assault weapon sales that would occur if the public had forewarning. The Appellate Division (New York State's first-level appeals court) affirmed. Federal and state courts dismissed several other pro se lawsuits.[49]

In March 2013, the NYSRPA, represented by Stephen Halbrook, one of the nation's foremost Second Amendment authorities, filed a federal lawsuit challenging the constitutionality of the Act's bans on assault weapons and large-capacity magazines. Although the District Court struck down the provision prohibiting individuals from loading a magazine with more than seven rounds of ammunition, it upheld the prohibition of magazines with greater than ten-round capacity and the prohibition of assault weapons. The US Second Circuit Court of Appeals affirmed.[50]

The Second Amendment Foundation, joined by the Shooters Committee for Political Education (SCOPE) and Long Island Firearms LLC, sought to enjoin the state from enforcing the restriction on magazines (and other ammunition-feeding devices) of more than seven rounds. The federal District Court resolved that issue in favor of the plaintiffs. (This case is discussed in detail in chapter 4.)

Post–SAFE Act Gun Control Proposals

Despite the fact that the SAFE Act was a wide-ranging omnibus gun control law, that followed a predecessor omnibus law enacted just twelve years before, it did not stem the tide of gun control bills in the state legislature. On January 17, 2013, three days after enactment of the SAFE Act, Senator Eric Adams introduced a bill to require manufacturers to mark firearms and ammunition with identifying codes. At the end of the month, he offered two more bills, one restricting sale of handgun component parts to handgun licensees and the other requiring mandatory safety training for handgun licensees. All told, Democratic legislators offered sixty-four bills to enhance gun controls during the 2013–2014 session. Things slowed down a bit in the 2015–2016 legislative session: forty-eight bills to strengthen gun controls were introduced. In the first six months of the 2017–2018 legislative session, twenty-five bills were introduced. Here is a sampling of those bills:

- April 2013: Requires state law to match federal law regarding imitation weapons; provides a private right of action for individual consumers injured due to the sale of a nonconforming imitation weapon.
- January 2014: Expands the term "disguised gun" to include any rifle, pistol, shotgun, or machine gun resembling a toy gun; prohibits the possession, manufacture, and design of toy guns.
- January 2014: Prohibits the sale of pistols or revolvers by any person, firm, or corporation in the retail business of selling guns that does not contain child-proofing features built into the design of the gun; establishes violations of this provision as a class A misdemeanor.
- January 2014: Prohibits individuals from carrying guns if their level of intoxication would make it unlawful to operate a motor vehicle under the law.
- January 2014: Requires owners of firearms to obtain liability insurance.
- January 2014: Limits an individual's firearm purchases to one per thirty days; establishes violating this provision as a class A misdemeanor.

- April 2014: Bans the sale, use, or possession of .50-caliber weapons.
- January 2016: Establishes procedures for issuance of gun-violence restraining orders and gun-seizure warrants.
- January 2016: Enhances illegal gun trafficking to a class D felony.
- January 2016: Prohibits firearm promotion and sale on public property.
- January 2016: Establishes a ten-day waiting period for the purchase of any firearm.

These are fewer than 8 percent of the gun control bills introduced into the New York State Senate or Assembly in the five years after the SAFE Act's enactment.

* * *

Once Governor Andrew Cuomo committed to passing a new omnibus gun law, the outcome was never in doubt. No compromises had to be made with Second Amendment advocacy groups and lobbyists. There were no legislative hearings. Republican senators from the Long Island suburbs, who could have forced changes or delayed the bill, were quiescent, perhaps fearing Governor Cuomo's retaliation, voter disapproval, or both. The Act was drafted, negotiated, passed, and signed thirty days after the Sandy Hook Elementary School massacre.

More interesting than the ability of a popular Democratic governor in a pro-gun-control state to pass more gun control legislation is what post-enactment events reveal about the strength of gun owners' opposition and Second Amendment advocacy. The governor's staff did not anticipate the breadth and intensity of post-enactment opposition to the SAFE Act. "Repeal the SAFE Act" became a rallying cry for gun owners. At the grass-roots level, gun owners expressed opposition more loudly than non–gun owners expressed support. They believe, not unreasonably, that the SAFE Act does not represent the end point of the gun control agenda, citing the stream of gun control bills introduced in every subsequent legislative session. This explains their noncompliance with many SAFE Act provisions.

The opposition of county officials and sheriffs who live and work where the law is unpopular posed obstacles to implementation and enforcement. As subsequent chapters explain, opposition to the SAFE Act caused the governor to back away from providing the resources and support, which effective implementation and enforcement require. Effective implementation and enforcement do not offer significant political rewards. From the governor's perspective, almost all the SAFE Act's political payoff was reaped at its passage. There is not much to be gained, and possibly much to be lost, by pressing unpopular implementation and enforcement measures on resistant gun owners.

2

Was the SAFE Act Necessary?

2013 began with New York passing a comprehensive upgrade of
its already strong gun laws in response to the tragic shooting at
Sandy Hook Elementary School. . . . The [SAFE Act] strengthened many aspects of New York's gun laws, including its ban
on assault weapons and large capacity ammunition magazines.
—Giffords Law Center to Prevent Gun Violence, January 7,
2014[1]

These gun control schemes have failed in the past and will
have no impact on public safety and crime. Sadly, the New
York Legislature gave no consideration to that reality.
—National Rifle Association, January 15, 2013[2]

Before examining each of the SAFE Act's specific initiatives, this chapter sets the stage by providing background on the status of New York's
gun problems, gun control laws, and "gun culture" in the period up
to mid-December 2012, when the Sandy Hook massacre occurred. We
first look at mass shootings, gun crimes, and firearm accidents and then
turn to the status of New York's gun control regime as of December 14,
2012.

New York's Gun Casualties

In 2012, New York ranked fourth lowest in the nation in combined
gun homicides, suicides, and accidents, 4.99 per 100,000 population.[3] If, after Sandy Hook, one was looking to identify a state that
needed to address gun casualties with immediate and dramatic actions,
New York would not have been at or near the top of the list. The
SAFE Act is a prime example of Frank Zimring's observation in the

foreword to this book that new gun controls are most likely in states that already have strong gun controls.

Mass Shootings

The FBI defines "mass murder" as the random fatal shooting of four or more victims (not including the shooter) without a "cooling off" period between the killings. This definition excludes, because no gun was used, bloodbaths such as the March 25, 1990, arson at the Happy Land Social Club in the Bronx (89 killed) and the September 11, 2001, terrorist airplane attack on Manhattan's World Trade Center (2,996 dead). It also excludes, because they are not random, "familicides" in which one family member uses a gun to kill other family members and "felony murders" such as the May 24, 2000, murder of five Wendy's employees in Queens, New York, in the course of a robbery. Consequently, according to the FBI definition, New York had experienced only two mass shootings in the twenty years prior to December 14, 2012.

On December 7, 1993, as a commuter train pulled into the Garden City (Nassau County, Long Island) Station, Colin Ferguson, who had a history of mental instability and violent episodes, randomly killed six and wounded nineteen fellow passengers before other passengers subdued him. He used a nine-millimeter pistol, which, though purchased legally in California, he was carrying illegally (that is, without a New York license). One of the fatalities was Dennis McCarthy. His son, Kevin, was badly injured in the attack. Carolyn McCarthy, Dennis's wife and Kevin's mother, successfully ran for Congress on a gun control platform and for almost two decades was one of the strongest gun control voices in the House of Representatives. Ferguson was convicted of murder and sentenced to life imprisonment.

On April 3, 2009, Jiverly Wong, a Vietnamese immigrant, used two pistols, for which he had a license to carry, to kill a teacher and twelve students and wound four others at the American Civic Association Immigration Center in Binghamton, where he had previously taken English classes. He then killed himself. (Shortly before embarking on his rampage, he sent a two-page delusional rant to a Syracuse television station, claiming that police were spying on him, sneaking into his home, and trying to crash into his car.)

Random mass shootings are, fortunately, *very rare events*. Determining what forms of firearms regulation would be most efficacious in preventing them, or at least in reducing the carnage that results from them, is no easy matter. The SAFE Act broadened and strengthened the assault weapons ban that New York had since 2000, but the perpetrators of the Long Island Railroad and the Binghamton Civic Center massacres used handguns.

Both Ferguson and Wong could be labeled mentally unwell (although that is almost a truism in cases involving motiveless attacks on strangers), but neither had been treated for mental illness. As an adolescent, Adam Lanza, the Sandy Hook shooter, had been diagnosed with mental health issues but, at the time of the attack, had not been in treatment for years. The SAFE Act includes a very aggressive provision that seeks to keep people identified as mentally ill and dangerous from acquiring or retaining guns. That provision would not have led to the identification of Ferguson, Wong, or Lanza but might identify other potential mass shooters. Of course, identifying someone as a risk is one thing; effectively keeping the person disarmed is another. This is the focus of chapter 6.

Gun Crime

The SAFE Act was rushed to passage at a time when, in New York State, violent crime generally and gun crime specifically had been declining for two decades. As table 2.1 shows, violent crime peaked in 1990, when there were 212,467 violent crimes and 2,608 homicides. That year, there were 806 gun murders. By 2012, violent crimes had fallen by more than

TABLE 2.1. Violent Crime (Crime Rate per 100,000 Population) in New York State, 1968–2012

Year	Population	Violent crime rate	Murder and nonnegligent manslaughter rate	Robbery rate	Aggravated assault rate
1968	18,113,000	544	6.5	330	193
1970	18,190,740	685	7.9	446	215
1972	18,366,000	754	11.0	470	250
1974	18,111,000	803	10.6	479	284

TABLE 2.1. (*cont.*)

Year	Population	Violent crime rate	Murder and nonnegligent manslaughter rate	Robbery rate	Aggravated assault rate
1976	18,084,000	868	10.9	529	302
1978	17,748,000	841	10.3	472	329
1980	17,506,690	1,029	12.7	641	345
1982	17,659,000	990	11.4	611	339
1984	17,735,000	914	10.1	507	366
1986	17,772,000	986	10.7	514	431
1988	17,898,000	1,097	12.5	544	510
1990	17,990,455	1,181	14.5	625	512
1992	18,119,000	1,122	13.2	597	483
1994	18,169,000	966	11.1	477	452
1996	18,185,000	727	7.4	340	357
1998	18,175,000	638	5.1	270	341
2000	18,976,457	554	5.0	214	317
2002	19,134,293	497	4.8	192	280
2004	19,280,727	440	4.6	174	243
2006	19,306,183	435	4.8	178	235
2008	19,490,297	398	4.3	163	216
2010	19,395,206	394	4.5	148	228
2012	19,576,125	406	3.5	146	242

Source: US Department of Justice, Federal Bureau of Investigation, *Uniform Crime Reporting Statistics*, www.ucrdatatool.gov (last visited December 18, 2018).

TABLE 2.2. New York State Firearm-Related Homicides, 2007–2012

	New York City		Non-New York City		New York State	
Year	Homicides	Firearm related	Homicides	Firearm related	Homicides	Firearm related
2007	496	328	311	176	807	504
2008	523	294	313	179	836	473
2009	471	302	313	181	784	483
2010	536	323	330	199	866	522
2011	515	315	255	133	770	448
2012	419	241	269	171	688	412

Source: New York State Division of Criminal Justice Services, *New York State Crime Report* (September 2015), www.criminaljustice.ny.gov.

half (79,479) and gun homicides by almost half (412) (see table 2.2). New York City had become the safest largest city in the United States.[4]

Gun crimes are overwhelmingly committed with handguns. By contrast, mass shootings are often committed with assault rifles (although Ferguson and Wong used handguns). Moreover, gun crime is not associated with mental illness. People suffering from mental illness are more likely to be victims rather than perpetrators of gun crime. The SAFE Act included provisions aimed at preventing both gun crime and mass shootings.

Gun Suicide

In justifying the need for the SAFE Act, Governor Cuomo did not mention suicide prevention, although the number of gun suicides has long been nearly as high or even higher than the number of gun homicides. Gun suicides in New York amount to about 30 percent of all New York suicides over the past thirty years (see table 2.3). Gun suicide was the only gun-fatality category that increased (albeit marginally) in New York from 2007 to 2012. Statewide, in 2012, there were 516 gun suicides compared to 412 gun homicides. No SAFE Act provision directly addressed suicide prevention, but the expanded firearm disqualification for persons reported mentally ill and dangerous has obvious relevance to suicide prevention as well to mass-shooting prevention.

TABLE 2.3. New York State Firearm-Related Suicides, 2007–2012

Year	Suicides	Firearm related	Number of firearm-related homicides (see table 2.2)
2007	1,396	441 (31.6%)	504
2008	1,409	429 (30.4%)	473
2009	1,417	422 (29.7%)	483
2010	1,547	459 (29.7%)	522
2011	1,658	505 (30.5%)	448
2012	1,708	516 (30.2%)	412

Source: Centers for Disease Control and Prevention, *Fatal Injury Reports: 1999–2015 National and Regional* (June 24, 2015), https://webappa.cdc.gov.

TABLE 2.4. New York State Firearm-Related Fatal Accidents, 2007–2012

Year	Fatal accidents	Firearm related (%)
2007	5,160	8 (0.2%)
2008	5,042	11 (0.2%)
2009	4,891	12 (0.2%)
2010	5,004	13 (0.3%)
2011	5,537	< 10
2012	5,786	< 10

Source: Centers for Disease Control and Prevention, *Fatal Injury Reports: 1999–2015 National and Regional* (June 24, 2015), https://webappa.cdc.gov.

Accidental Firearm Deaths

Governor Cuomo also did not mention accidental gun deaths as a justification for the SAFE Act. Indeed, accidental gun fatalities are a small part of the gun problem. The leading causes of accidental deaths in New York are traffic crashes, falls, and poisonings. There were fewer than ten accidental gun deaths in both 2011 and 2012 (see table 2.4). (By comparison, about twenty-eight New York children, from birth to age nineteen, die each year in drowning incidents.)

New York State's Pre–SAFE Act Gun Control Regime

The federal and state controls that were in effect on the eve of the Sandy Hook massacre already made New York one of the country's toughest gun control states. State laws prohibited carrying and possessing a handgun without a license, banned semiautomatic firearms with two or more specified military-like features, and banned magazines with greater than ten-round capacity. Firearms dealers were subject to state, as well as federal, licensing requirements, including the obligation to confirm purchasers' eligibility to possess firearms and the obligation to initiate purchaser background checks. In addition, state law required background checks for purchases at gun shows. Local jurisdictions were permitted to prescribe additional tougher gun regulations. In a number of ways, New York's City's gun regulations are more stringent than the state's.

Restrictive Handgun Licensing

New York's 1911 Sullivan Act established a system of restrictive handgun licensing that, with periodic amendments, remains the core of the state's gun control regime. One type of license is required to possess handguns (but not rifles or shotguns) at home or work, and another type is required to carry a concealed handgun in public. Except in New York City, no license is required to possess or carry a rifle or shotgun.

The two basic categories of handgun licenses are premises licenses and concealed carry licenses. (New York does not issue licenses to carry handguns openly.) A premises license restricts handgun possession to a particular residential or business location. State law provides that a handgun licensee must be at least twenty-one years old and a state resident. Minors under the age of sixteen are generally prohibited from possessing any type of firearm. The law disqualifies people from possessing a firearm if they have ever been convicted of a felony or other "serious offense," ever been involuntarily committed to a mental institution, or are currently subject to a domestic violence protection order. Eligibility does not guarantee a successful application. License applicants must submit fingerprints and four reference letters to their county licensing officer, who is a judge, except in New York City and a few other counties, where the police chief or commissioner holds that role. The licensee must demonstrate "good moral character," a standard that is not statutorily defined. The licensing officer can deny a license for "good cause" (also not defined). (In 2008, gun owners and gun rights groups unsuccessfully challenged this restrictive licensing scheme, immediately after the Supreme Court issued its seminal decision in *District of Columbia v. Heller*, recognizing an individual's Second Amendment right to keep and bear arms at home.)[5] In addition to these eligibility requirements that include minimal age and good character, an applicant for a concealed carry license must also show "proper cause" or "special need."[6] New York State courts have interpreted proper cause to mean "a special need for self-protection distinguishable from that of the general community or of persons engaged in the same profession."[7] Neither a generalized desire to carry a concealed weapon for self-protection nor living or working in a high-crime area constitutes proper cause.[8] The county licensing officer may restrict a concealed carry license to particular times and places, for example, to and from a shooting range or hunting venue.

A rejected handgun-license applicant can challenge the licensing officer's decision in a New York State Supreme Court (the trial-level court of general jurisdiction), but the challenger must convince the judge that the county licensing officer's decision was arbitrary and capricious.[9] In practice, reviewing judges rarely overturn a license denial.

A handgun license issued in one of the state's sixty-two counties is valid in all other counties, *except* in New York City (whose five "boroughs"—the Bronx, Brooklyn, Manhattan, Queens, and Staten Island—each constitute a county), which only recognizes licenses issued by the New York City Police Commissioner. County-based licensing administration inevitably means that licenses are more liberally issued in some counties than in others. While decentralized licensing recognizes that gun culture differs in urban and rural counties, it also means that persons who obtain handgun licenses in more-gun-friendly counties can keep or carry them in less-gun-friendly counties.

A handgun license is valid only for handguns listed (by model and serial number) on the license. Each time licensed gun owners want to purchase an additional handgun, they must get approval from the county licensing officer and have the new gun's model and serial number entered on their official license, which is held by the county clerk. The county clerk sends a copy of the license and any subsequent amendments to the State Police. There is no limit on the number of handguns that may be listed. In reality, there is no auditing of licensees to determine whether they possess unlisted handguns or whether they continue to possess the handguns listed on their license. (If a licensee is arrested for a crime, the police might discover that the license does not cover the gun he or she possesses.)

New York City's licensing application process is far stricter and more expensive than that of other counties. The city requires a license to possess a rifle or shotgun as well as a handgun. Both licenses must be renewed every three years. In comparison to the state requirements, license applicants must provide more information, such as whether they have undergone any treatment for psychological issues. Application vetting often takes several months. Historically, police commissioners have issued very few firearms permits; success usually requires a lawyer's assistance.

In 2011, out of a population of more than eight and a half million people, approximately thirty-three thousand New York City residents held premises-only firearms licenses, and only four thousand residents held a concealed carry license.[10] (No one knows how many unlicensed residents possess handguns and/or long guns.)

Licensing Firearms Dealers

"Firearm dealers," defined as persons engaged "in the business of purchasing, selling, keeping for sale, loaning, leasing, or in any manner disposing of handguns," must hold a state dealer's license as well as a federal firearms license (FFL). Applicants for a New York firearm dealer's license are subject to the same vetting process as applicants for a concealed handgun carry license. A dealer's license is valid for three years and only in the county where issued. The dealer is responsible for confirming a handgun purchaser's identity and that the purchaser holds a license authorizing acquisition of the gun to be purchased. Before consummating the sale, the dealer must also initiate an FBI (National Instant Check System) background check. As of October 2017, there were 3,949 FFLs in the state.[11]

New York's 2000 Gun Control Act

In 2000, a bipartisan omnibus gun control law greatly strengthened New York's gun control regime. At the signing ceremony, Republican Governor George Pataki hailed the new law as "the toughest in the nation." In words similar to Governor Cuomo's praise for the SAFE Act thirteen years later, Pataki said, "We hope this law serves as a national model. We hope other states will follow." The *New York Times* reported, "The law encompasses several measures, most of which have been tried in a few other states, though no state has as broad a combination of restrictions."[12]

BANS ON ASSAULT WEAPONS AND LARGE-CAPACITY MAGAZINES

The 2000 law, like the 1994 federal assault weapons ban, prohibited the manufacture, sale, and possession of assault weapons, defined as center-fire semiautomatic firearms (rifle, shotgun, or pistol) that accept a detachable magazine and have at least two of a list of military-like features. The law grandfathered assault weapons manufactured before September 15, 1994, the date that the federal assault weapons ban became effective; assault weapons manufactured before that date could be legally possessed. Grandfathering made the 2000 ban difficult to enforce, because police could not determine, and prosecutors could not prove, that a person *knew* that his or her assault weapon had been manufactured after 1994. (A gun's date of manufacture can be traced from its serial number, but that requires the manufacturer's assistance in matching the gun's serial number to a manufacture date; an individual gun owner could not count on that assistance, even if requested.)

The 2000 law also banned the sale and possession of "large capacity ammunition feeding devices" (most of which are detachable magazines) with capacity (or which could be readily restored or converted to accept) more than ten rounds of ammunition. Large-capacity magazines manufactured before 1994 were grandfathered. Since magazines are not stamped or engraved with a manufacture date or serial number, this provision was essentially unenforceable.

PURCHASER BACKGROUND CHECKS AT GUN SHOWS

Under federal law, a person who is "in the business of selling firearms" must obtain a federal firearms license from the Bureau of Alcohol, Tobacco, and Firearms. The 1993 federal Handgun Violence Prevention Act (Brady Law) required FFLs to initiate purchaser background checks to determine whether the purchaser is firearms-ineligible, but private sellers were under no such obligation. Often referred to as "the gun show loophole," it is more accurately a secondary-market loophole. Gun owners could legally advertise and sell or trade a small number of their personal guns as long as they were not engaged in the business of selling guns. Indeed, private sellers were not authorized to initiate FBI background checks on purchasers.

New York's omnibus 2000 gun control law partially addressed the secondary-market loophole by requiring anyone who transferred a handgun at a gun show to initiate a purchaser background check by processing the sale through an FFL. A gun show organizer had to assure that, at the show, there would be at least one FFL willing to initiate purchaser background checks on persons acquiring guns from private sellers. "Gun show" was defined as an

> event sponsored, whether for profit or not, by an individual, national, state or local organization, association or other entity devoted to the collection, competitive use, sporting use, or any other legal use of firearms, rifles or shotguns, or an event at which (a) twenty percent or more of the total number of exhibitors are firearm exhibitors or (b) ten or more firearm exhibitors are participating or (c) a total of twenty-five or more pistols or revolvers are offered for sale or transfer or (d) a total of fifty or more firearms, rifles or shotguns are offered for sale or transfer. The term gun show shall include any building, structure or facility where firearms, rifles or shotguns are offered for sale or transfer and any grounds used in connection with the event.[13]

In 2005, a federal District Court struck down this provision because its definition of "gun show" potentially applied to all gun club events, including political rallies.[14]

STRAW PURCHASERS

New York State's 2000 law criminalized (as a class A misdemeanor) purchasing a firearm for someone whom the purchaser knows is firearms-ineligible. Recruiting a straw purchaser is one of the principal ways that firearms-ineligible persons acquire guns (discussed in chapter 5).

BALLISTIC "FINGERPRINTING" DATABASE

The 2000 gun control law saw New York become the second state in the nation (following Maryland) to establish a digitized ballistics fingerprint database, the Combined Ballistic Identification System (CoBis). Every new handgun, before its first retail sale, had to be sent to the State Police for test firing. The State Police put images of the spent shell-case markings into a database. Proponents claimed that CoBis would enable police to match a shell recovered at a crime scene to the gun from which the shell had been fired, in turn leading to identification of the FFL who sold the gun and then to the gun's first retail purchaser. Unfortunately, despite three hundred thousand handguns having been tested over the next ten years, at a cost of $5 million a year, CoBis did not solve a single crime. The Cuomo administration terminated CoBis in April 2012. Maryland did the same in 2015.

MANDATORY TRIGGER LOCKS

The 2000 law required firearm dealers to include with every new handgun sale a trigger lock, defined as "an integrated design feature or an attachable accessory that is resistant to tampering and is effective in preventing the discharge of such rifle, shotgun or [other] firearm by a person who does not have access to the key combination or other mechanism used to disengage the device." The box containing the gun or the trigger lock must also include a warning label stating, "The use of a locking device or safety lock is only one aspect of responsible firearm storage. For increased safety firearms should be stored unloaded and locked in a location that is both separate from their ammunition and inaccessible to children and any other unauthorized person."[15] The law did not include a corresponding requirement that the device be affixed at the time of transfer or thereafter, although New York City, Albany, and a few other municipalities do impose that obligation on gun owners.

This provision aimed to prevent gun accidents, which were already rare. However, supplying a new gun purchaser with a trigger lock does not assure that the purchaser will use the device safely. The SAFE Act includes a provision that requires firearm owners who reside with firearms-ineligible individuals to lock the firearm in a safe, or use a trigger lock when the gun is not in their immediate possession. Unfortunately, the obligation is practically unenforceable and, in any case, defeats the ability to deploy the gun for self-defense at home, which, according to the Supreme Court, is the core purpose of the Second Amendment.

Domestic Violence Protection Orders

Before passage of the SAFE Act, New York law *required* family and criminal court judges to disarm the subject of a *permanent* domestic violence protection order. If the defendant (Criminal Court) or respondent (Family Court) held a handgun license, that license would be revoked or suspended, and the person would have to surrender all his or her guns to the police if the conduct that resulted in the order involved:

1. the infliction of [serious] physical injury;
2. the use or threatened use of a deadly weapon or dangerous instrument; or
3. behavior constituting any violent felony offense.

Suspension of the defendant's or respondent's firearm license was mandatory if the judge had "good cause to believe that":

1. the defendant had a prior conviction for any violent felony offense;
2. the defendant had previously been found to have willfully failed to obey an order of protection, and such willful failure involved:
   a. the infliction of [serious] physical injury;
   b. the use or threatened use of a deadly weapon or dangerous instrument; or
   c. behavior constituting any violent felony offense; or
3. the defendant had a prior conviction for stalking in the first through fourth degree.

New York law gave judges discretion to order that the defendant or respondent be disarmed if there is a "substantial risk" that the subject of a *temporary* protection order might use or threaten to use a firearm unlawfully against the order's beneficiary.

County and Municipal Gun Controls

The New York State Constitution gives local governments broad authority to adopt laws that promote the "protection, order, conduct, safety, health and well-being of persons or property."[16] Consequently, county and municipal gun control ordinances are only preempted if they conflict with a state law. (However, municipalities cannot create felonies; their ordinances are punishable as misdemeanors or administrative violations.) Courts have mostly upheld county ordinances that are more restrictive than state gun controls. For example, before the SAFE Act, state law did not require handgun licenses to be renewed. Nassau, Suffolk, and Westchester Counties had a five-year renewal requirement; New York City had a three-year renewal requirement. All these counties impose significant renewal fees.

New York City has a number of gun control ordinances that are more stringent than state law. A person who wants to possess a long gun must obtain a license from the New York City Police Department. A New York City firearms licensee may not purchase a handgun or a long gun more than once every ninety days. Upon purchase of a fifth handgun, the licensee must show evidence that the guns are stored in a safe. New York City also limits persons, including licensees, to possession of two hundred rounds of ammunition.

Other Criminal and Regulatory Gun Controls

On the eve of the SAFE Act, New York State's Penal Law constituted a gun control regime in its own right. It included many criminal laws covering illegal gun possession and criminal misuse of guns, such as criminal possession of a firearm (several degrees), criminal use of a firearm in the first degree, unlawful possession of a weapon on school grounds, and criminal sale of a firearm to a minor.

In sum, as of December 14, 2012, the date of the Sandy Hook Elementary School massacre, New York already had a strong gun control regime. The Brady Campaign to Prevent Gun Violence ranked New York the third-toughest gun control state in the nation. The Giffords Law Center to Prevent Gun Violence ranked New York sixth. In 2012, Jackie Hilly, then executive director of New Yorkers Against Gun Violence, praised the state's gun control laws as being "strong and effective."[17] In addition, counties and municipalities that wished to enact even stronger controls were free to do so. Gun control scholar, UCLA Law Professor Adam Winkler, said of New York City's gun control regime: "It's not a total gun ban, but it's awfully close."[18]

The Regulated Sector

While it is relatively easy to pass gun control legislation in New York, there are obstacles to implementing and enforcing these controls. Some are posed by lack of government resources and competence, others are posed by the noncompliance and resistance of gun owners and their advocates. The gun culture of many of the state's counties outside the New York City metropolitan area is not unlike that of western and southern states. Statewide, there are more than one million gun owners, four thousand licensed gun dealers, hundreds of shooting ranges, dozens of annual gun shows and shooting competitions, and several Second Amendment advocacy groups. In 2012, there were three hundred thousand retail gun sales in the state. Secondary-market and black-market firearms transfers probably added at least an additional one hundred thousand. Imposing unpopular regulations on these gun owners is a major and underappreciated challenge for gun controllers.

Gun Manufacture, Retail Sellers, and Gun Shows

New York is home to half a dozen major gun manufacturers. The biggest and best known are Remington Arms, American Tactical Imports (ATI), and Kahr Arms. These companies' thousands of employees and their families are likely to be supportive of gun owners' rights. In addition, there are approximately eleven hundred FFLs statewide.[19] FFLs range from behemoth vendors such as Walmart to small mom-and-pop gun shops. There is at least one gun show every week somewhere in New York State.[20]

Gun Owners

The number of New Yorkers who own guns or who have a gun in their household is hard to estimate. In 2010, the Westchester County's *Journal News* published a list of 1.3 million *handgun* licensees that the State Police disclosed in response to a Freedom of Information Law request. However, this figure exaggerates the number of *active* licensees because an unknown number of those on the list had died, moved out of the state, or no longer owned a gun. To try to approximate a reliable number, let us reduce the 1.3 million figure to 1 million. However, to estimate the total number of gun owners, we must take into account persons who possess long guns, for which no license is needed. Nationwide, there are approximately twice as many long guns as handguns in private hands, but many long-gun owners possess more than one. Let us conservatively assume an additional 1 million possessors. That brings us to 2 million. To this figure, we have to add an unknown number of *unlicensed handgun owners*. In the early 1990s, the US Office of Juvenile Justice and

Delinquency Prevention reported that "it has been estimated that there were approximately two million handguns in the hands of unlicensed owners in New York City in 1993," but it provided no source for this extraordinary estimate.[21] For our guestimate, let us put the number at 500,000 statewide, bringing us to a total of 2.5 million gun owners, out of a total (over-eighteen-years-old) population of 15 million. (In 2004, Jacob Bernstein in a *New York* magazine article, stated that 4.5 million New Yorkers own guns, but he also provided no source for that estimate.)[22] The Census Bureau estimates 2.6 persons per household in New York. Assuming each household includes only one gun owner, then 2.5 million gun owners would account for more than one-third of the state's 7.2 million households. Admittedly, this is a highly speculative calculation, but it suggests that the challenge of regulating firearms, even in this very gun-control-friendly state, is substantial.

Hunters and Target Shooters

Hunting is a significant recreational activity in New York State. According to the state's Department of Environmental Conservation, "Hunting is among the most popular forms of wildlife recreation in New York State. Nearly 700,000 New Yorkers and over 50,000 nonresidents hunt in the Empire State. New York offers many exciting opportunities to hunt a large variety of wildlife, including big game, small game, game birds and furbearers."[23] Much state-owned land, including wildlife management areas, state forests, forest preserve, and state parks hold hunting and trapping seasons. Nevertheless, over 90 percent of hunting occurs on private land, much of which is owned by hunting clubs. We can assume that practically every hunter owns at least one firearm, mostly long guns.

Competitive and recreational target shooting are also popular activities. The state has at least 230 shooting ranges; every county (including each of New York City's five boroughs) has one or more.[24] There is at least one shooting competition somewhere in the state every week. Noncompetitive recreational target shooting at a range is more common. In addition, many gun owners engage in casual shooting ("plinking") in backyards or other informal sites.

Gun Owners' Advocates

New York is home to two major organizations that lobby and litigate on behalf of gun owners: the New York State Rifle and Pistol Association (NYSRPA) and the Shooters Committee on Political Education (SCOPE). The NYSRPA, founded in 1871, is the oldest firearms advocacy organization in the United States and now an NRA affiliate. It is "dedicated to the preservation of Second Amendment rights, firearm safety, education and training, and the shooting sports."[25] Located in Albany, the state capital, it claims forty thousand members. Its political action committee, the Political Victory Fund, supports pro-gun-rights candidates for elective office.

SCOPE, founded in 1965 by activists in the western part of the state, characterizes itself as "an issues oriented organization" whose "function is to counter assaults on the right of firearms owners. This entails providing legislators and executives with timely and accurate information to support sound decisions."[26]

There are also numerous local gun rights organizations that share the NYSRPA's and SCOPE's goals, such as the Westchester County Firearms Owner Association, Gun Rights Across America—New York, New York Second Amendment Coalition, and Pink Pistols of the Twin Tiers (which provides firearms education and training to women and the LGBTQ community).

Gun owners' rights advocacy organizations raise money and recruit members by promising to protect gun owners' rights. They monitor, publicize, and lobby against gun control bills introduced into the legislature and gun control proposals offered by candidates and political incumbents. Lobbying goes far beyond trying to persuade legislators not to pass gun control laws. When lobbying is unsuccessful, these organizations bring court challenges to strike down or at least narrow the interpretation of gun control laws and regulations. Sometimes they encourage resistance and noncompliance.

* * *

New York led the nation's post-1990 decline in violent crime. Accidental firearms deaths were near an all-time low when the Sandy Hook massacre occurred. Gun suicides had risen slightly in the six years before the Sandy Hook massacre, but non-gun-related suicides, which constitute the majority of all state suicides, rose commensurately. None of those "gun problems" would have led to passage of a massive gun control law in 2013, especially since an omnibus gun control law had been enacted in 2000.

On the eve of the Sandy Hook massacre, New York had one of the most extensive state-level gun control regimes in the country. While more regulations can always be imagined, there were few glaring inadequacies in the state's gun control regime circa December 2012. Instead, as we saw in chapter 1, Sandy Hook presented the governor with a political opportunity, if he acted swiftly. There was no time for careful consideration of how each proposal would enhance the existing regime in order to further reduce gun crime or the risk of mass shootings. Indeed, many SAFE Act provisions had little, if anything, to do with preventing mass shootings.

3

Assault Weapons Ban and Registration

I believe that the vast majority of the American people agree
with us. The vast majority of gun owners agree with us.
That military-style assault weapons are—these are weapons
of war. They don't belong in the street, and the recent decision declaring the right of someone to own a weapon in
their home for self-protection, Justice [Antonin] Scalia ac-
knowledged that you can constitutionally ban certain types
of weapons. And, so, I haven't given up on this.
—Vice President Joe Biden, March 21, 2013[1]

While we don't get involved in campaigns to resist the law, I
will say this: Historic experience here and in Canada shows
that when you try to force gun owners into a registration and
licensing system, there's usually mass opposition and mass
noncompliance. . . . I think it's going to be very difficult for the
governor [Cuomo] to get mass compliance with this new law.
—David Keene, president of the National Rifle Association,
September 16, 2016[2]

New York's first assault weapons ban was part of the 2000 omnibus gun
control law. It defined a prohibited assault weapon as a semiautomatic
rifle, shotgun, or handgun that accommodates a detachable magazine
and has two or more specified military-style features: protruding pistol
grip, collapsible stock, bayonet mount, barrel shroud, spark suppressor.
The 2000 law classified sale or possession of an assault weapon manufactured after September 15, 1994 (the date that the federal assault weapons
ban became effective), as a class D felony, punishable by a maximum
seven-year prison term. Assault weapons manufactured before September 15, 1994, could be lawfully sold, purchased, and possessed. Between
2000 and December 14, 2012, New York did not experience any mass

shootings with an assault weapon, but many commentators blamed the Sandy Hook massacre on the availability of assault weapons.

Governor Cuomo's January 14, 2012, message, of necessity accompanying the SAFE Act, proclaimed that the state had an emergency need for a stronger assault weapons ban. According to the governor, "Some weapons are so dangerous, and some ammunition devices so lethal, that New York State must act without delay to prohibit their continued sale and possession in the state in order to protect its children, first responders and citizens as soon as possible. This bill, if enacted, would do so by immediately banning the ownership, purchase and sale of assault weapons and large capacity ammunition feeding devices, and eliminate them from commerce in New York State."[3]

Because New York already banned assault weapons, Cuomo's bill redefined "assault weapon" to cover guns with just one military-style feature. Henceforth, a prohibited assault weapon is defined as a center-fire semiautomatic rifle, shotgun, or pistol that accepts a detachable magazine and has *one or more* military-like features.[4] The listed features are the same as those in New York State's 2000 law, except for the addition of a "thumbhole stock" (referring to a hole in the butt or stock of a rifle or shotgun, into which the shooter can insert the thumb of his or her trigger hand.) The banned features are:

1. a folding or telescoping stock;
2. a pistol grip that protrudes conspicuously beneath the action of the weapon;
3. a thumbhole stock;
4. a second handgrip or a protruding grip that can be held by the nontrigger hand;
5. a bayonet mount;
6. a flash suppressor, muzzle break, muzzle compensator, or threaded barrel designed to accommodate a flash suppressor;
7. a grenade launcher.[5]

None of these "military-style" features, or even all of them together, makes a semiautomatic weapon more powerful, more lethal, or more dangerous than many semiautomatic firearms without these features. The military prefers these features because they make the automatic-fire

M-16 easier to use. Many consumers are enthusiastic about them for the same reason, insisting that a pistol grip and thumbhole stock make a rifle easier to hold and keep steady, that a folding stock makes the firearm easier and safer to carry and transport, and that a telescopic stock, like a folding stock,[6] makes a long gun easier to handle in a small space. Gun enthusiasts argue that a firearm that permits the user to adjust the length of the stock makes it more comfortable to use.[7] A flash suppressor—also called a flash guard, flash eliminator, flash hider, or flash cone—reduces the flash when the cartridge is fired, thereby reducing the risk that a shooter will be temporarily blinded in low-light conditions. Bayonet and grenade launcher mounts are purely decorative. Bayonets are collector's items and do not figure in mass murder, gun crime, gun suicide, or gun accidents.[8] Even if all these banned features were to disappear, semiautomatics would not be less dangerous, and the risk of mass casualties would not be diminished (see figure 3.1).

Figure 3.1. Photographic comparison of SAFE Act complicant and noncompliant assault weapons. (MMO Champion Forum [June 17, 2016], www.mmo-champion. com)

Grandfathering

The architects of any gun ban must decide whether to prohibit (by means of criminal sanction) current weapon owners or to grandfather their previously legal weapons. Logically, if assault weapons are a danger to the public, they should all be banned, whenever they were manufactured or acquired. In addition, it seems unfair to subject the owner of a 2013 assault weapon to *felony prosecution* for possessing the same gun that a neighbor purchased a year earlier and possesses legally on account of grandfathering. Nevertheless, to date, all federal and state assault weapons bans have grandfathered existing assault weapons or current assault weapon owners.[9] (Australia's 1996 ban on certain semi-automatics did not include grandfathering but did offer government compensation.)

The SAFE Act grandfathered assault weapon *owners* who registered their weapons with the State Police before April 15, 2014. A grandfathered owner may not transfer or bequeath an assault weapon to any New York resident. Should the owner want to dispose of an assault weapon, the options are to sell it to an in-state or out-of-state FFL, turn it over to the police, or destroy it. When the current generation of registered owners dies, there will be no more legally possessed assault weapons in the state. Assault weapon owners who do not register can be prosecuted for a felony.

One purpose of registration is to keep track of assault weapons so that, a generation from now, none will be lawfully possessed. A second purpose is to assure that every current assault weapon owner is assault-weapon-eligible. Since every registered assault weapon owner has to pass a background check as part of the registration process, a firearm-ineligible person's registration application will be rejected. A third reason is deterrence. A registered owner might hesitate to use a registered weapon to commit a crime because, if the weapon is found at the crime scene, it could be traced back to that person. Of course, few massacre perpetrators expect to escape; almost all commit suicide, are killed at the scene, or are apprehended immediately thereafter.

The massacre-prevention value of an assault weapons ban is limited because a would-be shooter who is unable to acquire an assault weapon could use a functionally equivalent non-military-style semiautomatic rifle, shotgun, or handgun. For example, in June 2018, Jarrod Ramos used a shotgun to kill four journalists and a staffer in Annapolis, Maryland. In April 2017, Seung Hui Cho used handguns to kill thirty-two students at Virginia Tech. In July 2018, Alek Minassian used a handgun to kill two and wound thirteen on a busy Toronto street. Indeed, manufacturers quickly began producing guns functionally identical to banned assault weapons but without the disqualifying military-style features. For example, some post–SAFE Act semiautomatics have an oblique pistol grip rather than the outlawed vertical pistol grip.

If, however, a would-be massacre perpetrator had his heart set on using a prohibited military-style assault weapon, he could assemble or make one from a commercial kit, aided by step-by-step instructions available in print or online.[10] Alternatively, he could look to the black market, where such weapons are plentiful because they are legal under federal law and in all but five states and the District of Columbia. He could travel to a nearby state where assault weapons are legally available and buy one from a private seller.

Assault weapons are very rarely used in "ordinary gun crime." The leading empirical evaluation of the federal assault weapons ban concluded that, at best, it made a negligible contribution to reducing gun crime and suicide because long guns of any kind were used in only 10 percent of gun crimes and gun suicides; assault weapons accounted for perhaps 1–2 percent of gun crimes and even fewer suicides.[11] Since New York State has experienced two public mass-murder events (defined as five or more fatalities in a public place) in the past twenty-five years (both killers used handguns), it is impossible to say whether the SAFE Act's one-military-feature assault weapons ban has saved lives.

Resistance, Noncompliance, and Circumventions

The SAFE Act gave current owners fifteen months from its passage (until April 15, 2014) to register their weapon(s) with the State Police. The registration procedure is not complicated.[12] The applicant downloads a one-page State Police registration form, fills in his or her name, date of birth, gender, race, residential address, Social Security number, and information about the assault weapon (manufacturer and model).[13] The State Police add the registrant's name to a database of assault weapon owners. Failure to register an assault weapon within one year of the registration deadline resulted in a warning and a thirty-day grace period during which the assault weapon owner was required to register or surrender the assault weapon. After April 15, 2014, possession of an unregistered assault weapon constitutes a class E felony.[14]

Some assault weapon owners (probably including the most dangerous) did not register, perhaps because they feared that they would not be approved. Others did not register because they feared that, sometime in the future, registration could facilitate assault weapon confiscation. It is hardly surprising that an assault weapon owner would worry that a future massacre, in New York or elsewhere, would spark a movement for complete assault weapon prohibition and confiscation. Indeed, the Sandy Hook massacre led to the expansion of the 2000 assault weapons ban to cover those one-military-feature semiautomatics that the 2000 law had declared lawful. The prominent *New York Times* columnist Thomas Friedman has already proposed "banning the manufacture and sale of *all semiautomatic* and other military-style guns, [coupled with a] government offer to buy back any rifle or pistol in circulation."[15]

After passage of the SAFE Act, assault weapon owners, at rallies around the state, urged noncompliance with registration. Some symbolically burned blank registration forms.[16] To demonstrate registration's failure and to encourage noncompliance, anti–SAFE Act activists deluged the State Police with Freedom of Information Law (FOIL) requests for data on the number of assault weapon registrants. The State Police refused to disclose that information until an Albany County Supreme Court judge ordered disclosure.[17]

The disclosed data revealed that, as of June 2015, 23,847 people (and businesses) had registered 45,000 assault weapons.[18] If, as estimates suggest, there are 750,000 to one million assault weapons in the state, registration compliance is 4–6 percent. (Assault weapon registration rates in California, Connecticut, and New Jersey are similarly low.)[19] Connecticut's assault weapon registration law, passed after the Sandy Hook massacre, also produced a very low compliance rate, albeit higher than New York's.[20]

It is no surprise that gun owners and Second Amendment advocacy organizations opposed the SAFE Act's assault weapons ban, but so did seventeen New York law enforcement agencies, mostly county sheriffs' departments. The New York Sheriffs' Association sharply criticized the ban, and a number of individual sheriffs vowed not to actively enforce it.[21] Schoharie County's sheriff said, "If you have an (assault) weapon, which under the SAFE Act is considered illegal, I don't look at it as being illegal just because someone said it was."[22] The Schuyler County sheriff posted the following statement: "I want to assure every resident of Schuyler County, that neither myself, nor any Deputy Sheriff from the Schuyler County Sheriff's Office will be coming to take your firearms from you. I believe in our rights under the Second Amendment, and the protections for our citizens under the Fourth Amendment."[23] Similarly, the Essex County sheriff announced, "I assure you that I have no intention of going door to door to pick up any weapons legally owned by any Essex County residents, nor does any other sheriff in New York State."[24] The Chemung County sheriff, Christopher Moss, said, "When I prioritize what I need to do as a sheriff, the SAFE Act comes in at the bottom of the list."[25] Such statements probably encouraged noncompliance. Leah Gunn Barrett, executive director of New Yorkers Against Gun Violence, the state's premier gun control advocacy organization, predicted that the SAFE Act's ban would not be vigorously enforced: "You're not going to have the State Police going door to door seeing if you have an AR-15 and if it's registered."[26]

Even if a police department wanted to enforce the SAFE Act's ban and registration requirement aggressively, it is not clear how that department would do it. Under New York's restrictive search-and-seizure law, it is probably not legal for an officer to ask an apparent assault weapon possessor to show proof of registration. In *People v. DeBour* (1979), the New York Court of Appeals held that, as a matter of state constitutional law, any approach by a police officer to a person constitutes a *seizure* that has to be justified by some level of probable cause. An officer must have a "credible reason" to approach a person for the purpose of asking an informational question. And the officer must have a "founded suspicion of criminality" to ask a "hostile question."[27] A court might consider an officer's request to see proof of assault weapon registration to be a hostile question. If so, the mere possibility that a person who possesses an assault weapon is an unregistered assault weapon possessor is unlikely to satisfy the founded suspicion threshold.

Prohibition on Bequeathing Assault Weapons

The SAFE Act prohibits registered assault weapon owners from bequeathing their firearm to an heir who resides in New York State. Upon the assault weapon owner's death, the estate's executor must, within fifteen days, sell the weapon to an out-of-state purchaser or surrender it to the police; possession beyond fifteen days is a class A misdemeanor, punishable by up to one year's imprisonment. The State Police or county sheriff to whom the assault weapon is surrendered can hold it for up to a year. During that period, the executor may sell the gun to a New York FFL or to an out-of-state purchaser. If there is no such transaction within a year, the law enforcement agency may destroy the gun.

Gun owners see the SAFE Act's prohibition on bequeathing assault weapons as violative of their Second Amendment and property rights. Alan Gottlieb, chairman of the Citizens Committee for the Right to Keep and Bear Arms, called the bequeathing prohibition "cold-hearted," "ghoulish," and "the kind of behavior one might expect in a police state."[28] This provision stoked fear that someday gun controllers will seek to confiscate all assault weapons or even all semiautomatics.

Some assault weapons owners sought to evade the bequeathing ban (at least for one generation) by registering their assault weapon in their child's name. The SAFE Act states that assault weapons have to be registered, but it does not say that the person who possesses the weapon must be the person to whom it is registered. Arguably, a father could have his child register his assault weapon, but maintain possession himself. However, the son or daughter could not, years later, follow that same strategy, because a registered owner cannot transfer the assault weapon to another New Yorker.

Legal Challenges

Shortly after the SAFE Act became law, the New York State Rifle and Pistol Association (NYSRPA) filed a constitutional challenge to the bans on assault weapons and large-capacity magazines. (The federal assault weapons ban withstood several constitutional challenges.) The NYSRPA argued that the Supreme Court's seminal decisions in *Heller* (2008) and *McDonald* (2010) guarantee the right to possess at home any type of firearm commonly used for self-defense.[29] Moreover, according to the NYSRPA, since possessing a firearm for self-defense in the home is a fundamental constitutional right, the state bears the burden of proving a compelling interest for prohibiting possession of popular firearm models such as the AR-15 and similar military-style semiautomatics.

Federal judge William Skretny, Chief Judge of the Western District of New York, adopted a three-step inquiry to determine whether the ban was constitutional: (1) whether assault weapons and large-capacity magazines prohibited by the SAFE Act are commonly used for lawful purposes, (2) whether New York's assault weapons ban substantially burdens Second Amendment rights, and (3) what the proper level of constitutional scrutiny to apply to the state's assault weapons ban is.[30] Chief Judge Skretny observed that "the legislature is far better equipped than the judiciary to make sensitive policy judgments (within constitutional limits) concerning the risks of possessing firearms and the manner of combatting those risks"[31] (to be sure, an ironic observation since New York's legislators had no time to read the SAFE Act before voting on it). Adopting an "intermediate scrutiny test," he held that for the ban to survive constitutional challenge, New York State had to demonstrate that its ban furthers an important government interest by means of a strategy substantially related to that interest.[32] He then reasoned that, unlike DC's handgun ban, which the Supreme Court struck down in *Heller*, the SAFE Act applies to a subset of firearms with characteristics that the legislature determined to be dangerous and unnecessary for self-defense. Given the huge number of other commercially available firearms models, he concluded that the Act "does not totally disarm New York's citizens and it does not meaningfully jeopardize their right to self-defense."[33] He explained that New Yorkers can still purchase, own, and sell "all manner of semiautomatic weapons" and that the "attributes of the banned weapons are 'present in easily-substituted unbanned, counterpart firearms.'"[34] (Gun owners agree that prohibited assault weapons are functionally identical to nonprohibited semiautomatics.) Chief Judge Skretny concluded that military-like features such as folding stocks and pistol grips may increase a firearm's utility for self-defense but that they also render the firearm "unusually dangerous, commonly associated with military combat situations and commonly found on weapons used in mass shootings."[35] He did not cite any evidence to support these empirical claims.[36]

Chief Judge Skretny found the SAFE Act's prohibition of "semi-automatic version[s] of fully automatic firearms" unconstitutionally vague because an ordinary person cannot know whether any single semi-automatic pistol is a "version" of an automatic one.[37] Less importantly, he struck down the SAFE Act's designation of a "muzzle break" as a military-like feature that qualifies a semiautomatic as an assault weapon because there is no such thing; the correct term is "muzzle brake." Even though the legislature could easily fix that error, it has not been amended.

A month after Chief Judge Skretny's decision in *NYPRSA v. Cuomo*, Chief Judge Gary Sharpe of the Northern District of New York upheld the SAFE Act against a pro se claim in *Kampfer v. Cuomo*.[38] Sharpe was even more emphatic than Skretny that the SAFE Act's assault weapons ban does not burden Second Amendment rights because a vast number of firearms remain available for self-defensive purposes.

Second Circuit Court of Appeals' Decision

The NYSRPA's appeal to the Second Circuit attracted considerable attention. A number of states and organizations weighed into the case at both the first instance and appellate stages. Twenty-two state attorneys general signed an amicus brief supporting the plaintiff's Second Amendment challenge.[39] Their brief argued that because the SAFE Act burdens the core right of self-defense, the Second Circuit should assess its constitutionality according to strict scrutiny review (which federal, state, and local statutes rarely survive).[40] Moreover, they insisted that semiautomatic "sporting rifles" are commonly used for self-defense, target shooting, and other lawful purposes; they are not "dangerous and unusual" weapons like machine guns and artillery. They sharply criticized Chief Judge Skretny's conclusion that a weapon that is easier to use is more dangerous: "The District Court concluded that features enabling a shooter to be more accurate are problematic. Under that logic, additional training for citizens designed to improve their accuracy could likewise be prohibited because such training would 'increase' the 'lethalness' of the weapons they used. Furthermore, a law-abiding citizen should be able to increase the accuracy of the weapon he or she uses for self-defense and other lawful purposes. Increased accuracy means more effective self-defense, less risk of danger for innocent bystanders, and, as a result, increased public safety."[41] The state attorneys general also argued that New York's assault weapons ban will not enhance public safety because criminals "who disregard the law will have firearms including the safety features banned by the Act, making it more difficult for law-abiding citizens to defend themselves."[42]

The New York State Sheriffs' Association emphasized how difficult it is for law enforcement officers to determine which semiautomatics qualify as prohibited assault weapons.[43] It warned that police, lacking firearms expertise, will rely on "subjective interpretations," inevitably resulting in unjustifiable stops, searches, and seizures: "Officers [will be] put in the unenviable position of guessing whether individuals exercising their Second Amendment rights should be arrested under the new laws. And while the laws are difficult for citizens to comprehend, they are worse for law enforcement. Officers are not only expected to enforce the laws against those seeking to exercise fundamental rights, they are likely to face suits for wrongful arrests and have prosecutions dismissed."[44] The NRA's amicus brief called the term "assault weapon" "a politically charged neologism that arbitrarily stigmatizes some semi-automatics that are functionally identical to many other semi-automatics."[45] The banned features, according to the NRA, increase accuracy, thereby enabling law-abiding citizens to defend themselves more effectively and to engage in other lawful activities such as target shooting and hunting.[46]

The National Shooting Sports Foundation (NSSF) argued that the SAFE Act's prohibition of a "semi-automatic version of an automatic rifle, shotgun or firearm" is unconstitutionally vague,[47] forcing gun owners to guess whether possessing a particular gun constitutes criminal conduct: "Exactly what constitutes a 'semi-automatic version' of an 'automatic firearm'? Does the same manufacturer have to make the same model in both automatic and semi-automatic versions for this provision to apply? If another manufacturer were to make an automatic version of a firearm, would all similar existing semi-automatic versions then become illegal 'assault weapons'? The only way NSSF's members can answer this question is by speculating, something the Due Process Clause mandates they not be forced to do. Simply put, what level of similarity rises to 'version'?"⁴⁸ The NSSF also challenged as unconstitutionally vague the SAFE Act's provision stating that a prohibited assault weapon can be brought into compliance with the law if military-like features are "permanently eliminated":

> For example, if a rifle is defined as an "assault weapon" pursuant to the New York SAFE Act simply because it has a "pistol grip that protrudes conspicuously beneath the action of the weapon" or a "thumbhole stock," would removing them and replacing them with an acceptable grip be sufficient to remove the rifle at issue from the definition of an "assault weapon"? What if the original pistol grip or thumbhole stock could simply be put back on the rifle, does that mean it would still be an "assault weapon"? If so, would any semi-automatic rifle with the ability to accept a detachable magazine potentially be considered an assault weapon if a prohibited pistol grip or thumbhole stock could be installed on it?⁴⁹

The Empire State Arms Collectors Association, which represents New York's licensed gun dealers, complained that the SAFE Act significantly diminished the value of firearm retailers' inventories.⁵⁰

Nine states and the District of Columbia filed an amicus brief supporting the SAFE Act's ban (and Connecticut's assault weapons ban, which the Second Circuit considered at the same time). That brief's principal argument was that since states are free to enact firearms regulations to promote public safety, the SAFE Act represents a policy choice that New York State is entitled to make:

> As with all other rights guaranteed by the Constitution, the Second Amendment limits, but "by no means eliminates," the ability of states to experiment with reasonable firearms regulations. . . . In light of the different challenges facing different states, and the daunting challenges that states and local law enforcement encounter in preparing for the next active shooter incident, it is critical that states have the opportunity to experiment with different policies to attempt to reduce the negative effects of firearms violence. Such policy experimentation, as long as it does

not transgress the limitations imposed by the constitutional right, must be allowed to proceed as the Supreme Court promised it would.[51]

New York City's amicus brief in support of the SAFE Act argued that the Second Amendment does not protect assault weapons because, in *Heller*, the Supreme Court made clear that the Constitution does not create "a right to keep and carry any weapon whatsoever in any manner whatsoever and for whatever purpose."[52] New York City asserted, without explanation or evidence, that the SAFE Act's assault weapons ban enhances the safety of innocent bystanders and law enforcement officers because assault weapons have the "capacity for rapid discharge of large numbers of rounds of ammunitions."[53] This is incorrect. Assault weapons do not discharge bullets more rapidly than many other semiautomatic nonassault weapons. If the speed at which rounds are discharged is what makes some firearms more dangerous than others, that should be the objective criterion for labeling guns legal or illegal.

In support of the SAFE Act's ban, the Brady Center to Prevent Gun Violence argued that the Second Amendment does not protect "secondary characteristics" unrelated to the weapon's functionality for self-defense purposes:[54]

The SAFE Act covers certain characteristics that do not relate to the utility of the weapons for self-defense (or even sporting) but to improving the utility of guns for mass slaughter. . . . Restricted and unrestricted weapons serve equally well for purposes of self-defense. . . . In fact, a semiautomatic weapon with, for example, a large detachable magazine may be more dangerous (and therefore less suited for self-defense) given that the ability to fire a burst of bullets in a short period of time increases the risk of accidental shootings of innocent bystanders. Given that the prohibited weapons are not of greater utility than permitted weapons for purposes of self-defense, or for any other identified "core" lawful purpose, the regulation cannot implicate the Second Amendment.[55]

This is a strange argument to make for an organization that is in favor of the assault weapons ban because it echoes the NYSRPA's argument that military-style features that distinguish a semiautomatic assault weapon from a semiautomatic nonassault weapon have no functional significance. In effect, the Brady Center argued that the military-style features that distinguish an assault weapon from a nonassault weapon affect the gun's offensive but not defensive capability. But it is hard to accept that assault weapons are particularly well suited for criminal activity when they are so rarely used to commit ordinary gun crimes. Although assault weapons are used in rampage shootings more frequently than their percentage of the entire gun stock would predict, they do not fire "bursts of bullets" and are no more useful to a rampage perpetrator than a comparable semiautomatic with no military-style features. The impetus to ban them is based on their intimidating appearance.

The Second Circuit Court of Appeals, like Chief Judge Skretny, assessed the SAFE Act's constitutionality according to an intermediate scrutiny test, reasoning that because assault weapons bans are "both broad and burdensome. . . . They impose a substantial burden on Second Amendment rights and therefore trigger the application of some form of heightened scrutiny." The court held that the SAFE Act's assault weapons ban survives intermediate scrutiny review because it is "substantially related to the achievement of an important governmental interest." The "fit between the challenged regulation [and the government interest] need only be substantial, not perfect."[56]

The Second Circuit's three-judge panel then found that "the dangers posed by some of the military-style features prohibited by the ban—such as grenade launchers and silencers—are manifest and incontrovertible."[57] "Manifest and incontrovertible" is rebutted by the fact that the large majority of states do not prohibit silencers; indeed, congressional Republicans are currently pushing the Hearing Protection Act, which would remove silencers from the list of heavily regulated "destructive devices."[58] As for "grenade launchers," some assault weapons have a mount to which a grenade launcher could theoretically be affixed. This is essentially ornamental because federal law define grenades as "destructive devices" that are, for all practical purposes, forbidden to civilians.

The SAFE Act, and assault weapons bans in other jurisdictions, prohibit firearms from being fitted with a flash suppressor, protruding grip, or barrel shroud. According to the Second Circuit panel, "the net effect of these military combat features is a capability for lethality, more wounds, more victims, far beyond that of other firearms in general, including other semiautomatic guns," but it offered neither evidence nor explanation for that conclusion.[59] These military-style features are functionally irrelevant. Some semiautomatic models with no military-style features are functionally identical to a semiautomatic model with one or more such features.

The Second Circuit reversed the portion of Chief Judge Skretny's opinion striking down, on vagueness grounds, the SAFE Act's prohibition of "semiautomatic versions of automatic rifles, shotguns and firearms." The court said that similar language in the 1994 federal assault weapons ban had not caused confusion.[60] Moreover, the Second Circuit held that the SAFE Act's provision authorizing creation of a website listing firearm models covered by the "semiautomatic version" language provides additional notice to gun owners. The court also rejected the plaintiffs' argument that giving state authorities unguided discretion to list a firearm as "a prohibited *version* of an automatic weapons" violates due process.

The plaintiffs decided against filing a certiorari petition to the US Supreme Court because, after Justice Antonin Scalia's death, the NYSRPA was unable to count on five votes for reversal. The president of the NYS-RPA said, "It's just the wrong time. . . . The Second Amendment is our client and that's what we have to protect."[61] An affirmance, even by an equally divided bench, would have established a worrisome precedent.[62]

* * *

The SAFE Act's assault weapons ban broadened the definition of prohibited assault weapon by covering center-fire semiautomatics with detachable magazines and one, rather than two, military-style features. Under this definition, many firearms that New York State's 2000 ban had treated as lawful became unlawful. Existing owners of those assault weapons can keep them provided that they are firearms-eligible and register them with the State Police. However, they can never sell, give, or bequeath them to another New York resident.

The SAFE Act's assault weapons ban drew more protest from gun owners and Second Amendment advocates than any other SAFE Act provision. They argued, persuasively, that the ban will not contribute to making New York safer because what distinguishes semiautomatic assault weapons from semiautomatic nonassault weapons is appearance, not function. They do not fire more quickly or fire larger-caliber bullets. Moreover, they are rarely used in crimes and offer no special advantage for mass shootings. Assault weapons are not more danger-ous than other semiautomatics. This is especially true of firearm models with one military-style feature (for example, a bayonet mount). Firearms should not be considered more dangerous simply on the basis that they are more comfortable and thus easier to use.

If weapons with one or more military-like features were more danger-ous, they should all be prohibited, rather than permitting existing own-ers to register and keep theirs. Registration undercuts the dangerousness argument and establishes vastly unequal treatment between new and existing assault weapon owners. New owners are subject to a maximum seven-year prison term, while existing owners who register are legal gun possessors.

That fewer than 10 percent of New York's assault weapon owners registered their weapons provides important support for our argument that the gun control debate has to move beyond just passing laws. It is too often assumed that once a law is passed, the problem animating the law is on its way to being solved. We should have learned from the war on drugs that this is often not the case. Many assault weapon own-ers strongly believe they have a right to own these weapons and that the government's labeling of them as especially dangerous is not based on empirical evidence. Sheriffs in upstate counties, where assault weap-ons are popular, have been reluctant, even unwilling, to enforce such a law. The consequence is that there has been practically no enforcement against nonregistrants. Where anti–SAFE Act sentiment is strong, the successful prosecution of unregistered, but otherwise law-abiding, as-sault weapon owners may be frustrated by jury nullification.[63]

New Yorkers who did not own an assault weapon at the time the SAFE Act's ban became effective can legally purchase a slightly modified and functionally identical firearm that is not covered by the SAFE Act definition. According to one news report, "New York lawmakers passed the SAFE Act last year, and announced with fanfare that it effectively banned the sale of 'assault weapons.' But AR-15s, the most popular type of guns often referred to as assault weapons, are sold in Empire State gun shops, freely and legally. The gun is being marketed by Stag Arms as a 'New York-compliant AR-15,' and features a slightly modified stock and no bells and whistles. The gun does not have a pistol grip, for instance— one of the features banned by the Act."[64] While the shooter has to hold the firearm differently, the modified gun is functionally equivalent to a SAFE Act–prohibited assault weapon.[65] Some state firearm retailers also sell kits to remove or modify outlawed military features.

A person who is determined to acquire a prohibited assault weapon and is willing to violate New York State law has several options. He or she could obtain one illegally: (1) from a New York State owner who is willing to make the transfer in violation of the law; (2) from a corrupt out-of-state dealer in a state where assault weapons are legal; (3) from a private owner in a state where assault weapons are legal, who is willing to overlook the purchaser's out-of-state status (assuming the New York purchaser does not have phony identification or the assistance of an in-state straw purchaser); (4) from a black-market dealer in New York or another state; (5) using a commercially available kit; or (5) by making one with 3D printer.

Given these realities, redefining prohibited assault weapons from two military-like features to one feature should not have been a priority, particularly given the intense opposition that redefinition provoked. A more careful consideration of what characteristics actually make some semiautomatics more dangerous than others is needed in order to make such bans effective.

4

The Ban on Large-Capacity Magazines

Bans on large capacity ammunition magazines are often adopted in concert with bans on assault weapons. However, large capacity ammunition magazine bans reduce the capacity, and thus the potential lethality, of any firearm that can accept a large capacity ammunition magazine, including a firearm that is not an assault weapon. Crime data also suggests that a ban on large capacity magazines would have a greater impact on gun crime than a ban on assault weapons alone.
—Giffords Law Center to Prevent Gun Violence[1]

Both handguns and long guns are used for personal defense. Such instances tend to be sudden and violent events that have to be dealt with using the weapon at hand. A high magazine capacity increases the defender's odds. Not all shots are hits nor do all hits stop an attacker. And, according to the Justice Department, one third of aggravated assaults and robberies involve more than one assailant. When your life is on the line, more is better.
—Shooters Committee on Political Education, *Position on New York State Bill to Prohibit Large Capacity Magazines*[2]

Assault weapons bans, including the SAFE Act's, are invariably coupled with bans on large-capacity ammunition-feeding devices. What counts as "large capacity" varies, but recent state and federal bans on large-capacity magazines have mostly specified ten rounds as the permissible maximum capacity. Proponents of bans on large-capacity magazines plausibly argue that, in a mass-shooting situation, when a shooter pauses to switch a detachable magazine, even if it takes just a few seconds, potential victims can subdue the shooter or escape. Gun owners' rights advocates insist that limiting the number of rounds in a magazine needlessly limits effective self-defense; they conjure the specter of a law-abiding victim with a ten-round magazine having to stop to reload while under attack.

When it comes to defending against "ordinary gun crimes," there is little reason to support bans on large-capacity magazines. Ordinary gun crimes almost never involve more than ten shots.[3] However, mass shootings are a different story. Perpetrators routinely fire dozens of rounds. In a few cases, perpetrators have been subdued when they paused to reload. Undoubtedly, potential victims may escape when a shooter pauses to reload.

Assuming that banning large-capacity magazines is desirable, there is the challenge of effectively implementing and enforcing such a ban when there are tens of millions of such magazines in private hands and new ones are easy to manufacture even in home workshops. A ban on large-capacity magazines will not deter a would-be mass shooter, who expects and often intends to die in the attack. And for a state like New York, attempts to prevent a potential mass murderer from acquiring a large-capacity magazine may be frustrated by the fact that a majority of states and the federal government do not ban them.

TABLE 4.1. Mass Murders in Which Shooters Used Large-Capacity Magazines

Case and location		Weapons involved	Magazines involved	Dead	Injured	Total
Sandy Hook Elementary, Newtown, CT	12/14/2012	10 mm Glock, 9 mm SIG Sauer P226 semi-automatic handguns; .223-caliber Bushmaster XM15-E2S semiautomatic rifle; Izhmash Saiga-12 12-gauge semiautomatic shotgun	15- to 20-round magazines (handguns); 30-round magazines (rifle); two 70-round magazines (shotgun)	28	2	30
Accent Signage Systems, Minneapolis, MN	9/27/2012	9 mm Glock semiautomatic handgun	Two 15-round magazines	7	1	8

TABLE 4.1. (*cont.*)

Case and location		Weapons involved	Magazines involved	Dead	Injured	Total
Sikh temple, Oak Creek, WI	8/5/2012	9 mm Springfield Armory XDM semiautomatic handgun	Three 19-round magazines	7	3	10
Movie theater, Aurora, CO	7/20/2012	Two .40-caliber Glock semiautomatic handguns; .223-caliber Smith & Wesson M&P15 semiautomatic rifle; 12-gauge Remington 870 pump-action shotgun	40-round extended magazine (handgun); 100-round magazine (rifle)	12	58	70
IHOP, Carson City, NV	9/6/2011	AK-47 Norinco Arms variant, AK-47 Romarm Cugir variant automatic rifles; .38-caliber Colt revolver	30-round magazines (rifles)	5	7	12
Shooting, Tucson, AZ	1/8/2011	9 mm Glock 19 semiautomatic handgun	Two 15-round magazines, two 33-round magazines	6	13	19
Hartford Distributors, Manchester, CT	8/3/2010	Two 9 mm Ruger SR9 semiautomatic handguns	Two 17-round magazines	9	2	11
Massacre, Fort Hood, TX	11/5/2009	FN Five-seveN semiautomatic handgun	One 20-round magazine, one 30-round magazine	13	30	43
Immigration center, Binghamton, NY	4/3/2009	9 mm Beretta, .45-caliber Springfield semiautomatic handguns	Multiple magazines including at least one 30-round magazine	14	4	18
Northern Illinois University, DeKalb, IL	2/14/2008	9 mm Glock 19, Hi-Point CF380, 9 mm Kurz SIG Sauer P232 semiautomatic handguns; 12-gauge Remington Sportsman 48 sawed-off shotgun	15- and 33-round magazines (handguns)	6	21	27
Westroads Mall, Omaha, NE	12/5/2007	WASR-10 Century Arms semiautomatic rifle	Two 30-round magazines	9	4	13
Virginia Tech, Blacksburg, VA	4/16/2007	9 mm Glock 19, .22-caliber Walther P22 semiautomatic handguns	Seventeen 10- to 15-round magazines	33	23	56

TABLE 4.1. (*cont.*)

Case and location		Weapons involved	Magazines involved	Dead	Injured	Total
Post office, Goleta, CA	1/30/2006	9 mm Smith & Wesson 915 semiautomatic handgun	15-round magazine	8	0	8
Edgewater Technology, Wakefield, MA	12/26/2000	.32-caliber Retolaza semiautomatic handgun; AK-47 variant semiautomatic rifle; 12-gauge Winchester 1300 pump-action shotgun	60-round magazine (rifle)	7	0	7
Xerox office, Honolulu, HI	11/2/1999	9 mm Glock 17 semiautomatic handgun	Three 15- to 17-round magazines	7	0	7
Wedgwood Baptist, Fort Worth, TX	9/15/1999	.380-caliber, 9 mm Ruger P85 semiautomatic handguns	Three 15-round magazines	8	7	15
Columbine High School, Littleton, CO	4/20/1999	9 mm Intratec DC-9 semiautomatic handgun; 9 mm Hi-Point 995 carbine rifle; 12-gauge sawed-off Savage Stevens 311D, 12-gauge sawed-off Savage Springfield 67H pump-action shotguns	Thirteen 10-round magazines, one 28-round magazine, one 32-round magazine, one 52-round magazine (various guns)	15	24	39
Thurston High School, Springfield, OR	5/21/1998	9 mm Glock, .22-caliber Ruger semiautomatic handguns, .22-caliber Ruger rifle	30-round magazine (handgun); 50-round magazine (rifle)	4	25	29
Westside Middle School, Jonesboro, AR	3/24/1998	FIE 380, .380-caliber Star semiautomatic handguns; .44 Magnum Ruger, .30-06 Remington 742, .30-caliber Universal M-1 carbine replica rifles; .38-caliber Charter Arms, .357-caliber Ruger Security Six, .38-caliber Smith & Wesson revolvers; .22-caliber Double Deuce Buddie two-shot, .38-caliber Davis Industries two-shot derringers	15-round magazines, three 30-round magazines (various guns)	5	10	15

TABLE 4.1. *(cont.)*

Case and location		Weapons involved	Magazines involved	Dead	Injured	Total
Connecticut Lottery, Newington, CT	3/6/1998	9 mm semiautomatic handgun	19-round magazine	5	1	6
Caltrans maintenance yard, Orange, CA	12/18/1997	7.62 mm AK-47 Chinese variant semi-automatic rifle	Five 30-round magazines	5	2	7
Fairchild Air Force Base, WA	6/20/1994	MAK-90 semiauto-matic rifle	70- to 75-round magazine	5	23	28
Long Island Rail Road, Garden City, NY	12/7/1993	9 mm Ruger P89 semi-automatic handgun	Four 15-round magazines	6	19	25
101 California Street, San Francisco, CA	7/1/1993	Two Intratec DC-9, .45-caliber Colt semi-automatic handguns	30-round magazine (.45-caliber), 40- and 50-round magazines (Intratecs)	9	6	15
Luby's, Killeen, TX	10/16/1991	9 mm Glock 17, 9 mm Ruger P89 semiauto-matic handguns	15- and 17-round magazines	24	20	44
GMAC, Jacksonville, FL	6/18/1990	.30-caliber Universal M1 carbine rifle; .38-caliber revolver	30-round magazine (rifle)	10	4	14
Standard Gravure, Louisville, KY	9/14/1989	Two Intratec MAC-11, 9 mm SIG Sauer semi-automatic handguns; AK-47 Chinese variant semiautomatic rifle; .38-caliber revolver	30-round magazines (unclear)	9	12	21
Schoolyard, Stockton, CA	1/17/1989	9 mm Taurus semi-automatic handgun; AK-47 Chinese variant semiautomatic rifle	Four 35-round magazines, two 75-round magazines (unclear)	6	29	35
Shopping centers spree, Palm Bay, FL	4/23/1987	Sturm, Ruger Mini-14 semiautomatic rifle; 20-gauge Winchester pump-action shotgun; .357 Ruger Blackhawk revolver	Five 30-round magazines (rifle)	6	14	20

TABLE 4.1. (cont.)

Case and location		Weapons involved	Magazines involved	Dead	Injured	Total
McDonald's, San Ysidro, CA	7/18/1984	9 mm Browning P35 Hi-Power semiautomatic handgun; 9 mm Israeli Military Industries Uzi Model A carbine semiautomatic rifle; 12-gauge Winchester 1200 pump-action shotgun	25-round magazines (unclear)	22	19	41
Nightclub, Dallas, TX	6/29/1984	9 mm Smith & Wesson 459 semiautomatic handgun	Two 14-round magazines	6	1	7

Source: Mark Follman & Gavin Aronsen, "A Killing Machine": Half of All Mass Shooters Used High-Capacity Magazines, Mother Jones (January 30, 2013).

Ammunition-Feeding Devices

The vast majority of semiautomatic firearms are loaded by means of either a fixed or detachable magazine. The magazine holds cartridges under spring pressure, feeding a fresh cartridge into the gun's firing chamber each time the shooter pulls the trigger. Energy from the exploding gunpowder advances the next cartridge into firing position. A "fixed magazine," built into the firearm, is loaded by means of a multicartridge "clip" that inserts into the magazine. A shooter can carry multiple clips. A "detachable magazine" is a freestanding ammunition-loading device that is manually inserted into the firearm; it makes reloading faster. When all the detachable magazine's cartridges have been fired, the shooter expels it by pressing a button and quickly replaces it by inserting a fresh magazine into the gun. Detachable magazines can have more cartridge capacity than fixed magazines. Thus, detachable magazines arguably have more destructive potential than fixed magazines.

Historically, detachable and fixed magazines could be easily distinguished; a fixed magazine was part of the firearm and could only be removed (and replaced) with tools. However, in response to the 1994 federal assault weapons ban that prohibited military-like semiautomatics, which accommodated a detachable magazine, manufacturers started producing firearms with fixed magazines that can be removed by pressing a button on the firearm's frame with a pin or even a bullet (hence the name "bullet button"). This technological innovation, blurring the distinction between fixed and detachable magazines, is a good example of how gun control laws stimulate changes in firearm design and technology, in turn stimulating new regulatory responses. Today, proponents of large-capacity magazine bans urge redefinition of "detachable magazine" to include fixed magazines that can be removed with "bullet buttons."

Regulating magazines according to cartridge capacity is more complicated than might first appear because "magazine capacity" is somewhat flexible. A magazine's capacity depends on the size (caliber) of the cartridges it is loaded with. (Some magazines can also accommodate ammunition designed for both handguns and long guns.)

A magazine's capacity can be increased by adding to its length. A ten-round magazine, for example, can with some adaptation be transformed to a fifteen-round magazine. Likewise, a fifteen-round-capacity magazine can be reduced to ten-round capacity by means of a "pin" or plate that renders some of the magazine's capacity unusable. If the ten-round capacity limitation were actively enforced, magazine owners would need clear guidance on whether inserting a pin or plate would constitute compliance. The SAFE Act, as amended (see later in this chapter), permits ten-round-capacity magazines that cannot be readily restored or converted to greater than ten-round capacity, but what does that mean? What if a magazine's modification can be reversed? If magazine bans were actively enforced, these questions would need to be hashed out in the courts. However, since arrests and prosecutions are extremely rare, gun owners must decide for themselves.

The History of Bans on Large-Capacity Magazines

Efforts to limit the capacity of magazines and other ammunition-feeding devices are not new.[4] In 1927, Michigan prohibited "any machine gun or firearm which can be fired more than sixteen times without reloading," and Rhode Island banned "any weapon which shoots more than twelve shots semi-automatically without reloading."[5] In 1932, a District of

Columbia law prohibited possession of a firearm that "shoots automatically or semi-automatically more than twelve shots without reloading."[6]

New Jersey enacted the first modern ban on large-capacity magazines in 1990; it prohibited magazines that hold more than fifteen rounds.[7] In 1991, New York City banned possession of magazines "designed for use in a rifle or shotgun . . . capable of holding more than five rounds of . . . ammunition."[8] The following year, Hawaii banned possession of handgun magazines with greater than twenty-round capacity, but in 1993, it reduced the legal maximum to ten rounds.[9] In 1994, Maryland banned the manufacture and sale, but not possession, of magazines with greater than twenty-round capacity.[10]

The federal 1994 assault weapons ban prohibited the manufacture, sale, and possession of *new magazines* with greater than ten-round capacity. Tens of millions of existing large-capacity magazines were therefore grandfathered. This not only assured that large-capacity magazines would be readily available for decades to come, but it rendered the ban more or less unenforceable against possessors because magazines are not stamped with a date. Thus, there is no way for magazine owners, purchasers, or police officers to determine whether a particular magazine is grandfathered. However, the ban could be enforced against a manufacturer who continued to produce large-capacity magazines after the date that such production became illegal.

The federal ban on large-capacity magazines expired in 2004. Since then, there has been no federal limit on magazine capacity. Bills to renew the federal ban were unsuccessfully introduced into Congress in 2004, 2005, 2008, and after the Sandy Hook massacre in 2013.[11] Even if a federal ban was enacted, new large-capacity magazines could be illegally imported from abroad or produced in small workshops.[12] More importantly, the existing stock, numbering in the tens of millions, would remain available for many decades.[13]

California passed the first state ten-round limit on magazine capacity in 1999 in the wake of the Columbine massacre. New York's omnibus 2000 gun control law followed suit. Both states grandfathered magazines manufactured prior to September 13, 1994, the effective date of the federal ban, thereby rendering their bans just as unenforceable as the federal ban. As of summer 2018, eight states plus the District of Columbia have such bans.[14]

The SAFE Act's Ban on Large-Capacity Magazines

Governor Andrew Cuomo wanted the SAFE Act to establish New York as the most restrictive magazine-capacity jurisdiction in the country. His biographer explains, "States at the vanguard of gun control law—including New York—had set ten-bullet-or-more maximums for gun magazines. So New York's maximum would be seven, Andrew ruled. The Republican staffers tried to explain the problem with that. Gun clips were designed to hold ten bullets at least."[15] The SAFE Act made it (at a maximum) a class D felony (two-year minimum sentence; seven-year maximum sentence) to possess any "magazine, belt, drum, feed strip, or similar device" that either contains more than seven rounds of ammunition or could be "readily restored or converted to accept more than seven rounds of ammunition." This makes sense politically as Governor Cuomo's bid to be the most pro-gun-control governor in the nation, but it does not make practical sense since there are few, if any, seven-round-capacity magazines on the market that would fit the vast majority of long-gun and handgun models. Gun owners' vociferous protests quickly persuaded the governor and legislature to replace the seven-round limit with a ten-round limit, but with the face-saving proviso that a ten-round magazine may not be loaded with more than seven cartridges.

Possession of certain large-capacity ammunition-feeding devices remains legal if the magazine is an attached tubular device designed to accept, and capable of operating only with, .22-caliber rimfire ammunition or if the magazine qualifies as a curio or relic (i.e., manufactured at least fifty years prior to January 15, 2013, and capable of being used exclusively in a weapon manufactured at least fifty years prior to January 15, 2013). Possession of a curio or relic magazine is lawful only if it is registered with the State Police and if the possessor is not otherwise prohibited from possessing a firearm.

No Grandfathering

Unlike the 1994 federal ban on large-capacity magazines, the SAFE Act does not provide for grandfathering.[16] It allowed owners of large-capacity magazines one year (until January 16, 2014) to dispose of their large-capacity magazines, either by destruction, permanent modification, surrender to police, transfer to a licensed dealer, or sale to an out-of-state buyer. An out-of-state sale, exchange, or disposal must be reported to the local county clerk's office "within seventy-two hours."[17] After January 16, 2014, possession of a previously lawful large-capacity magazine constitutes a class A misdemeanor (punishable by up to one year in jail and $1,000 fine).[18] It is an affirmative defense that the defendant (1) reasonably believed that the magazine was lawfully possessed and (2) within thirty days of notification disposes of the magazine. Since magazines are not marked with a manufacture date, any arrestee could claim that he or she reasonably believed that the magazine was previously grandfathered and lawfully possessed.[19]

Protests

Gun owners excoriated the governor and SAFE Act proponents as ignorant and politically opportunistic. (Governor Cuomo later said that the seven-round magazine issue caused the "biggest blowback" to the Act.)[20] Gun rights activists argued that the ban interfered with their ability to defend themselves effectively. For example, Chris W. Cox, executive director of the NRA Institute for Legislative Action, said, "Anyone who's thought seriously about armed self-defense knows why honest Americans—private citizens and police alike—choose magazines that hold more than 10 rounds. Quite simply, they improve good people's odds in defensive situations."[21] The Shooters Committee on Political Education charged, "There appears to be no real purpose for this restriction other than to impose additional burdens and risk on legal firearms owners in the State of New York under a vague and ill-defined premise that somehow it will make us safer."[22] Gun owners disputed that magazines with greater than ten-round capacity should be labeled too large, given how common they are (e.g., the popular Glock 17 handgun comes with a seventeen-round magazine; twenty- to thirty-round magazines are standard for the AR-15 rifle).[23] Manufacturers insisted that they would not respond to the SAFE Act by producing seven-round magazines for their various firearm models.[24]

Within months of the SAFE Act's passage, Governor Cuomo agreed to a legislative amendment to increase lawful magazine capacity from seven to ten rounds, provided that the ten-round magazine is not loaded with more than seven cartridges (except at firing ranges and target-shooting competitions).[25] Cuomo rejected the charge that the seven-round limitation was a blunder caused by the Act's secretive drafting process and the rush to passage. According to the governor, "There are always inconsistences in a complicated piece of legislation . . . once it's out and once its second-guessed. With total hindsight, you will find grammatical errors and you will find confusing things."[26] Amending the SAFE Act to permit possession of ten-round-capacity magazines if they are loaded with no more than seven rounds did not satisfy the anti–SAFE Act protesters. They derided the ban's underlying assumption that a criminal, much less a would-be mass murderer, would comply with the seven-round loading restriction.[27]

Exempting Retired Police Officers

Law enforcement officers criticized the ban for not exempting retired officers, who had carried fifteen-round magazines during their years of active service. The president of the NYPD Captains Endowment Association explained, "it puts retired officers in a position that the [fifteen-round] clip they were issued by the NYPD, carried for their careers and for which they were fully trained, is now considered contraband."[28] State senator Martin Golden (R-Brooklyn), a former police officer, argued that retired officers "are an experienced class of people. They know how to deal with the criminal element, so if anybody deserves to have a greater than ten-round magazine [they do]."[29] Presumably not wishing to add retired police officers, and perhaps active police officers as well, to the ranks of SAFE Act critics, Governor Cuomo quickly agreed to an amendment allowing retired officers to retain assault weapons and large-capacity magazines acquired during law enforcement employment.[30]

Constitutional Challenge

Gun owners' rights advocates are often very active litigators. Gun control proponents can expect every new law to be challenged in court. The New York State Rifle and Pistol Association (NYSRPA) filed a federal lawsuit attacking both the ten-round magazine capacity limit and the seven-round loading limit (as well as the assault weapons ban discussed in chapter 3). The NYSRPA argued that prohibiting a person from loading more than seven rounds violates the Second Amendment right to keep and bear arms in the home for self-defense, because it "put[s] law-abiding citizens at a grave disadvantage to criminals," who will not comply with these limits. "It is not a viable option to say that persons may obtain multiple magazines and change magazines if confronted with a sudden home invasion, robbery or other attack. There are members of [plaintiffs' class] who only have one magazine for their firearms; own obsolete models of firearms for which extra magazines are no longer available; do not keep extra loaded magazines with their firearms; could not change magazines while under the extreme stress of a criminal attack; and could not change magazines quickly due to old age, major disability, arthritis, and other physical conditions."[31] The Second Amendment Foundation (SAF), in its amicus curiae brief in support of the plaintiffs, echoed that argument: "Magazine capacity restrictions increase the chance that an individual's gun will become empty before he or she can stop an attacker (or attackers), forcing him or her to stop and reload—if, that is, extra ammunition is available. All things being equal, an individual forced to defend himself or herself with a gun is more likely to survive if he or she has more ammunition at the ready."[32]

The plaintiffs also charged that the SAFE Act's ban on large-capacity magazines was unconstitutionally vague in making it criminal to possess a magazine that can be "readily restored or converted" to more than ten-round capacity. They complained that they must guess whether possessing a large-capacity magazine would be unlawful if the chambers for rounds greater than ten are pinned or plated. According to the National Shooting Sports Foundation (NSSF), gun owners are "expected to guess about what magazines are capable of being 'readily converted' to hold more than 10 rounds. Even worse, the answer to that guess turns on, among other things, another question: readily converted by who[m]? An engineer? A gunsmith? An individual who has never handled and has no experience with a firearm? Someone with access to normal household tools, or to a full machine shop?"[33] The plaintiffs claimed that they wanted to be able to modify their large-capacity magazines in a way that would allow them to be restored to their original capacity if the SAFE Act's ammunition-loading provision were to be repealed or struck down as unconstitutional. In light of Congress having permitted the federal ban on large-capacity magazines to sunset, this hope was not fanciful.

The plaintiffs also challenged as unconstitutionally vague the ten-round magazine restriction as it applied to tubular magazines, because the capacity of these magazines depends on the caliber of the cartridges they are loaded with. According to the New York State Sheriffs' Association's amicus brief, tubular magazine owners have to:

> guess as to whether liability should be triggered where the capacity of tubular magazines for rifles and shotguns varies with the length of cartridges used. . . . If an officer encounters one of these firearms, is the officer to seize the firearm and arrest the individual . . . because it is capable of holding more than ten rounds of one type of ammunition? . . . What if the firearm is unloaded, or if the individual is unaware that it can hold eleven rounds of a different type of ammunition? Inevitably, officers will be forced to decide on a case by case [basis] which firearms trigger confiscation and arrest, according to their own interpretation of the laws, and according to their varying knowledge of firearms and ammunition.[34]

Federal District Court Chief Judge William Skretny upheld the ten-round capacity ban because it is based on "reasonable inferences from substantial evidence."[35] It is unclear how he reached this conclusion since there was no trial or cross-examination of experts' affidavits submitted by the parties. Instead, Chief Judge Skretny decided the case on cross motions for summary judgment. He cited *Mother Jones* magazine's finding that "more than half of the mass shootings since 1982" involved large-capacity magazines.[36] Skretny correctly pointed out that the perpetrators of at least "five of the six mass shootings" in 2012 used large-capacity magazines, including the Sandy Hook massacre perpetrator, Adam Lanza, who fired 150 bullets from several fifteen- and twenty-round magazines.

Chief Judge Skretny rejected the plaintiffs' argument that prohibiting magazines that can be "readily restored" to more than ten-round capacity is unconstitutionally vague: "Surely the Legislature, intent on reaching assault weapons which could be altered in minor ways or disassembled to avoid the purview of the other assault weapon definitions, did not have to specify in hours and minutes and with reference to specific tools and degrees of knowledge the parameters of what 'readily assembled' means."[37] He also held that the term "tubular magazine capacity" was "neither impermissibly vague in all its applications, nor permeated with vagueness."[38]

Chief Judge Skretny *struck down* the seven-round loading limit on substantive due process grounds. He opined that it would have no effect on reducing the prevalence and accessibility of large-capacity magazines, because "10-round magazines remain legal."[39] Moreover, he agreed with the plaintiffs that since prospective mass murderers and other criminals will not comply with the seven-round loading limit, the provision might perversely result in "pitting the criminal with a fully-loaded magazine against a law-abiding citizen with seven rounds. . . . It stretches the bounds of this court's deference to the predictive judgments of the legislature to suppose that those who are intent on doing harm (whom, of course, the Act is aimed to stop) will load their weapon with only the permitted rounds of ammunition."[40]

Second Circuit Court of Appeals' Decision

The Second Circuit Court of Appeals substantially affirmed Skretny's decision.[41] The three-judge panel agreed that New York State had demonstrated a "substantial relationship between the prohibition of [large-capacity magazines] and the important, indeed, compelling, state interest in controlling crime."[42] (This is an interesting observation given that large-capacity magazines are rarely used in ordinary gun crime.) It accepted the state's claim that large-capacity magazines are disproportionately used in mass shootings and result in "more shots fired, persons wounded, and wounds per victim than other gun attacks." The court relied on George Mason University criminologist Christopher Koper's conclusion that the ban on large-capacity magazines has the greatest "potential to prevent and limit shootings [the number of shots and victims] in the long-run."[43] Koper may be right, but since the challenge to the SAFE Act's provision was adjudicated without a trial, the plaintiffs did not get to cross-examine him. The Second Circuit also affirmed Skretny's conclusion that the prohibition on magazines that can be "readily restored" to hold more than ten rounds is not unconstitutionally vague: "Plaintiffs' purported concern—that this provision might be unfairly used to prosecute an ordinary citizen for owning a magazine that only a gunsmith equipped with technical knowledge and specialized tools could 'readily convert'—is implausible. Should such a prosecution ever occur, the defendant could bring an 'as applied' vagueness challenge, grounded in the facts and context of a particular set of charges. That improbable scenario cannot, however, adequately support the *facial* challenge plaintiffs attempt to bring here."[44] The Second Circuit struck down the state's seven-round loading limit, on the ground that:

> It will not decrease [ten-round magazines'] availability or in any way frustrate the access of those who intend to use ten-round magazines for mass shootings or other crimes. . . . New York has failed to present evidence that the mere existence of this load limit will convince any would-be malefactors to load magazines capable of holding ten rounds with only the permissible seven. To be sure, the mere possibility of criminal disregard of laws does not foreclose an attempt by the state to enact firearm regulations. But on intermediate scrutiny review, the state cannot "get away with shoddy data or reasoning."[45]

Noting the Second Circuit's decision, several New York district attorneys have since issued public statements affirming that their offices will not prosecute anyone for violating the seven-round loading limit.[46]

Compliance

If the SAFE Act's ban on large-capacity magazines worked as envisioned, the number of magazines with a capacity exceeding ten rounds in New York State would, over time, significantly diminish due to (1) cessation of in-state sales of new or used large-capacity magazines and (2) gun owners destroying their large-capacity magazines, selling them to out-of-state purchasers, or surrendering them to the police. There are no empirical data on the extent to which this has occurred.

It is implausible that the SAFE Act will deter people, especially potential mass shooters, from acquiring large-capacity magazines since a conviction for possession may result in as little as a low-level misdemeanor. It is also unlikely that the SAFE Act will make it difficult to acquire a large-capacity magazine since a New York resident can purchase a large-capacity magazine in person from a store (or private seller) in adjacent Pennsylvania or Vermont or order one by mail from an out-of-state seller. While federal law makes it illegal to sell a firearm to someone whom the seller knows does not have in-state identification, there is no similar prohibition on knowingly selling a large-capacity magazine to an out-of-state person.

If more states were to enact magazine bans similar to New York's, it might in time become more difficult for New York residents to acquire large-capacity magazines. However, the existing national stock of tens of millions of large-capacity magazines would supply the secondary market and black market for many years to come. Moreover, people could make their own large-capacity magazines in home workshops, using instructions downloaded from the internet. In January 2013, Defense Distributed Inc. unveiled blueprints for a 3D-printable thirty-round ArmaLite AR-15 magazine made from a plastic filament similar to the type of material used to manufacture Lego blocks;[47] the company provactively named it "The Cuomo Mag." If larger than ten-round magazines become difficult to acquire, individuals could print them on a 3D printer that they own or borrow. 3D printing is a technological innovation that will have major future implications for gun, magazine, and ammunition controls.[48]

Enforceability

Other than apprehending a suspect using a large-capacity magazine at a crime scene, it is unlikely that a police officer will encounter an unlawful magazine possessor. Magazines are usually transported in a bag, box, or pocket, which cannot be searched without a search warrant or consent. Police could, of course, monitor shooting ranges, but the SAFE Act contains an exception permitting large-capacity magazines to be possessed and used on those premises.[49] As of July 2016, there had been only sixty-four arrests and arraignments statewide for possession of a large-capacity magazine. Six of these arrests occurred in New York City. There are no available data on how these arrests arose or how they were resolved.

The Efficacy of Banning Large-Capacity Magazines

There has not been an empirical evaluation of the impact of the SAFE Act's ban on large-capacity magazines. Indeed, it is not clear what the dependent variable would be: How many times a large-capacity magazine is used in a gun crime? How many large-capacity magazines are in circulation? Because federal and state bans are principally motivated by the goal of limiting casualties in mass-shooting events, the most relevant evaluation should focus on whether there has been a decrease in the use of large-capacity magazines in mass shootings after the SAFE Act's passage. Fortunately, there have been no random public mass shootings in New York State since the Binghamton mass shooting in 2009. (In that incident, the shooter used several ten-round magazines and one thirty-round magazine.)

Something can be learned from two studies of the federal ban on large-capacity magazines (in place from 1994 to 2004) and from a recent study in Maryland. In an analysis of the first two years of the federal ban (1994–1996), Jeffrey Roth and Christopher Koper concluded that there had been no reduction in the average number of victims per gun-murder incident and no reduction in the number of multiple-gunshot-wound victims.[50] A second evaluation, carried out by Koper, concluded that the federal ban failed to reduce the number of large-capacity magazines in private hands due to a pre-ban surge in production and sales and a post-ban surge in imported and grandfathered large-capacity magazines. Over four million large-capacity magazines were imported between 1994 and 2000 (amounting to an estimated 19 percent of all large-capacity magazines prior to the 1994 federal assault weapons ban).[51] In fact, during this period, the Bureau of Alcohol, Tobacco, Firearms, and Explosives approved importation of forty-seven million large-capacity magazines.[52]

Koper also conducted a study of trends in criminal use of large-capacity magazines, using data from four different jurisdictions: Baltimore, Milwaukee, Anchorage, and Louisville.[53] He concluded that "because the [federal ban] had not yet reduced the use of large capacity magazines in crime, we [could not] clearly credit the ban with any of the national decline in gun violence."[54] The ban's exemption of millions of pre-ban assault weapons and large-capacity magazines ensured that the law would, at best, have a gradual impact. The 2004 sunsetting of the federal ban precluded analysis of long-term effects.

Koper found that the federal ban increased the market price of large-capacity magazines. Four years after the ban was implemented, (grand-fathered) large-capacity magazines sold for 22 percent more than in the first year after the ban and 80 percent more than the year before the ban. He predicted that the ban would gradually result in higher prices and fewer sales, meaning "more would-be criminal users would be unable or unwilling to pay the higher prices"; others would be "discouraged by the increasing non-monetary costs (i.e. search time) of obtaining the weapons." But since large-capacity magazines are not necessary and rarely used to commit crimes, it seems highly unlikely that even if all large-capacity magazines disappeared, there would be a reduction in casualties per gun crime. However, Koper did find, based on data from four jurisdictions, that the criminal use of large-capacity magazines actually *increased* during the ten-year life span of the federal ban. Moreover, although criminal use of assault weapons had declined after the 1994 ban, this reduction was offset, through at least the late 1990s, by increased use of nonassault weapons equipped with large-capacity magazines.[55] Koper did not address the use of large-capacity magazines in suicides, but it seems implausible that suicide ever involves more than one or two bullets. A recent analysis of law enforcement records in Baltimore (where state law prohibits magazines with a capacity exceeding ten rounds) is consistent with Koper's evaluations. It concluded that that Maryland's ban on large-capacity magazines had done little to reduce the use of large-capacity magazines. In 2016, 22 percent of recovered firearms accommodated a high-capacity magazine, a 4 percent *increase* over 2013, the year Maryland enacted its ban on large-capacity magazines.[56]

* * *

We have not found any media reports about crime victims who were injured or killed after exhausting their ten-round magazine in an unsuccessful attempt to defend themselves against an attacker with a larger-capacity magazine. If public policy with respect to appropriate civilian weaponry were based on improbable hypotheticals such as that, citizens would have access to the same weapons and ammunition as the heaviest-armed criminal imaginable. Since we can *imagine* a criminal or terrorist armed with all manner of military weapons, all limitations on civilian weaponry would have to be rejected; for example, civilians would have to be permitted to possess machine guns and grenades because one or more criminals or terrorists *might attack* with one of those weapons or with multiple lesser weapons. For much the same reason, that is, that detachable ten-round magazines are sufficient for self-defensive purposes, we do not find persuasive the argument that the SAFE Act's ten-round magazine capacity limitation violates the Second Amendment right to keep and bear arms in the home for defensive purposes.

The problem remains, however, that New York's ten-round capacity limit is not enforceable. Tens of thousands of gun owners who possess larger magazines have little incentive to surrender them. Eleven- to twenty-round and larger magazines continue to be legally sold in the large majority of states. (For states considering a ban on large-capacity magazines, a federal law prohibiting sale of large-capacity magazines to residents of other states would be desirable, albeit largely unenforceable.)

Given the number of eleven- to twenty-round-capacity magazines already in civilian hands, their widespread availability in more than forty states, and their production for many popular firearms, it probably would have been easier to enforce a ban on the largest, and least common, ammunition-feeding devices, such as one-hundred-round drums and fifty-round belts. Of course, a modest policy initiative such as that would not have made a big political splash. It bears reemphasizing that the SAFE Act's initial ban on magazines with more than seven-round capacity and the subsequent seven-round loading limit reinforced gun owners' belief that New York's gun controllers were not really focused on crime control.

The likelihood that the SAFE Act's limit on magazine capacity will prevent or deter a prospective mass shooter from obtaining a large-capacity magazine is remote, given the modest punishment for a violation of the ban and the easy availability of large-capacity magazines.

In any event, a shooter with a large-capacity magazine is only marginally more dangerous than a shooter with multiple ten-round magazines. We need to keep in mind that mass shootings have more often been perpetrated with multiple non-large-capacity magazines and/or multiple weapons rather than with large-capacity magazines. The Binghamton shooter managed to kill thirteen people and wound four others by using two semi-automatic pistols (a .45-caliber Beretta and a nine-millimeter Beretta).

5

Universal Background Checking

Requiring a criminal background check for all gun sales is
the single most effective policy for keeping guns out of the
hands of dangerous people and saving lives.
—Everytown for Gun Safety, 2014[1]

Numerous studies conducted by academic researchers and
by the federal government have shown that criminals do not
use legal markets to obtain guns. . . . They do not buy guns in
gun stores. They do not get guns at gun shows. They do not
buy them from Internet sources. The study even found that
criminals only rarely steal guns.
—National Rifle Association Institute for Legislative Action,
September 4, 2015[2]

Purchaser background checking is the United States' principal strategy
for keeping guns out of the hands of dangerous and unreliable people.
The federal Gun Control Act of 1968 disqualified certain categories of
persons (ex-felons, involuntarily committed mental patients, dishonorably discharged military personnel, and others) from purchasing any
firearm or ammunition from a federally licensed firearms dealer (FFL).
The Act made it a felony for persons falling into these categories of ineligibility to possess a gun. A person purchasing a gun from an FFL had
to sign a Bureau of Alcohol, Tobacco, Firearms, and Explosives (ATF)
form attesting that he or she was not firearms-ineligible. Lying on the
form was a federal crime.

The 1993 Brady Law (Handgun Violence Prevention Act) imposed
on FFLs an obligation to send the prospective purchaser's identification
information to the FBI's National Instant Criminal Background Check
System (NICS) and to abide by NICS's determination as to whether or not
to complete the sale. However, the Brady Law's background checking

requirement left a huge loophole: individuals could, without being subject to any background check, purchase a firearm from a "private seller" (non-FFL) whom they met at a gun show or whose gun-for-sale advertisement they saw on a bulletin board or in a newspaper, or online. Gun control activists call this the "gun show loophole," but it is actually a private-sale loophole. After the Sandy Hook massacre, President Obama and the Democratic Party leadership made universal background checking their number-one gun control priority, but they were unable to persuade Congress to pass it. The SAFE Act accomplished for New York State what Congress was unable to do for the whole country. This chapter explains how the SAFE Act, building on the federal Brady Law, extends background checking to all gun purchasers and analyzes how implementation and enforcement works (and does not work). There is much about the potential and the limitations of universal background checking that other states can learn from this SAFE Act initiative.

The FFL's Background-Checking Role

Federally licensed firearms dealers serve as the linchpins of the federal firearms regulatory system. The 1938 Federal Firearms Act required persons in the business of selling firearms to obtain a federal license and obliged FFLs to verify that a firearm purchaser was age-eligible (older than eighteen for a long gun and older than twenty-one for a handgun) and was an in-state resident. The 1968 Gun Control Act required FFLs to supervise completion of a federal form on which purchasers must affirm, under penalty for making a false statement, that they are not subject to a federal firearms disqualification and are not purchasing the gun for someone else. (The FFL must retain the completed form for twenty years and make it available to police, upon request.)

The 1993 Brady Handgun Violence Prevention Act strengthened the federal regulatory regime by adding a background-checking procedure for verifying the purchaser's claim to be firearms-eligible. Under the interim Brady Act procedure (1994–1998), before selling a handgun, an FFL had to inform the chief law enforcement officer (CLEO) in its jurisdiction of a pending handgun sale.[3] The CLEO had five business days to conduct a purchaser background check and block the sale if the purchaser was found to be firearms-ineligible. If, within five days, the CLEO did not instruct the FFL not to complete the sale, the FFL could complete it.

In November 1998, the FBI's National Instant Criminal Background Check System became operational,[4] thereby extending background checking to long-gun purchasers and eliminating the CLEO's role.[5] The FFL must transmit (by fax or phone) the prospective purchaser's name and other identifying information (not fingerprints) to NICS, whose personnel (located in West Virginia) check the prospective purchaser's identifying information against various databases of firearms-ineligible persons. Although most sales are approved within minutes, NICS has three business days to block the sale. If NICS does not respond or claim a short time extension to investigate further, the FFL can complete the sale.

Limitations of the Federal Purchaser Background-Checking Regime

The Brady Law does not apply to "secondary gun market" sales.[6] In other words, private gun sellers (non-FFLs) are not required, and indeed are not authorized, to initiate purchaser background checks. It has been estimated that 40 percent of all firearms that are acquired each year are acquired pursuant to private sales.[7] The private seller is not obliged to verify the purchaser's age or in-state residency, but it is a federal crime to knowingly transfer a firearm to someone whom the transferor knows to be firearms-ineligible.

A second problem with the federal background-checking regime is that FFLs are lightly vetted, not trained, and infrequently monitored. To become an FFL, one need only apply to ATF for a license, provide a set of fingerprints, and pay a small fee ($10 until 1994 and $200 since then for a three-year license).[8] Fifteen states (including New York) and the District of Columbia require firearm dealers to obtain a state-issued license. California, Hawaii, Massachusetts, New Jersey, Pennsylvania, Rhode Island, Washington State, and the District of Columbia require licensing for the sale of *all* firearms. Alabama, Connecticut, Delaware, Indiana, Maryland, and New Hampshire require licensing for the sale of handguns and other specified firearms. New York requires a license for the sale of handguns, assault weapons, and large-capacity-ammunition devices. The process is so straightforward and inexpensive that, historically, tens of thousands of persons with no business premises obtained a license in order to enjoy the convenience of receiving guns directly from out-of-state manufacturers, wholesalers, and retailers. (It would be simple for an enterprising criminal gun trafficker himself to obtain a FFL license in his own name—provided he has no criminal record—or in someone else's name.) By the 1990s, there were estimated to be over 300,000 FFLs nationwide. The Clinton administration reduced the number of FFLs by increasing the license fee to $200 and making a business premises a license prerequisite. In early 2015, there were approximately 140,000 FFLs.[9] Even so, while ATF is supposed to audit FFLs to make sure that records are properly kept, lack of sufficient resources makes it impossible for that agency to meet its goals of auditing each FFL every three to five years. Between 2007 and 2012, the ATF inspected fewer than half of all FFLs.[10]

While FFLs serve as the front line of the federal effort to keep firearms out of the hands of dangerous persons, they receive no training in spotting false identity documents. Ineligible gun purchasers have been known to buy guns using borrowed, counterfeit, or stolen identification. It would not be a surprise to find that some, perhaps many, FFLs are not competent vetters of identity documents—that is, matching the customer to the customer's photo identification. Others, perhaps for a premium or just to make a sale, will turn a blind eye to suspicious buyers. Still others are corrupt.

Firearms-ineligible individuals also acquire guns with the assistance of "straw purchasers," who buy a gun in their own name for the benefit of a person who cannot pass a background check. The beneficial gun owner may accompany the straw purchaser on a visit to one or more gun stores, examine various guns, and decide on the desired gun. The straw purchaser may then go to a different store to make the purchase.

In 2006, New York City Mayor Michael Bloomberg hired private investigators to carry out sting operations on FFLs in Georgia, Ohio, Pennsylvania, South Carolina, and Virginia. Investigators entered a store in pairs and, in the least subtle form of straw purchasing, the beneficial purchaser gave the straw purchaser money and instructions about what gun to buy. New York City subsequently sued twenty-seven FFLs for facilitating straw purchases.[11] Those lawsuits were settled, the defendants promising to follow best sales practices, to be monitored, and in some cases to be supervised by a special monitor. In 2009, Bloomberg sent undercover investigators to seven gun shows in three states (Nevada, Ohio, and Tennessee). Ninety-four percent of the sellers approached by investigators "failed the integrity test" by selling guns to investigators who told them that they could not pass a background check.[12] This time New York City did not sue but urged ATF to take action.

Gun control advocates often urge a crackdown on straw purchasers, but that is easier said than done. If the actual purchaser does not accompany the straw purchaser into the store, it will usually be impossible for the store clerk to determine that a particular customer is a straw purchaser. Even if both the straw and true purchaser shop together, the store clerk may lack the confidence or competence to challenge the straw purchaser's role (i.e., in effect, to call the customer a liar) and deny him or her service. Indeed, the storeowner may be wary of being accused of wrongful discrimination. Moreover, purchasers who are denied service can adjust their tactics and try other stores. Eventually, they are likely to succeed.

Critiquing Federal Firearms Disqualifications

When an FFL transmits a prospective gun purchaser's name and identifying information (fingerprints are not used) to NICS, NICS personnel search several databases of firearms-ineligible persons. If they find a match, they block the sale. Background checking can only be an effective gun control initiative if the federal law's firearm-disqualifying categories accurately identify subgroups in the population that pose a higher risk of firearms violence and if the databases are reliably populated with the identities of persons who meet the disqualification criteria.

Defining of Dangerous Persons Categories

It is a federal felony for a person to possess a firearm if he or she has ever been convicted of a federal or state felony or domestic violence misdemeanor; has ever been involuntarily committed to a mental institution or adjudicated as "mentally defective";[13] has ever been addicted to or is using controlled drugs; is unlawfully in the United States; has renounced his or her US citizenship; has ever been subject to a domestic violence restraining order; has been dishonorably discharged from the armed forces; or is a fugitive from justice.[14]

These categories are underinclusive because there are many persons who would be irresponsible and dangerous gun possessors who do not fall into any of these categories. Indeed, the perpetrators of most mass shootings were not firearms-ineligible.[15] Anomalously, federal law does not render as firearms-ineligible persons whom the FBI designates as potentially dangerous, for example, those in the Terrorist Screening Database.[16]

The federal statutory firearms-ineligible categories are also overinclusive because many people with such disqualifications are not currently dangerous. For example, individuals with very old convictions, especially for non-firearm offenses, do not, many years later, present an above-average risk of gun violence. In fact, in recent years, Ban the Box activists and other reformers who focus on alleviating the collateral consequences of conviction have strenuously and persuasively argued that it is unfair and inaccurate to treat convicted persons as dangerous and unreliable once they complete their sentence, much less for the rest of their lives.[17]

Although federal law prohibits a person who is "a drug addict or unlawful user of any controlled substance" from possessing a firearm, it is not true that persons (much less middle-age users) who currently use marijuana, for example, pose a significantly greater risk of gun violence than persons who do not use marijuana.[18] (Statistically, alcohol is the substance most highly correlated with violent crime.)

A minuscule number of people renounce their US citizenship, almost always for tax purposes.[19] (In 2014, 3,145 individuals renounced citizenship.)[20] There is no reason to believe that these tax avoiders would be particularly dangerous if armed. Congress probably intended forfeiture of Second Amendment rights as a penalty for citizenship renunciation.

The most contentious federal disqualification applies to persons ever involuntarily committed to a mental hospital, or adjudicated mentally defective. Psychiatrists, psychologists, social workers, and advocates for the mentally ill insist, with considerable empirical evidence, that persons who have suffered (even serious) episodes of mental illness at some point in their lives are not, for that reason, more dangerous for the rest of their lives when compared to the general population.[21]

Incomplete Databases

Even if federal firearms-disqualification categories accurately identified population subgroups that pose an unacceptably high risk of firearms violence, background checking will not be successful unless these databases are accurately populated. As of December 31, 2016, there were 15,810,039 individuals in the NICS index of firearms-ineligible persons.[22] (This does not include the national criminal record database, which NICS also searches.) The index is made up of records submitted by local, state, tribal, and federal agencies. Table 5.1 shows the number of people in each of these databases.

At present, the relevant federal databases are vastly underpopulated, undermining the reliability of background checking. For example, even if people who have ever used illegal drugs forever pose a significantly higher than average risk of gun violence (a dubious assumption), there is no reliable system for reporting drug addicts, much less drug users.

TABLE 5.1. Total Active Records in the NICS Index (as of December 31, 2016)

Category of ineligibility	Number of records
Illegal/unlawful alien	7,071,484
Adjudicated mental health	4,658,676
Convicted of a crime punishable by more than one year or a misdemeanor punishable by more than two years	2,940,921
Fugitive from justice	518,670
State prohibitor	296,705
Convicted of a domestic violence misdemeanor	142,402
Protection/restraining order for domestic violence	66,892
Under indictment/information	42,375
Renounced US citizenship	38,003
Unlawful user / addicted to a controlled substance	22,831
Dishonorable discharge	11,080
TOTAL:	15,810,039

Source: FBI, *National Instant Criminal Background Check System (NICS) Operations Report* (2016), www.fbi.gov.

According to a 2011 report by Mayors Against Illegal Guns, forty-four states submitted *fewer than ten names* of controlled-substance addicts/ users to the NICS database; thirty-three had not submitted any names at all.[23] Even some federal agencies, such as the Veteran's Administration, do not submit to NICS the names of illegal drug users known to the agency.[24] Only three federal agencies (the FBI, the US Coast Guard, and the Court Services and Offenders Supervision Agency [CSOSA]) had submitted any names. The Drug Enforcement Administration (DEA) had not submitted a single substance abuser's name to NICS.

To take another example, NICS holds the names of only a fraction of persons who have ever been involuntarily committed to a mental hospital or been adjudicated mentally defective. Adjudications of persons as mentally defective are rare. In 2011, twenty-three states and the District of Columbia submitted fewer than one hundred names in these categories to NICS.[25] Seventeen states submitted fewer than ten names; four states submitted none.[26]

Are Purchasers Blocked by NICS Actually Disarmed?

Even if the NICS databases were reliably and comprehensively populated with a significant percentage of people who meet the federal firearms-disqualification criteria and an FFL abided by NICS's order not to complete the transaction, we cannot assume that the rejected customer would be disarmed. Since most gun purchasers are repeat purchasers, more likely than not, the rejected purchaser already owns a gun. First-time purchasers blocked by NICS may acquire a gun from a private seller, who, under federal law, is not required nor authorized to initiate an NICS purchaser background check. Other rejected purchasers may acquire a gun with assistance from a straw purchaser. Still others will buy a gun from a black-market seller. In short, it should not be assumed that NICS background checking keeps guns out of the hands of dangerous and unreliable persons.

New York State Closes the Gun Show Loophole

In 2000, New York State extended purchaser background-checking responsibility to *private sellers* at gun shows. Gun show "operators" (organizers) have to "conspicuously post signs" at the show stating that a background check must be completed prior to all firearm sales or transfers, and they must ensure that an FFL is available to process background checks for individuals purchasing guns from private sellers. A private seller who wants to make a sale at the gun show must take the gun, along with the prospective purchaser, to the on-site FFL for initiation of a NICS background check on the purchaser.

The Shooter's Committee on Political Education (SCOPE) immediately filed a constitutional challenge.[27] SCOPE argued that the law's definition of "gun show" was so broad that it would cover any gun or hunting club event, such as a pig roast or political rally (thus requiring the host to assure that an FFL was on-site to initiate background checks).[28] Federal District Court Judge Charles Siragusa agreed that the "[the law] essentially declares any assembly of gun owners for any purpose a 'gun show.'"[29] He rejected the state's argument that prosecutorial discretion could be relied on to curb abusive enforcement of the statute:

> COURT: If I'm at the pancake breakfast sponsored by a gun club and I say to you, gee, I heard you have this nifty gun that is for sale. And you say to me, yeah, it's in my car, wouldn't the gun show background checking provision apply?
>
> PROSECUTOR: At the risk of taxing the Court's patience, because we say it doesn't. Because we are not going to prosecute (seek) civil actions or enforcement under that situation . . .
>
> COURT: With due respect, it is not the wisdom of the Attorney General that controls, but the plain text of the statute.[30]

Judge Siragusa concluded that New York State did not have a compelling interest that justifies such a broad definition of "gun show." Thus, the gun show loophole was not closed.

The SAFE Act's Universal-Background-Checking Provisions

The SAFE Act requires every firearm transfer, no matter where it takes place, to be processed through a federally licensed dealer.[31] Prospective firearm transferors and transferees, except those falling under the "immediate family" exception, must take the gun to be transferred to a licensed dealer, who can initiate an NICS background check on the purchaser.[32] The exception applies to transfers between "spouses, domestic partners, children and step-children," provided that the transferor does not know or have reasonable cause to believe that the transferee is prohibited from receiving or possessing a firearm under Federal, State, or local law.[33]

Eight other states (California, Colorado, Connecticut, Delaware, Nevada, Oregon, Rhode Island, Washington) and the District of Columbia require background checks at point of sale for transfers of all classes of firearms, including purchases from unlicensed sellers; Maryland and Pennsylvania do the same for handgun purchases only. Four states (Hawaii, Illinois, Massachusetts, and New Jersey) require any firearm purchaser, including from an unlicensed seller, to obtain a permit issued after a background check. Four states (Iowa, Michigan, Nebraska, and North Carolina) do the same only for handgun purchases. Illinois requires a background check for sales at gun shows.[34]

Purchasers' Compliance

Since 1911, New Yorkers have been required to hold a license to possess a handgun. (In New York City, a license is also necessary to possess a rifle or shotgun.) Unlicensed possession of a handgun is a class A misdemeanor. Persons who have already passed a background check in order to obtain a handgun license are likely to comply with the SAFE Act's requirement that a new handgun acquisition be processed through an FFL.[35] If persons are purchasing a handgun, they are required to alert the county clerk's office and have that new gun added to their license. (The FFL is required to verify the amended license before completing the sale.)

Persons who cannot pass the background check necessary for obtaining a handgun license could not pass an NICS background check. If such persons are determined to acquire a handgun, they could seek out a corrupt FFL, a black-market dealer, or a private seller willing to ignore the SAFE Act's universal-background-checking requirement. Alternatively, they could recruit a firearms-eligible straw purchaser (perhaps a friend, relative, or significant other) to purchase a firearm for them. (Although straw purchasing is unlawful, a 2000 ATF study found straw purchasing in 46 percent of firearms-trafficking investigations.)[36]

A firearms-ineligible person could also avoid a background check by "borrowing" a gun; borrowing is not subject to background checking. Alternatively, a firearms-ineligible individual could, without undergoing a background check, acquire a gun from a family member as a gift, loan, or sale. However, the family transferor commits a crime if he or she "knows that [the transferee] is prohibited by law from possessing a firearm . . . because of a prior conviction or because of some other disability which would render him or her ineligible to lawfully possess a firearm."[37] Realistically, however, the police are unlikely to find out, and prosecutors will find it difficult to prove, that the seller had such knowledge. Another option for the firearms-ineligible person is to steal a gun or to buy a stolen gun. (More than two thousand firearms are reported stolen each year in New York.)[38]

An indication of the extent to which gun acquirers have complied with the SAFE Act's universal-background-checking provision can be obtained from NICS background-checking data. NICS reports that in 2013 New York State FFLs initiated 2,909 NICS background checks emanating from private gun sales. This compares with 353,000 total background checks for that year. By 2016, there were 5,560 background checks emanating from private sales out of 404,700. This works out to under 1 percent of all NICS background checks in New York in 2013 and just over 1 percent in 2016. Researchers estimate that, nationwide, non-FFLs account for between 22 percent and 40 percent of all gun transfers. If the actual number of private gun transfers in New York State is anything like these estimates, the vast majority of private transfers are not being processed through an FFL and thus not generating a purchaser background check.

Private Sellers' Compliance

Because the SAFE Act's universal-background-checking provision is aimed at private (non-FFL) gun sellers, their compliance is crucial to the law's success. Nevertheless, there are several reasons why a private seller might ignore the SAFE Act's requirements. First, the seller may wish to avoid the inconvenience of locating an FFL willing to process the sale, especially in rural counties where there is no willing FFL close by.[39] Second, the private seller may be ideologically opposed to the SAFE Act's regulation of private sales or even to gun control generally. Third, the prospective purchaser might only be willing to purchase the gun without a background check.

A 2011 undercover investigation conducted by New York City Mayor Michael Bloomberg's office contacted 125 sellers from fourteen states advertising guns for sale on different online websites; 77 (62 percent) of those sellers agreed to make the sale after the faux purchaser said that he or she "probably could not pass a background check."[40] Eighty-two percent of sellers on Craigslist agreed to sell to the ineligible purchaser, despite Craigslist formally banning firearms sales on its site. While the 2011 sellers were not subject to universal-background-checking laws, it was a federal felony to sell a gun to someone the seller had reason to believe was a prohibited purchaser. If this sting operation is indicative, seller noncompliance represents a major problem for universal background checking.

Black-market gun sellers are also a threat to the efficacy of universal-background-checking laws. Their business is selling guns to firearms-ineligible persons such as gang members, drug dealers, and others who do not want to create a paper trail. They may meet prospective purchasers on street corners or on the dark web.[41] These sellers might even benefit from universal background checking if some purchasers switch to the black market because secondary-market sellers require compliance with the law.

More than four years after passage of the SAFE Act, *no one in New York State* had been arrested for selling a firearm that has not been processed through an FFL. Thus, most private sellers will probably assume that the risk of getting caught for ignoring universal background checking is very low. The most likely way for the police to identify a violator is to persuade an unlicensed person arrested for a gun offense to name the person who sold him or her the crime gun. But while prosecutors may be willing to make plea-bargaining concessions with the perpetrator of an armed crime, in order to catch *a major gun trafficker*, they will probably be unwilling to make such concessions to apprehend a one-time or casual seller who has ignored the SAFE Act's universal-background-checking provision. Moreover, even if the gun-crime arrestee claims to know the seller's name and whereabouts, and even if that alleged seller can be located (both big "ifs"), the accused seller will surely deny having made the sale. What proof is there? Certainly not a signed receipt!

Voluntary FFL Participation

The SAFE Act's universal-background-checking strategy relies on FFLs volunteering to process private sales.[42] An FFL who chooses to do so may charge the transacting parties no more than ten dollars per gun.[43] We conducted phone interviews with fifty randomly selected New York State FFLs to assess their willingness to process secondary firearms sales. (As of May 2016, there were 1,191 FFLs in New York State.)[44] Of the fifty FFLs contacted, forty-two (84 percent) said that they would process at least some private sales; they are more willing to provide the service to regular customers than to strangers. Only eight respondents (16 percent) said they would not act as an intermediary for private sales. Most of them strongly opposed the SAFE Act, especially its assault weapons ban.[45] Some believe that furthering private sales will reduce their own sale of new guns. In addition, many respondents criticized the ten-dollar fee cap as inadequate compensation for the time (twenty to thirty minutes) and effort required to process a secondary sale.[46] An FFL in East Rochester complained, "The store has to take the gun in, book it in, give you a receipt for selling it, give them a receipt for taking it, do a background check, book it out of our logbooks, save the background check forever in our records, and give them a lock with it, all for $10."[47]

No doubt, the SAFE Act's drafters wanted to keep the FFL's processing charge low in order to encourage universal-background-checking compliance. By comparison, FFLs typically charge thirty to forty dollars for facilitating an interstate firearms transfer for someone who purchases a firearm from an out-of-state manufacturer, wholesaler, or retailer. The ten-dollar cap may dissuade some FFLs from processing secondary sales. Empire State Arms Collectors, an association to which many FFLs belong, explained in an amicus brief:

> The State wants FFLs [to] facilitate private firearm sales for $10. To say "facilitate" is a misnomer. Taking just the two core elements of the NICS federal background check and the A&D book into consideration, the FFL has significant federal compliance to perform in order to conduct the background check in the context of the private firearm sales.... Generally speaking, in a private firearm sale a proposed seller places the firearm into the FFL's inventory, requiring the FFL to process the firearm into

the Acquisition & Disposition book, assume liability for the firearm, and be potentially unable to clear the firearm back out of inventory. If the proposed buyer fails a background check, the FFL is then required to run a background check on the proposed seller. (Once a firearm is placed in the FFL's inventory, it cannot be released without the next owner, even the original seller passing a NICS background check.) If the proposed seller likewise fails the background check, the FFL is not permitted to release the firearm from its inventory.[48]

Similarly, the National Shooting Sports Foundation complained, "The universal background check is a pure cost to the retailer, most of which are small 'mom-and-pop' businesses. . . . Licensed retailers would be forced to use paid staff hours or to hire additional infrastructure to accommodate such transactions, including, but not limited to additional surveillance equipment, secure firearm storage, parking, IT infrastructure, and acquisition and distribution (A&D) records."[49]

A few FFL respondents volunteered that they (unlawfully) circumvent the fee cap by charging an additional twenty- to thirty-dollar "paperwork" fee; others buy the firearm from the seller and then resell it to the purchaser for fifty or sixty dollars more than they paid. Others claimed not to process secondary gun sales for fear of becoming embroiled in a police investigation if the gun turns out to have been stolen. Walmart, the nation's largest firearms retailer, does not process private firearm sales, pointing to the danger to customers and employees posed by private firearm sellers bringing possibly loaded firearms into their stores.[50]

Universal Background Checking's Crime-Reducing Potential

Evaluating the impact of purchaser background-checking laws on crime and suicide presents a significant challenge. There may be other variables, singly or in combination, that affect gun-crime and gun-suicide rates. Even during periods when there have been no changes in gun laws or enforcement, there have been significant variations in rates of gun crime and gun suicide.

Some researchers have compared firearm homicides and suicides in years before and after enactment of a background-checking law. For example, the economists Jens Ludwig and Philip J. Cook's empirical study of the impact of the Brady Law's background-checking requirements found no relationship between background checks and firearm crimes and homicides.[51] This is not surprising given that the Brady Law left the secondary gun market entirely unregulated and that only a small minority of convicted criminals report having obtained a gun from an FFL. That does not mean that a universal-background-checking law would also be ineffective. Notably, Ludwig and Cook found a negative correlation between background checks combined with waiting periods, and suicide rates for persons over fifty-five years old. The clinical psychologists Michael and Joyce Anestis, studying the impact of changes in background-checking laws in Connecticut and Missouri, confirmed Cook and Ludwig's findings regarding the suicide-reducing effect of background checking.[52]

A 2001 study by public-health researcher Garen Wintemute found that a 1991 California law that classified a wider group of convicted misdemeanants as firearms-disqualified had a "moderate impact" on reducing gun crime.[53] Wintemute compared two groups of people, all with at least one prior violent misdemeanor conviction in the ten years prior to their application for a state permit to purchase a gun. People in the "purchaser" group acquired a gun before passage of the 1991 law. People in the "denied" group were barred under the 1991 law from obtaining a permit. Wintemute found that within three years of the purchase or attempted gun purchase, those in the purchaser group were *slightly more likely* than those in the denied group to be arrested for a "new gun and/ or violent crime" (23.9 percent versus 20.1 percent) but not for a "new non-gun and/or non-violent crime" (21.3 percent versus 22.8 percent).[54] These are very small differences. Moreover, the data did not allow Wintemute to distinguish between violent crimes committed with a gun and violent crimes committed without a gun, hence the somewhat confusing "new gun and/or violent crime" dependent variable.[55] Further, since the "purchasers" and the "denied purchasers" were not randomly assigned, it is possible that the statistically significant difference in gun-crime arrest rates between the two groups is attributable to an uncontrolled variable. Indeed, the "purchaser group" included a slightly higher percentage of people who had committed two or more violent misdemeanors prior to firearm purchase. The study could not control for prior gun crimes.

Thus, this study does not provide strong support for the gun-crime-reducing potential of purchaser background-checking laws.

The public-health professor Daniel Webster and colleagues examined the impact of Missouri's 2007 repeal of its firearms permit-to-purchase law.[56] They claim that the repeal was responsible for much of the 34 percent increase in firearm homicides from 2007 to 2008. Prior to repeal, the licensing authority conducted background checks on permits-to-purchase applicants. Since repeal, permits are no longer required, but gun purchasers who buy a gun from an FFL are still subject to an NICS background check. It seems highly unlikely to us that Missouri's universal-background-checking repeal could have had such a huge impact on increasing gun homicides in just one year. For that to have happened, one would have to believe that many potential murderers prior to repeal did not have and were not able to acquire a gun because they could not pass a background check. For all the reasons discussed earlier (straw purchasing, black markets, theft, borrowing), that seems highly implausible. Moreover, surveys of persons convicted of gun crimes show that the vast majority do not apply for licenses and do not buy guns from retail dealers.

Webster supports his interpretation of the sharp increase in homicides by pointing to a "relatively stable" Missouri firearm homicide rate from 1999 to 2007. He contends that the 2008 spike could only, or at least most plausibly, be explained by repeal of the permit law. The data do not support this claim. The firearm homicide rate in Missouri also spiked by 32 percent from 2003 to 2005. If permit-repeal caused the 2007–2008 spike in firearm homicides, what explains the 2003–2005 spike? While Webster does not present data on gun suicides, the gun-suicide rate *decreased by 8 percent after universal-background-checking repeal.*

Clayton Cramer also examined Missouri's monthly homicide data after repeal and observed that there was a gap of eight months between repeal and the spike in firearm homicides.[57] This delay, Cramer argues, casts doubt on a causal relationship.[58] He further observes that the spike in homicides during the spring and summer of 2008 coincided with increased gang violence in the St. Louis area.[59] It seems unlikely to us that, before repeal, gang members could not acquire guns because they could not get permits or that, following repeal, it took eight months to find a gun.[60]

Cramer examined homicide rates in eight states with some version of universal background checking. He compared the first full year the background-checking law was in effect with the average murder rate in the five years before and the five years after the law became effective.[61] His results, presented in table 5.2, show statistically significant declines in murder rates for two of the eight states but increased murder rates for six states. In three out of the eight states, the changes in murder rates were not statistically significant.[62]

These studies do not support the hypothesis that a universal-background-checking requirement reduces gun crime or gun suicide. Of course, the negative is not proven either. It is possible that universal background checking does have a depressing impact on firearm violence but that its impact is masked by other variables that cannot be, or at least have not so far been, controlled for. It is also possible that while present-day universal background checking has not been effective, better-designed and better-enforced background checking could have a depressing effect on gun crime and gun suicide.

New York State's homicides declined from 2009 to 2014. The question is what part, if any, of this decline is attributable to the SAFE Act, and if

TABLE 5.2. Average Murder Rates before and after Universal-Background-Checking Laws Were Passed

State	First full year	Murder-rate average before (T–5)	Std. Dev.	Murder-rate average after (T+5)	Std. Dev.	Change	Statistically significant?	Type of firearms
California	1991	11	0.60	12	0.78	12%	Y	All
Illinois	1968	6	1.02	9	0.65	49%	Y	All
Iowa	1978	2	0.22	2	0.20	6%	N	Pistols
Maryland	1997	12	0.46	9	0.88	−24%	Y	Pistols
Massa-chusetts	1969	3	0.57	4	0.37	44%	Y	All
Nebraska	1992	3.1	0.49	3	0.61	9%	N	Pistols
Pennsyl-vania	1998	6.1	0.44	5	0.20	−17%	Y	Pistols
Rhode Island	1991	4.2	0.68	4	0.30	−11%	N	Long guns

the SAFE Act did have an impact, what part of the impact is attributable to the universal-background-checking provision rather than the Act's many other gun control provisions? To begin, the state's declining homicide rate is almost totally accounted for by New York City's homicide decline, but the SAFE Act's universal-background-checking provisions probably had little, if any, effect on New York City, where gun crime had already plummeted almost 75 percent since the early 1990s.[63] For the SAFE Act's universal-background-checking laws to have played a causal role in the post-2012 decline in homicides, there would need to have been an acceleration of this long-term gun-crime decline due to the SAFE Act's universal background checking requirements. However, the homicide rate did not show a uniform trend. In 2013 and 2014, gun and nongun homicides in New York City fell, but there was a homicide spike in 2015 (more dramatically in gun than in nongun homicides). But this increase did not continue. In 2016, the city's homicide rate fell again (but was still higher than in 2014). Importantly, gun homicides as a percentage of all homicides remained relatively constant.

The SAFE Act's universal-background-checking provisions could affect gun suicides if background checking prevents persons with suicidal intentions from obtaining a gun. However, there is no reason to think that suicidal people have a greater rate of firearms-ineligibility than the

TABLE 5.3. New York State and New York City Firearm-Related Homicides, 2009–2016

	New York City		Non–New York City		New York State	
Year	Homicides	Firearm related (%)	Homicides	Firearm related (%)	Homicides	Firearm related (%)
2009	471	302 (64%)	313	181 (58%)	784	483 (67%)
2010	536	323 (60%)	330	199 (60%)	866	522 (61%)
2011	515	315 (61%)	255	133 (52%)	770	448 (58%)
2012	419	241 (57%)	269	171 (64%)	688	412 (60%)
2013	335	194 (58%)	309	172 (56%)	644	366 (57%)
2014	333	188 (56%)	283	160 (56%)	616	348 (56%)
2015	352	235 (67%)	266	151 (58%)	618	386 (62%)
2016	335	203 (61%)	293	164 (56%)	628	367 (58%)

Source: New York State Division of Criminal Justice Services, *New York State Crime Report: Crime in New York State 2016 Final Data* (September 2017), www.criminaljustice.ny.gov.

TABLE 5.4. New York State Firearm-Related Suicide, 2009–2016

Year	Firearm suicides	Rate per 100,000	Total suicides	Rate per 100,000	State population
2009	422	2.2	1,417	7.3	19,307,066
2010	459	2.4	1,547	8.0	19,378,102
2011	505	2.6	1,658	8.5	19,521,745
2012	516	2.6	1,708	8.7	19,607,140
2013	465	2.4	1,687	8.6	19,695,680
2014	474	2.4	1,700	8.6	19,746,227
2015	421	2.1	1,652	8.4	19,747,183
2016	490	2.5	1,679	8.5	19,745,289

Source: Center for Disease Control and Prevention, WISQARS, *Fatal Injury Reports, National and Regional 1999–2016*, https://webappa.cdc.gov.

general population in respect of many of the disqualifying categories, for example, felony or misdemeanor domestic violence convictions.[64] More relevantly, the SAFE Act's provisions requiring mental health professionals to report patients whom they believe pose a substantial risk of serious injury to self rendered at least eighty-five thousand persons firearms-ineligible between 2013 and 2016. Table 5.4 shows that both total suicides and gun suicides increased from 2009 to 2012 but were lower in the years 2013–2016 than they were in 2011 and 2012.[65] The increase in both gun and nongun suicides during this period does not support the hypothesis that the SAFE Act prevented suicidal individuals from acquiring guns.

* * *

The hypothesis that universal background checking will reduce gun crimes and suicides depends on several assumptions: that some characteristics or events reliably indicate a person's dangerousness for one's entire life; that those characteristics or events are reliably recorded in accessible databases; that FFLs and private sellers will initiate government-conducted background checks and abide by negative decisions; and that rejected gun purchasers who are blocked by the background-checking system will be disarmed if they already have a gun and be prevented in the future from acquiring firearms. The validity of these assumptions is doubtful.

It is challenging enough to run a background-checking regime through federally licensed dealers, who are self-selected, are weakly vetted, untrained, largely unmonitored, and have conflicting incentives. When responsibility for initiating background checking is placed on private sellers, at least insofar as they have to take the gun to a licensed dealer, intentional and inadvertent noncompliance is much more likely, especially if those who do not comply face a negligible chance of apprehension and punishment. NICS background checks data do not indicate a high rate of private sellers' compliance in New York State.

Despite the SAFE Act's universal-background-checking provisions, firearms-ineligible individuals still have many options for obtaining a gun.[66] They can seek out rogue FFLs, private sellers willing to ignore the SAFE Act's universal-background-checking requirements, or black marketeers. They can also circumvent the universal-background-checking requirement by recruiting a straw purchaser. It is not surprising, then, that, to date, New York's gun statistics do not support the hypothesis that universal background checking has reduced gun homicides or gun suicides.

This skepticism does not mean that universal background checking is a bad policy. Closing the private gun sale loophole is necessary to make the Brady Law regime coherent. It makes no sense to require background checking for purchasers from FFLs but not from non-FFLs. But there are major obstacles to effective implementation, compliance, and enforcement. Background checking would be much more efficacious if coupled with mandatory registration, which would establish a comprehensive record of every gun's ownership. However, creating a national or even statewide gun registry in a nation where over three hundred million unregistered firearms are in civilian hands would be a monumental challenge. Still, future policy makers considering universal-background-checking proposals should give a great deal of thought to linking this policy to firearm registration. They should also consider using both carrots and sticks to encourage private sellers to initiate background checks on their purchasers.

Finally, imposing lifetime categorical firearm disqualifications needs to be reexamined. The crude federal disqualification regime is only weakly connected, at best, with firearm dangerousness and unreliability. It also reinforces the stereotype that people convicted of crimes and experiencing mental illness will be forever dangerous. Some kind of case-by-case assessment would be more accurate and fairer but of course vastly more expensive. Moreover, after *Heller* and *McDonald*, lifetime forfeiture of Second Amendment rights is likely to become a vigorously contested constitutional issue.

6

Disarming the Mentally Ill

Like most rights, the right secured by the Second Amendment is not unlimited. . . . Nothing in our opinion should be taken to cast doubt on longstanding prohibitions on the possession of firearms by felons and the mentally ill, or laws forbidding the carrying of firearms in sensitive places such as schools and government buildings, or laws imposing conditions and qualifications on the commercial sale of arms.
—Supreme Court of the United States, *District of Columbia v. Heller*, June 26, 2008[1]

While much of the national dialogue around recent mass shootings has focused on the relationship between mental illness and violence, the research evidence shows that the large majority of people with mental illness do not engage in violence against others and most violence is caused by factors other than mental illness.
—Consortium for Risk-Based Firearm Policy, December 2, 2013[2]

Perpetrators of practically every mass shooting in recent years, including the Sandy Hook shooter Adam Lanza, have had a history of mental illness, although it was often not professionally diagnosed or treated. Therefore, it is not surprising that the SAFE Act, precipitated by the Sandy Hook massacre, included an aggressive effort to disarm people identified as mentally ill and dangerous. In this chapter, we ask whether the SAFE Act casts too wide a net and how successfully it keeps those who are caught in the net from acquiring or keeping a gun.

The federal 1968 Criminal Justice Act declared persons who had ever been involuntarily committed to a mental hospital or ever adjudicated "mentally defective" to be firearms-ineligible for life or until they obtained a Relief from Disabilities Order (a court-issued certificate that removes restrictions on employment, public housing, and certain licenses).[3] However, the number of individuals who are involuntarily committed to a mental hospital has declined drastically since the 1950s. Today, voluntary hospital commitments are far more common than involuntary commitments.[4] Adjudications of mental defectiveness have always been rare, usually triggered by a family's desire to prevent an elderly relative from endangering themselves or dissipating their assets.

The 1986 Firearm Owners Protection Act established a "relief from disabilities" program whereby individuals who were prohibited from possessing firearms could petition the Bureau of Alcohol, Tobacco, Firearms, and Explosives (ATF) to have their gun rights restored.[5] The applicant had to persuade an ATF examiner that he or she "will not be likely to act in a manner dangerous to public safety and that granting relief would not be contrary to the public interest."[6] Denial of relief was subject to judicial review. In 1992, Congress ceased funding and the ATF stopped operating the program. It has never been revived.

The 1993 Brady Law (Handgun Violence Prevention Act) required states (beginning in 1998) to submit to the National Instant Criminal Background Check System (NICS) the names of state residents who had ever been involuntarily committed to a mental hospital or adjudicated mentally defective. However, only a few states did much reporting.[7] States, often intentionally, do not collect this information because mental health professionals object to reporting information about their patients to state officials and indirectly to the FBI. They cite empirical studies showing that mental illness is not a good predictor of gun violence or of violence generally and object to even implicitly equating mental illness with criminality. To the contrary, they argue, persons suffering from mental illness are more likely to be the victims than the perpetrators of violence.

In April 2007, the Virginia Tech student Seung-Hui Cho massacred thirty-two and wounded seventeen fellow students. A state judge had previously found him to be a danger to himself but decided to order community treatment rather than hospitalization. The state did not submit his name to NICS because it did not consider a community treatment order to be an involuntary commitment. A little over a year later, Cho purchased a semiautomatic pistol from an FFL. After the massacre, federal and state lawyers disagreed about whether the community treatment order should have been treated as an "involuntary commitment," triggering reporting to NICS.

Congress responded to the Virginia Tech massacre with the 2007 NICS Improvement Amendments Act (NIAA), which authorized withholding federal funds from states that do not meet federal reporting standards.[8] The NIAA did improve state reporting. A 2012 Government Accountability Office (GAO) report found that "the total number of mental health records that states made available to the NICS Index increased by approximately 800 percent—from about 126,000 records in October 2004 to about 1.2 million records in October 2011."[9] However, the report found that "many states have made little progress providing critical information records for gun background checks" and that "the substantial increase in mental health records coming mostly from 12 states serves to demonstrate the great untapped potential within the remaining states and territories."[10]

Congress next addressed state underreporting to NICS with the Fix NICS Act of 2017, directing the Department of Justice (DOJ) to collaborate with state governments to establish an implementation plan "to ensure maximum coordination and automated reporting" of individuals prohibited by law from possessing firearms to the NICS (including mental health records).[11] DOJ must periodically issue reports on states' compliance; the most compliant states will receive preference in obtaining federal grants. (No grant money has ever been withheld from a state for failing to meet the 2007 NICS Improvement Act's reporting requirements.)

Even if states reported all civil commitments and mental-defective adjudications, huge numbers of mentally unstable individuals would remain firearms-eligible. In a recent study, Jeffrey Swanson, a prominent psychiatric commentator, concluded that "the federal prohibiting criteria themselves, as defined in the 1968 Gun Control Act and mirrored in many states' statutes, tend to correlate poorly with actual risk of violence and suicide. The rules are both over- and under-inclusive insofar as they prohibit many people at a very low risk of violence from owning guns while also failing to identify many others who are at a high risk of violence."[12] While most massacre perpetrators had, at least in retrospect, shown signs of severe mental illness, few of them had substantial engagement with mental health professionals; none of them had been civilly committed or adjudicated mentally defective.

James Holmes, the Aurora, Colorado, movie theater shooter, legally purchased guns, although he had told a school psychiatrist that he fantasized about killing people.[13] Jared Loughner ignored his mother's pleas to get treatment for mental illness, before acquiring a gun with which he shot Rep. Gabrielle Giffords and nineteen others at a Tucson, Arizona, shopping center.[14] Nikolas Cruz, the nineteen-year-old Parkland, Florida, school shooter (February 2018) had been transferred to a school for emotionally disturbed students in the eighth grade. Police had been called to his home more than a dozen times on account of his disturbing behavior. He ignored high school officials' recommendation to enter therapy. He posted to the internet messages about aspiring to perpetrate a school massacre, but he had never been involuntarily committed to a mental hospital or adjudicated mentally defective.[15]

In the waning days of the Obama administration, the Social Security Administration (SSA) proposed an administrative rule that would have authorized that agency to report to NICS the names of Social Security recipients who were determined, due to mental incompetence, to require a representative payee to handle their benefits.[16] Both the NRA and the American Civil Liberties Union (ACLU) opposed the proposed rule, predicting that it would result in tens of thousands of persons losing their Second Amendment rights. According to the ACLU:

> We oppose this rule because it advances and reinforces the harmful stereotype that people with mental disabilities, a vast and diverse group of citizens, are violent. There is no data to support a connection between the need for a representative payee to manage one's Social Security disability benefits and a propensity toward gun violence. The rule further demonstrates the damaging phenomenon of "spread," or the perception that a disabled individual with one area of impairment automatically has additional, negative and unrelated attributes. Here, the rule automatically conflates one disability-related characteristic, that is, difficulty with managing money, with the inability to safely possess a firearm.[17]

In early 2017, both houses of Congress voted to reject SSA's proposed rule; President Trump concurred.[18]

While in hindsight it is obvious that a mentally ill mass shooter should have been rendered firearms-ineligible, it is difficult to distinguish the future massacre perpetrator from others who appear odd, unwell, and even frightening but who will never act violently. How much risk should society have to tolerate before requiring the forfeiture of Second Amendment rights by someone suffering mental illness? How large is the pool of people who are too dangerous to have access to guns but not dangerous enough to be civilly committed? Who should decide how much risk a particular person represents?

The SAFE Act's Mandatory Reporting Obligation for Mental Health Professionals

The SAFE Act greatly expands the pool of people suffering from a mental illness who may lose their Second Amendment rights, albeit for a maximum of five years. It provides that a mental health professional who, in the exercise of reasonable professional judgment, believes that a patient is likely to engage in conduct that would result in serious harm to self or others *must*, "as soon as practicable," transmit a report to a director of community services (DCS) in the patient's county of residence.[19] (DCSs are appointed pursuant to the New York Mental Hygiene Law. They are responsible for developing and administering local services for persons suffering from a mental illness or developmental disability.)[20] "Likely to result in serious harm" is defined to mean (a) a substantial risk of harm to the person as manifested by threats of or attempts at suicide or serious bodily harm or other conduct demonstrating that the person is dangerous to him- or herself or (b) a substantial risk of physical harm to other persons manifested by homicidal or other violent behavior by which others are placed in reasonable fear of serious physical harm.[21] Using the online Integrated SAFE Act Reporting Site (ISARS), the mental health professional must select a diagnosis from a diagnostic list and briefly (fifty to five hundred characters) explain why the reported person poses a specific threat.

A county DCS who has never met the reported patient, and almost certainly has not communicated directly with the reporting health care professional who prepared the report, is very unlikely to disagree with the clinician's judgment due to the negative professional consequences he or she might suffer if the reported person were to commit a future gun crime.[22] The *New York Times* reported that so many patients' names are reported to DCSs (approximately five hundred per week statewide) that DCS review is necessarily cursory. The Dutchess County DCS explained that, at first, he carefully scrutinized every report sent to him, but he soon realized that he was just "a middleman." Consequently, he began simply checking necessary boxes, sometimes without even reviewing the report: "Every so often I read one just to be sure. . . . I am not going to second guess. I don't see the patient. I don't know the patient."[23]

The SAFE Act protects a medical professional who fails to report someone who later engages in violent conduct under a caveat provision that says, "Nothing in this section shall be construed to require a mental health professional to take any action which, in the exercise of reasonable professional judgment, would endanger such mental health professional or increase the danger to a potential victim or victims."[24] Moreover, a medical professional who reports someone is shielded from criminal and civil liability if the report was filed "reasonably and in good faith."

If the DCS accepts the clinician's report, he or she sends the reported individual's name and identifying information (i.e., date of birth, race, gender, Social Security number, residential address) to the New York Division of Criminal Justice Services (DCJS), which will forward it for inclusion in the Office of Mental Health's database, where it will remain for up to five years.[25] Because there is no notification requirement, reported persons who do not have a firearms license (and thus will not be subject to revocation) are unlikely to be aware that they have been rendered firearms-ineligible unless they apply for a firearms license.

If the reported person already has a firearms license, revocation is not assured. (Only a very small percentage of reported persons are licensed handgun owners. According to the New York Times, as of October 2014, of the 41,247 reported persons in the SAFE Act database, only 278 held a handgun license.)[26] DCJS is supposed to "periodically" check the statewide firearms license database against the database of mentally disqualified persons to identify individuals who are no longer firearms-eligible.[27] If DCJS personnel identify an individual who has been disqualified due to a clinician's report, they should notify the relevant county firearms licensing officer who should initiate license revocation.

While the SAFE Act did not provide procedures for a county clerk to follow after receiving notice that one of that county's licensees is the subject of a clinician's report, according to the Office of Court Administration's "uniform protocols to comply with the legislative mandates and intent of . . . § 9.46," the county clerk who receives a notification should inform the county licensing officer, who should immediately order the reported person to show cause as to why his or her license should not be revoked at a hearing within ten days. If the order includes a temporary license suspension, the sheriff or local police serving the order should seek the surrender of all the licensee's firearms. At the hearing, the licensing officer should determine whether the respondent "is in fact the individual identified in the § 9.46 notice; possesses any firearms, rifles, shotguns, firearm licenses, . . . [and] should be subject to a license suspension/revocation order."[28] To overturn the licensing officer's revocation decision, the licensee must prove that the revocation decision was arbitrary or capricious. Historically, judges have been very deferential to county firearm licensing officials, who in practically all counties are judges themselves.

If the county licensing officer revokes the license, the local police department or sheriff must dispatch an officer to the revoked licensee's residence to confirm that he or she no longer has *any* firearms (long guns as well as the licensed handguns). However, the police, other than in New York City, have no way of knowing whether the individual has one or more long guns, since outside New York City there is no licensing requirement for long guns. As for the handguns listed on the person's license, he or she might claim to have misplaced, lost, sold, or given them away, perhaps to a relative who resides in another state. Indeed, the revoked licensee may legally transfer his or her guns to another person, provided that he or she does not have access to them (a proviso all but impossible to monitor or enforce). Alternatively, he or she may hide all or some of the guns.

A police officer who is dissatisfied with the handgun licensee's cooperation could apply for a judicial warrant to search the licensee's house, grounds, vehicles, and workplace. However, judges are reluctant, to say the least, to issue such sweeping warrants.[29] Even executing a more limited warrant is likely to be very time-consuming. In short, we cannot be confident that the revoked licensee will be disarmed. Even if disarmed, he or she could easily buy or borrow new guns. Purchasing a rifle or shotgun from an FFL should not pose a problem because NICS does not search New York's DCJS database.

Criticism by Advocates for the Mentally Ill

The strongest critics of the SAFE Act's provisions for disarming people suffering from mental illness are advocates for the mentally ill, who argue that these provisions (1) stigmatize mental illness, (2) encourage over-reporting, (3) deter people with psychological and emotional problems from seeking treatment and/or from continuing in treatment, (4) under-mine the relationship between therapist and patient, (5) infringe on the privacy of personal health information, and (6) impose an unfunded mandate on New York State counties.

Stigmatizing Mental Illness and the Mentally Ill

Mental health professionals and advocates for persons with mental illness dispute the assumption that a person suffering from a men-tal illness necessarily carries a heightened risk of violence.[30] Citing the MacArthur Foundation's comprehensive study of the relationship between mental disorders and violence, they contend that mental ill-ness is, at most, a weak predictor of violence.[31] People with diagnosed mental illnesses, as a group, are less dangerous than drug and alcohol abusers, gang members, perpetrators of domestic violence, and persons convicted of violent misdemeanors or felonies before the age of eigh-teen.[32] According to the executive director of the National Alliance on Mental Illness:

> There is a strong belief that people with serious mental illness are danger-ous and are responsible for a significant amount of the violence in this country. The vast majority of Americans with mental health conditions are not violent. According to a 2006 *American Journal of Psychiatry* study, only 5 percent of violent crimes—defined by the FBI as murders, robber-ies, rapes, and aggravated assaults—can be attributed to people with men-tal illness. The remaining 95 percent of violent crimes are committed by individuals without mental health problems. If we are seeking to address the problem of violence in America, we must look elsewhere. Associat-ing violence with people with mental illness serves to exacerbate stigma. Stigma isolates individuals and their families, makes them feel ashamed and to blame, and prevents them from seeking treatment when needed.[33]

In contrast to New York's focus on mental illness as a risk factor, Connecticut's law authorizes police to temporarily remove guns from any individual who "poses a risk of imminent personal injury to himself or herself or to other individuals." As Jeffrey Swanson et al. explain, "As the draft of the law evolved, it was written deliberately to exclude mental illness per se from among the reasons attributing risk sufficient to remove someone's guns. . . . In the end, the proposal for a gun removal scheme based solely on 'imminent risk' regardless of mental health history was seen as less stigmatizing."[34] The individual from whom the gun was seized has the right to a court hearing within fourteen days to determine whether the gun should be returned or held for up to one year. The court must be satisfied that the state has proven by clear and convincing evidence that the person poses a risk of imminent personal injury to him- or herself or to others and that there is no reasonable alternative to prevent the person from causing harm.

Connecticut's law for disarming at-risk individuals is preferable to New York's SAFE Act provision. It does not equate mental illness with dangerousness; rather, it makes dangerous conduct the criterion for suspending Second Amendment rights and seizing guns. Indeed, the Consortium for Risk-Based Firearm Policy and the American Psychiatric Association have recommended firearm-disqualification criteria based on documented dangerous conduct rather than on an individual clinician's subjective prediction. They propose temporarily disarming persons who have exhibited prior episodes of violence (e.g., a conviction for a violent misdemeanor or having been subject to a temporary domestic violence restraining order) and those with documented incidents of loss of control while intoxicated.[35]

Overreporting

By October 2014, just over eighteen months after the SAFE Act's reporting requirement took effect, over forty thousand people had been reported by the end of 2016, that number had swelled to eighty-five thousand.[36] (Figure 6.1 shows by year the number of persons reported by mental health professionals and the number approved by DCSs and forwarded to the New York SAFE Act database.)

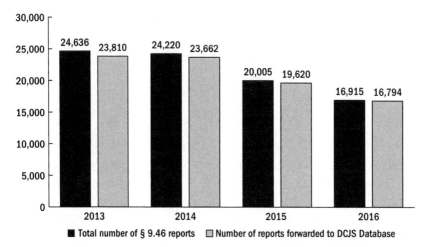

Figure 6.1. Total number of § 9.46 reports, 2013–2016. (New York State Office of Mental Health, *Response to Freedom of Information Law Request*, cited in Paloma Capanna, *More than 85,000 Secret Reports Made by Doctors to the NYS Police*, Law-Policy.com (March 16, 2017), http://law-policy.com)

According to the chair of the American Psychiatrist Association's Committee on Judicial Action, mental health professionals are unlikely not to report a patient about whom they harbor any suspicion of dangerousness: "If my patient acts on their impulses in a horrendous way, what happens when everyone starts pointing fingers at me?"[37] Hospitals are risk averse, on account of incurring liability and reputational injury, for a clinician's failure to report a patient who, after a hospital contact, commits a gun crime or gun suicide. State-operated psychiatric centers alone filed one thousand new reports in April 2014:

Some DCS are receiving reports that appear to be made by someone other than the [Mental Health Professional] treating the patient. This might be a person designated by the hospital to make such reports or in some cases by a computer generated report. Technically such a report is neither made by an MHP who is currently treating the subject nor is it based on reasonable professional judgment . . . we have been advised that the State has taken the position that all persons admitted to a State Psychiatric Center meet the criteria of 9.46 simply by virtue of their admission and, for at least some period of time, all such admitted persons were apparently being reported en mass by computer generated reports not based on the reasonable professional judgment of a treating clinician as the statute requires.[38]

Deterring People from Seeking or Continuing Treatment

New York City's Veterans' Mental Health Coalition charged that the SAFE Act's mandatory reporting provision deters military veterans suffering from posttraumatic stress and other disorders from seeking mental health treatment. A RAND Corporation study found that more than one in five veterans suffer from posttraumatic stress disorder (PTSD) or major depression, rates two to four times higher than the general population for major depression and eight times higher for PTSD.[39]

Paul Appelbaum, director of the Division of Law, Ethics, and Psychiatry at Columbia University, similarly observed, "Lots of people, because of the stigma associated with mental illness, don't want anybody to know that they're in treatment. . . . They don't use their insurance coverage. They pay out of pocket, so their employer and their insurer won't know. They may not even tell their spouse. The SAFE Act reporting provisions may be enough to scare them away forever."[40]

The US Department of Veterans Affairs announced that, as a federal agency, it is not required and would not report persons under the SAFE Act.[41] The New York State Mental Health Association's director of public policy predicted that the SAFE Act would have a "chilling effect on people getting care": "We're particularly concerned about veterans . . . [because] we have a hard enough time getting veterans in for PTSD. Veterans are a prime example of someone who would have a disincentive to go."[42]

Undermining the Doctor-Patient Relationship

Psychiatrists' and psychologists' organizations charge that by assigning therapists a quasi-policing role, the SAFE Act undermines the therapist-patient relationship. According to the New York State Psychiatric Association (NYSPA), "Psychiatry is unique among medical specialties in that patients' disclosure of their inner thoughts and feelings including angers, hostilities and resentments, is often essential to the treatment of mental illness. If patients do not feel secure that the information they provide to the psychiatrist will be kept confidential, they may be reluctant to enter into treatment or continue with on-going treatment. In this regard, the SAFE Act's mandatory reporting requirement may dissuade individuals from pursuing needed treatment precisely because they feel that their confidences will not be kept confidential."[43] NYSPA therefore proposed that the SAFE Act be amended *to permit but not require* medical health professionals to report patients to government authorities when the health professional believes that the patient poses a serious and imminent danger to themselves or others. Further, when a warning is issued, the NYSPA proposes that it be communicated directly to those who are in danger and/or to local police. According to NYSPA, these amendments would provide a more expeditious and targeted strategy for protecting potential victims and would significantly reduce infringement of Second Amendment and privacy rights.

Privacy of Personal Health Information and Conflicting Reporting Requirements

Some mental health professionals argue that the SAFE Act's reporting obligation conflicts with the protections for personal health information in the federal Health Insurance Portability and Accounting Act (HIPAA).[44] HIPAA provides, with a few limited exceptions, that an individual's protected health information may not be disclosed without that individual's consent.[45] HIPAA permits protected health information to be disclosed "when required by law."[46] There is disagreement about whether clinician reporting under the SAFE Act falls within that exception.

To resolve that issue, the first question is whether a clinician's report that a named individual is mentally ill and potentially dangerous constitutes "protected health information." The answer would seem to be yes because the clinician's report to the DCS contains information "relate[d] to the individual's past, present, or future . . . mental health."[47] If a report is "protected health information," the next question is whether it is "required by law." New York State argues that reports, prescribed by the SAFE Act, are "required by law."[48] However, NYSPA disagrees because, "unlike a compulsory mandate," the SAFE Act does not require mental health professionals to report patients if they believe it would "endanger such mental health professional or increase the danger to a potential victim."[49] Thus, according to NYSPA, the SAFE Act report is not "required." So far, the state's position has prevailed, at least with hospitals.

Arguably, SAFE Act reporting may be permissible in some cases under HIPAA's exception for information necessary "to prevent or lessen a serious and imminent threat to the health or safety of a person or the public."[50] Nonimminent threats do not fall under this HIPAA exception. While the SAFE Act requires a clinician to report a patient assessed to pose a threat to the general public, the threat need not be imminent; indeed, if it is imminent, the clinician should petition to have the patient civilly committed.

In April 2013, the US Department of Health and Human Services (HHS) issued advanced notice of proposed rule making to clarify that the reporting to NICS of persons who have been civilly committed or adjudicated mentally defective does not violate HIPAA.[51] Some commentators argued that the final rule should permit the disclosure of information about individuals who are subject to state mental illness firearm disqualifications on a different basis from the federal criteria. Otherwise, broader state firearm disqualifications on mental illness grounds (such as under the SAFE Act) would be frustrated. Other commentators argued, to the contrary, that state laws, such as the SAFE Act, violate HIPAA. Ultimately, HHS ruled that HIPAA restrictions do not prevent law enforcement agencies from reporting individuals disqualified under state law. That HHS rule permits New York's DCJS to notify county licensing officers and police agencies that a named individual is listed in the New York SAFE Act reporting database but does not give mental health professionals a green light to send reports to DCSS. The issue is still not free from doubt.[52]

In addition to the confusion caused by conflicting state and federal laws on permissible disclosure of mental health information, the Medical Society of the State of New York (MSSNY) complained that the SAFE Act subjects its members to inconsistent state laws.[53] A pre–SAFE Act law (which remains in effect) authorizes (but does not require) a health care professional working for an Office of Mental Health (OMH) or an Office for People with Developmental Disabilities' (OPWDD) licensed or operated facility to disclose to an endangered individual and/or to the police a patient's threat if "a treating psychiatrist or psychologist determines that a patient or client presents a serious and imminent danger to that individual."[54] By contrast, the SAFE Act *requires* mental health professionals to report a patient whom the therapist believes is "likely to engage in conduct that would result in serious harm." Thus, according to MSSNY:

> We are concerned that the existence of two standards will cause significant confusion among health care professionals and could result in the reporting of persons who do not pose a serious and imminent threat to society. MSSNY supports an amendment to the SAFE Act, which would assure that only those who present a "serious and imminent threat to self or others" are reported. Moreover, MSSNY supports an amendment to the Act, which would clearly do away with the private right of action, which will result in litigation over the question of whether the reporter exercised reasonable professional judgment in the exercise of their duty. MSSNY seeks an amendment which would assure that the decision of a mental health professional to disclose or not to disclose, if exercised without malice or intentional misconduct, shall not be the basis for any civil or criminal liability.[55]

Yet another disclosure issue is whether the names of persons reported under the SAFE Act are discoverable under New York's Freedom of Information Law (FOIL). New York State takes the position that disclosure would violate FOIL's bar on disclosing confidential information amounting to an "unwarranted invasion of personal privacy."[56] This issue may require judicial resolution.

The Shooters Committee on Political Education (SCOPE), a staunch SAFE Act opponent, urged both gun owners and non-gun owners to file FOIL requests seeking to ascertain whether they have been the subject of a SAFE Act report. This would, SCOPE's leaders hoped, illuminate another SAFE Act problem and ignite more protest. The State Police, based on FOIL's protection for private information, refused to disclose whether the petitioner had him- or herself been reported. The petitioners obviously argued that disclosing information to a petitioner about him- or herself does not violate that petitioner's privacy.

County Officials Object to Unfunded State Mandates

The New York State Conference of Local Mental Hygiene Directors (CLMHD), the statewide organization for DCSs, criticized the SAFE Act for imposing on counties the burden of reviewing tens of thousands of reports without providing funds for additional staff. The conference complained that prolific hospital reporting has generated huge workloads for county mental hygiene directors.[57]

Second Amendment Challenges

In *Heller* (2008) and *McDonald* (2010), the US Supreme Court held that the Second Amendment right to keep a firearm at home for self-defense is not inconsistent with disqualifying people from firearms possession on account of mental illness.[58] However, the court did not say how mental illness should be defined, who should determine it, or, more critically, what process is due to a person facing forfeiture of Second Amendment rights.

Since *Heller* and *McDonald*, there have been several constitutional challenges to state laws that disarm people deemed to be mentally ill and dangerous.[59] In *United States v. Rehlander* (2012), the First Circuit US Court of Appeals held that Second Amendment rights cannot be extinguished on mental illness grounds without a due process hearing at which the respondent has an opportunity to contest the determination that he or she is mentally ill and dangerous.[60] Rehlander, a Maine resident, had been involuntarily hospitalized for suicidal impulses. Maine's procedure for involuntary commitment to a mental hospital required an application from a health care professional or a law enforcement officer supported by a medical examination. The application had to be endorsed by a judge or justice of the peace confirming that the proper procedure was followed.[61] Rehlander was released after a court found that the state had not met its burden of proving that he posed a risk sufficient to justify long-term involuntary commitment.[62] The trial judge found that although Rehlander needed treatment, he did not pose a risk of serious harm. Nevertheless, Rehlander's short-term hospitalization resulted in automatic revocation of his firearms license.

Twenty months later, Rehlander was convicted of violating federal law prohibiting a statutorily disqualified person from possessing a firearm. He challenged the indictment on the ground that his license revocation violated the Second and Fourteenth Amendments. The First Circuit overturned the conviction, holding that Rehlander had been "permanently deprived of the right to bear arms based solely on procedures suitable for temporary hospitalization under emergency conditions. . . . Nothing in those procedures provided an adversary proceeding to test whether the subject was mentally ill or dangerous [and] there is also no effective post-hospitalization means to recover the right to bear arms if the subject had in fact never been mentally ill or dangerous."[63] The court said further, "Although the right established in *Heller* is a qualified right . . . the right to possess arms (among those not properly disqualified) is no longer something that can be withdrawn by government on a permanent and irrevocable basis without due process. Ordinarily, to work a permanent or prolonged loss of a constitutional liberty or property interest, an adjudicatory hearing, including the right to offer and test evidence if facts are in dispute, is required. It is evidently doubtful that a [temporary commitment hearing] provides the necessary process for a permanent deprivation."[64]

In *Tyler v. Hillsdale County Sheriff's Department* (2014), the Sixth Circuit US Court of Appeals heard a challenge to a Michigan statute that imposed a lifetime firearms disqualification on persons who had ever been civilly committed to a mental hospital. The court struck down the statute because it did not include a procedure for restoring Second Amendment rights. "It is certain that there is a non-zero chance that a previously institutionalized person will commit gun violence in the future, but that is true of all classes of persons. . . . The government . . . has offered not an iota of evidence that prohibiting the previously institutionalized person from possessing guns serves its compelling interests."[65]

A court following the reasoning in *Rehlander* or *Tyler* would almost certainly reach the same conclusion regarding the SAFE Act's reporting provision, which lacks any procedure for challenging the determination that an individual is mentally ill and dangerous. No matter how stable the reported person's conduct after issuance of a SAFE Act report, he or she will be regarded for up to five years as too dangerous to possess a gun.[66] By contrast, New York provides more procedural protection to a person facing firearms disqualification on account of civil commitment. The state provides for a due process hearing to determine whether the individual is currently mentally ill and dangerousness. Upon release from the hospital, the previously committed person may petition the Commissioner of Mental Health for relief on the ground that "the person's record and reputation are such that the person is not likely to act in a manner contrary to public safety."[67] An individual whose Second Amendment rights are suspended based on a SAFE Act report is not authorized to petition the commissioner for relief.

The SAFE Act's procedural deficiencies are illuminated by comparison with California's law for reporting and disarming mentally ill and dangerous persons. California provides that individuals may, for five years, be deprived of their right to possess a gun if they communicate to a licensed psychotherapist a "serious threat of physical violence against a reasonably identifiable victim or victims."[68] When a licensed therapist notifies the police that a patient has made a credible threat to a specified individual, the police must notify the patient that he or she has a right to a court hearing to challenge the firearms disqualification. At that hearing, the state "bears the burden of showing by a preponderance of evidence that the reported person would not be likely to use firearms in a safe and lawful manner."[69]

Red-Flag Laws

Since the February 14, 2018, massacre at Marjory Stoneman Douglas High School in Parkland, Florida, so-called red-flag laws that authorize gun seizure based on a court order have attracted a great deal of attention. Like Connecticut's law, discussed earlier in this chapter, these schemes require a judge to find probable cause for the petitioner's or police's assertion that an individual poses an "extreme risk" to him- or herself or to others. If the judge agrees with the petitioner, he or she may issue a temporary extreme-risk protection order (sometimes ex parte) to prohibit the respondent from purchasing or possessing a firearm and order the person to surrender any firearms. The respondent is then entitled to an expedited court hearing with an opportunity to rebut the risk allegation. The judge will determine after the hearing whether to grant a final extreme-risk protection order. Florida and a number of other states passed similar laws after the Parkland massacre.[70]

In June 2018, Governor Cuomo began a statewide bus tour to promote passage of New York's version of a red-flag bill, which, not surprisingly, the governor boasted would go further than comparable bills in other states. According to his press office:

> Governor Andrew M. Cuomo today kicked off a statewide campaign to pass the Red Flag Gun Protection Bill, also known as the Extreme Risk Protection Order Bill. . . .
>
> The bill would prevent individuals determined by a court to have the potential to cause themselves or others serious harm from purchasing, possessing, or attempting to purchase or possess any type of firearm, including hand guns, rifles, or shotguns. This legislation builds on New York's strongest in the nation gun laws and prior legislative efforts, and, if passed, would make New York the first in the United States to empower its teachers and school administrators to prevent school shootings by pursuing court intervention.
>
> New York will not stand by and wait for Washington to take action against the gun violence and school shootings that have become all too common in this country. . . .
>
> "If a fellow colleague or student poses a demonstrable threat or danger to others, we should not enable them to own a gun," said Lieutenant Governor Kathy Hochul. "With this legislation, we're continuing our push for common sense gun measures by providing teachers and administrators with a right to report and possibly prevent a terrible tragedy. Gun violence has had an enormous toll on our communities, and New York is leading the nation in an effort to protect our students and save lives."[71]

The red-flag law will be a valuable addition to the New York State gun control regime. It does not require much in the way of implementation since its procedure is principally initiated by private parties (family, friends) who are concerned about a relative's or friend's mental state. Admittedly, the court may have to issue a temporary extreme-risk protection order, the police will have to serve the order and seize the respondent's firearms, and the court has to hold a hearing to determine whether to issue a final order. Still, this requires less administrative effort than the SAFE Act's reporting provision. Of course, the success of red-flag laws in preventing mass shootings and suicides depends on the private parties actually using them. In the states that have such laws, usage has been minimal. Connecticut has had a red-flag law since 1999, and it obviously was not invoked to stop the perpetrator of the Sandy Hook massacre. Moreover, like the SAFE Act reporting provisions, extreme-risk protection orders may give rise to civil liberties concerns, including the breadth of police powers to search the property of an individual subject to an order and the legality of seizing firearms owned by householders other than the target of the warrant.

Kendra's Law

In 1999, in response to two separate incidents in which mentally ill persons pushed strangers in front of New York City subway trains, "Kendra's Law" (named for one of the victims) authorized courts to issue assisted outpatient treatment (AOT) orders for potentially violent individuals suffering from mental illness. While the SAFE Act's amendments to Kendra's Law do not explicitly disarm persons subject to AOT orders, these provisions aim to facilitate the monitoring of potentially dangerous mentally ill persons living in the community. The SAFE Act's drafters probably assumed that such persons would also be reported under the SAFE Act's reporting provision.

Assisted Outpatient Treatment (AOT)

An individual is eligible for AOT if a court finds that he or she meets all of the following criteria:

- Is at least eighteen years old
- Is suffering from mental illness
- Is unlikely to survive safely in the community without supervision, based on a clinical determination
- Has a history of lack of compliance with treatment for mental illness that has

- prior to the filing of the petition, at least twice within the last thirty-six months been a significant factor in necessitating hospitalization in a hospital, or receipt of services in a forensic or other mental health unit of a correctional facility or a local correctional facility, not including any current period, or period ending within the last six months, during which the person is or was hospitalized or incarcerated; or
- prior to the filing of the petition, resulted in one or more acts of serious violent behavior toward self or others or threats of, or attempts at, serious physical harm to self or others within the last forty-eight months, not including any current period, or period ending within the last six months, in which the person was or is hospitalized or incarcerated
- Is, as a result of his or her mental illness, unlikely to voluntarily participate in the outpatient treatment that would enable him or her to live safely in the community
- In view of his or her treatment history and current behavior, is in need of assisted outpatient treatment in order to prevent a relapse or deterioration which would be likely to result in serious harm to the person or others
- Is likely to benefit from assisted outpatient treatment[72]

An AOT order is initiated by a court petition filed by a parent, spouse, or adult (eighteen years or older) roommate, sibling or child, director of a hospital where the person is hospitalized, director of a charitable organization or home providing mental health services, treating or supervising psychiatrist, licensed psychologist or licensed social worker, DCS or social services official in the person's county, or supervising parole or probation officer.[73] The petition must be supported by a sworn affidavit from a physician who has examined the person within the past ten days. The subject of the AOT petition must be notified of his or her rights to legal representation, to testify, to call and examine witnesses, and to appeal. The judge may grant the AOT petition if satisfied that AOT is "the least restrictive alternative available for the person" and that there is "clear and convincing evidence" establishing the AOT criteria.[74] If the AOT subject fails to comply with the treatment order, he or she may be hospitalized for up to seventy-two hours while a civil commitment determination is made.[75]

The SAFE Act's Amendments to Kendra's Law

The SAFE Act strengthened Kendra's Law by

- extending the law until June 30, 2017 (which was then subsequently extended until June 30, 2022);
- extending the duration of an initial AOT order from six months to one year;
- establishing procedures whereby an AOT order follows the patient from one state county to another, in the event that the patient moves residence;
- requiring a DCS, thirty days prior to the expiry of the order, to evaluate whether the order should be extended, in which case the DCS may petition for an additional year's treatment and supervision;
- authorizing a DCS to file a petition in the supreme or county court to renew an expiring AOT order in circumstances where the subject of the order cannot be evaluated prior to the order's expiration; and
- authorizing the sharing of information between Office of Mental Health–operated and Office of Mental Health–licensed facilities.[76]

Since the AOT petitioner must prove that the order is necessary "to prevent a relapse or deterioration which would be likely to result in serious harm to the person or others," a SAFE Act report should also be filed (particularly if the petitioner is a mental health professional). However, many AOT subjects will already have been rendered firearms-ineligible on account of previous criminal convictions or civil commitments.

Most advocacy groups and practitioner organizations, including the National Alliance on Mental Illness, the American Psychological Association, and the American Psychiatric Nurses Association, supported these SAFE Act AOT provisions. However, the New York Association of Psychiatric Rehabilitation Services, a coalition of more than one hundred community-based mental health services, criticized the provisions because they enlist physicians "to act as state control agents."[77] The New York Civil Liberties Union also opposes extending the duration of an AOT order from six months to one year, on due process grounds.[78]

* * *

The SAFE Act's mandatory reporting provision was a direct response to the Sandy Hook massacre, which was widely attributed to Adam Lanza's mental illness. The Act disqualifies from firearms possession a much-larger pool of people on mental illness grounds than federal or other states' laws. Essentially, it assigns mental health care professionals, broadly defined, the responsibility and obligation to report to county officials the names of patients whom they believe pose a risk of future violence. After county officials perfunctorily approve these clinician reports, the reported persons' names are added to a database of firearms-ineligible people. The problem is that neither FFLs nor NICS personnel have access to that database, a major implementation failure. This regulatory gap could be closed if (1) NICS were amended to allow states to report as firearms-ineligible a broader category of mentally ill persons who are not covered by the federal involuntary commitment and mentally defective criteria or (2) the state required FFLs to get approval from DCJS or the State Police before completing a firearms sale. The first option would be easier and cheaper. The second option would require creation of an information system connecting FFLs to DCJS and/or to the State Police. This ought to be done, but New York State was unable, for reasons of cost, to create such a system for conducting state-level background checks on ammunition purchasers.

If the reported person is a licensed handgun owner, that fact needs to be detected by DCJS and called to the attention of the relevant county licensing officer. DCJS claims to regularly match names in the New York SAFE Act reporting database to the database of licensed gun owners, but we have been unable to confirm how effectively this is done. When the county clerk receives notification that one of its handgun licensees has been reported under the SAFE Act, it should move to revoke the license and request local police to seize the reported individual's guns. As we have discussed in previous chapters, this is not an easy task because the police may not know about all the reported person's handguns and certainly not about his or her rifles and shotguns. The reported person may choose to hide some or all of his or her guns. Lack of licensing for long-gun ownership is a significant gap in New York State's gun control regime.

If the reported person is an unlicensed gun owner, the county licensing officer will not be involved. DCJS should, but as far as we know does not, notify the local police that the person has been added to the firearms-ineligible database. Police do not have the resources to investigate possible gun ownership in respect to the tens of thousands of persons who have been reported as mentally ill and potentially dangerous pursuant to the SAFE Act's reporting requirement. Indeed, the reported person is not even notified that he or she has been reported and therefore should not acquire or continue to possess a gun.

Mental health professionals, or at least the hospitals where they work, have not been reluctant to report patients to county DCSs, who overwhelmingly pass the names of reported persons to DCJS. If anything, unlike other SAFE Act provisions, the reporting provision has been "overimplemented." More than eighty-five thousand New York residents have been reported and may have had their Second Amendment rights suspended or revoked without due process. Given that after *Heller* and *McDonald* the right to keep and bear arms is a fundamental constitutional right, it is questionable whether this provision will ultimately survive legal challenge.

7

Disarming Persons Subject to Domestic Violence Protection Orders

New York State must stand strong against domestic violence by protecting victims and making sure those convicted of such crimes cannot inflict further damage.
—Governor Andrew Cuomo (August 1, 2011)[1]

Orders of protection are a significant way to shield domestic violence victims from any further attacks at the hands of their abuser. . . . While New York State has taken many steps to ensure that orders of protection are strongly and effectively enforced, we have a long way to go.
—Assemblywoman Helene Weinstein (November 4, 2016)[2]

In 2012, the year that the Sandy Hook massacre occurred, New York State law already authorized disarmament orders in domestic violence cases, in addition to temporary and final protection orders. In fact, the courts' standard protection-order form required the judge either to check or to leave blank a box ordering the protection-order respondent to surrender all firearms. New York anti-domestic-violence advocates were more concerned about implementation of gun-surrender orders than about amending the law to cover more protection-order subjects ("respondents"). There was little the SAFE Act drafting team could do to ensure the efficient execution of disarmament orders and to prevent respondents from acquiring guns. Disarming domestic violence abusers, both those who hold handgun licenses and those who possess guns illegally, is challenging because the massive number of protection orders (293,525 issued by state judges in 2015) overwhelms law enforcement resources.[3] This does not mean that laws prohibiting domestic violence protection-order respondents from possessing guns are not desirable. It does mean that such laws, while necessary, are not nearly sufficient to achieve their aim.

Federal Law on Disarming Domestic Violence Abusers

The 1994 Violence Against Women Act (VAWA) prohibited persons subject to domestic violence restraining orders from purchasing or possessing a firearm.[4] VAWA made it a federal felony (punishable by a maximum ten-year prison term) for a person to possess a firearm if he or she is subject to a court order restraining the respondent from harassing, stalking, or threatening an intimate partner, or the child of an intimate partner.

The Act only applies to orders (1) that are issued pursuant to an adversarial hearing for which the subject received actual notice and an opportunity to be heard and (2) that include a finding that the defendant represents a credible threat to the physical safety of the victim or victim's child. or by its terms explicitly prohibits the use, attempted use, or threatened use of physical force against an intimate partner or child that would reasonably be expected to cause bodily injury.[5] This excludes a large percentage of temporary protection orders issued at the request of a prosecutor or an alleged victim at a hearing, at which the alleged abuser is not present or represented. Intimate partners include persons who are coparents and persons who currently or previously lived together; the law does not cover violence between persons in a noncohabitating relationship.

A person who is federally disqualified from gun possession on account of a domestic violence conviction or a protection order will not pass an NICS background check and will thereby be unable to purchase a gun from an FFL. The only question is whether NICS receives notice of the protection order and, if so, receives it in time to block the sale. We cannot assume that this automatically occurs, as the Devin Kelly case in Southerland Springs, Texas, demonstrates. Although Kelly was convicted of beating up his wife and cracking his child's skull, the military did not notify NICS. Kelly subsequently murdered twenty-six and wounded twenty at the town's First Baptist Church in November 2017. Although we have been unable to confirm how efficiently NICS receives protection-order information from New York's various family, criminal, and trial courts, all of which issue protection orders, knowledgeable observers are confident that NICS is reliably notified of criminal convictions; family court protection orders are less reliably transmitted. As we have discussed in previous chapters, a person whom NICS blocks from purchasing a firearm from an FFL can still acquire a gun with the assistance of a straw purchaser or on the black market.

Although a firearms-ineligible person who is apprehended with a firearm commits a federal crime, prosecutions are extremely rare. In 2012, federal prosecutors nationwide charged fewer than fifty persons for unlawfully possessing a firearm on account of a domestic violence conviction or protection order.[6] The reality is that federal resources are drastically inadequate to investigate, prosecute, and adjudicate persons who possess firearms in violation of a protection order. Moreover, federal law enforcement agencies and prosecutors regard apprehending and prosecuting protection-order violators as the job of local police and district attorneys. Unfortunately, local police resources are also inadequate.[7]

Firearm Seizure Prior to Issuance of Protection Order

Federal law has no procedures for seizing guns. When and how to seize guns from firearms-ineligible persons is left to state law and police discretion. Unlike many states, New York does not require police officers to seize firearms at the scene of a domestic violence incident.[8] Local police thus act pursuant to departmental policy or to their own individual judgment. For example, the Nassau County Sheriff Department's policy states that officers should remove, when warranted, "all firearms, rifles and shotguns . . . from persons involved in domestic incidents."[9] In New York City, even if no arrest is made and the police do not seize guns at the scene, a licensee is required to notify the New York Police Department's Licensing Division that he or she has been "involved in a situation which [has come] to the attention of any police department, or other law enforcement agency." Failure to so notify may itself constitute grounds for license revocation.[10]

A responding police officer may seize a gun in plain view, perhaps in the alleged abuser's or victim's hands. The victim may also volunteer information about the guns owned by the alleged abuser. A judge may find such information sufficient to grant a search warrant. However, unless the officer arrests the apparent aggressor or remains at the scene, the gun's owner may hide it or park it with a friend. Search warrants are usually limited to specified areas and rarely give police authority to scour an entire premises, inside and out. Even if the police find a gun, they may fail to find others. Even if a domestic violence abuser is disarmed, how much that adds to the safety of family members and current and former intimate partners is unknown. As New York State statistics on intimate homicides bear out, abusers more often kill their victims with knives, other weapons, and their hands than with guns. (In New York, from 2007 to 2012, about 25 percent of domestic homicides were perpetrated with a firearm. In 2016, the proportion of domestic homicides perpetrated with a firearm was the same.)

Disarmament Pursuant to a Protection Order

New York's criminal and family court judges have long had authority to issue temporary and permanent domestic violence protection orders that include gun-surrender orders. After a police officer makes an arrest in a domestic violence incident, the arrestee is promptly arraigned in criminal court. The judge must fill out a standard form that, among other things, requires a decision on whether to issue a temporary order of protection. The judge must also decide whether to check the box ordering revocation of the arrestee's firearms license. In misdemeanor cases, the temporary protection order must be renewed at each court appearance. Upon plea or conviction, the judge may issue a final order of protection as part of the sentence. The final order's duration varies with the seriousness of the underlying offense: one year for violations, three years for misdemeanors, and five years for felonies. Criminal court judges must immediately notify the New York Division of Criminal Justice Services (DCJS) about the protection orders they issue. DCJS records them on a database available to state, county, and local law enforcement personnel.[11]

A person who fears imminent victimization by a current or former intimate partner or a family member may, on his or her own, or with assistance from an anti-domestic-violence advocate or lawyer, file a petition in family court asking for an order that the respondent stay away from and avoid contacting the petitioner. The petitioner must be a "member of the same family or household" or in an intimate or dating relationship with the alleged abuser. This definition includes persons who are related by blood, are legally married to each other, were formerly married to each other regardless of whether they still reside in the same household, or have a child in common regardless of whether such persons have been married or have lived together at any time.[12] The definition does not include partners who have never lived together and have not had children together. The family court judge, relying solely on the petitioner's allegations, can issue a temporary protection order. However, the protection order only becomes effective when it is served on the respondent, usually by a sheriff's deputy, a local police officer, or a private process server hired by the victim.[13] The judge must schedule a final protection order hearing within two weeks.[14] If the petitioner does not appear at that hearing, perhaps because he or she has reconciled with the abuser, the temporary order expires. If the victim does appear in court to press his or her petition but the alleged abuser does not appear, the judge may issue the final order, but it must be served on the respondent to be effective.[15] A family court final order of protection is generally valid for two years. Family court personnel are required to report temporary and final protection orders to the New York State Protection Order Registry, maintained by the Office of Court Administration (OCA).

Prior to the SAFE Act, when criminal and family court judges issued a temporary order of protection, they were required to suspend the alleged abuser's firearms license if there was good cause to believe that:

1. the defendant/respondent had a prior conviction for any violent felony offense; or
2. the defendant/respondent had previously been found to have willfully failed to obey a prior order of protection and such willful failure involved
   a. the infliction of serious physical injury;
   b. the use or threatened use of a deadly weapon or dangerous instrument; or
   c. behavior constituting any violent felony offense; or
3. the defendant had a prior conviction for stalking in the first to fourth degree.[16]

New York law also required criminal and family court judges to strip the subject of a permanent order of protection of his or her firearms, by prohibiting the person from acquiring firearms and revoking any license held by him or her. If a permanent protection order was issued by the family court, license revocation and firearms surrender was mandatory if the underlying conduct involved:

1. the infliction of serious physical injury;
2. the use or threatened use of a deadly weapon or dangerous instrument; or
3. behavior constituting any violent felony offense.

Even if those criteria were not met, a judge had a discretion to order suspension of the alleged abuser's license (in the case of a temporary order of protection) or revocation (in the case of a permanent protection order) if there was a "substantial risk" that the respondent might use or threaten to use a firearm unlawfully against the intimate partner or family member for whom the protection order was issued. Anti-domestic-violence activists believe that New York City judges routinely exercised their discretion to order gun surrender, but they are not as confident about judges in upstate counties where guns are far more common. They are also doubtful about judges' gun-surrender orders being regularly carried out.[17]

The SAFE Act's Domestic Violence Provisions

The SAFE Act made it mandatory for criminal and family court judges to revoke or suspend the protection-order respondent's firearm license in the event that the judge finds "substantial risk that the respondent may use or threaten to use a firearm unlawfully" against the protected party. The Act also lowered the threshold for license suspension from "serious physical injury" to "physical injury."[18] However, the judge still retains substantial discretion to determine whether there is a "substantial risk" and whether that risk involves "physical injury." Additionally, the Act gave family court judges authority to revoke, rather than suspend, the firearms license of a temporary order of protection respondent who willfully disobeys the temporary order's terms.

Determining Whether Respondent Has a Gun

Both criminal court and family court judges can check the gun-surrender box on the protection-order form regardless of whether they have reason to believe that the defendant actually has a gun. At first blush, it makes sense to order all domestic violence abusers who threaten violence to surrender their guns, but on reflection, this creates a huge workload for police charged with investigating and disarming several hundred thousand protection-order respondents. Ideally, from the police perspective, it would be desirable to know which protection-order defendants and respondents should be investigated.

Police and county prosecutors can query the State Police to find out whether a defendant charged with a domestic violence offense is a handgun licensee but not whether he or she possesses a rifle or shotgun. The victim may provide information about the abuser's guns. There is no reliable way to determine whether the domestic violence defendant is an unlicensed handgun possessor. Of course, the judge can ask the defendant, but unless the judge first advises the defendant that he or she need not answer and that confession to illegal gun possession can and will be used against him or her, that would violate the Fifth Amendment rights of an unlicensed gun possessor.

A family court judge is in a less advantageous position with respect to finding out about the respondent's possible gun possession because there is no prosecutor involved and the judge does not have access to the State Police's handgun-licensee database. Because not all protection orders are firearms disqualifying under federal law, OCA has developed an algorithm that identifies and passes along to NICS those orders that meet the federal criteria.

Implementing the Firearm Surrender Order

The defendant (criminal court) and the respondent (family court) must be given notice of the protection order and instructed that he or she may not possess a gun and, if he or she already has guns, where and how to surrender them. Surrender is not without its own complexities. If police officers serve a protection order that includes a firearm-surrender order, they will order the respondent to surrender his or her firearms on the spot; several officers are usually assigned to the task. More frequently, the gun owner is instructed to arrange to bring the guns to a police station. The surrender is considered voluntary, thereby immunizing the respondent from prosecution for unlawful firearms possession. For up to one year after the respondent surrenders his or her gun to the police, the owner is permitted to sell it to a licensed dealer. However, if a year passes without the gun owner having made a transfer arrangement, the police chief can declare the gun a nuisance and destroy it. Police complain that finding room for, keeping track of, and safely holding surrendered firearms is challenging.[19]

What if, as is frequently the case, the defendant or respondent falsely claims not to possess a gun or admits to possessing fewer firearms than the police believe he or she has? If the police have probable cause to believe that the defendant or respondent has guns at his or her residence or somewhere else, they can apply for a warrant to search the premises. The judge might be hesitant to issue a wide-ranging search warrant covering the respondent's entire property. (That is the kind of search likely to infuriate a gun owner, much more a wrongly suspect non–gun owner.) If the judge issues the search-warrant request, its execution can be intrusive and time-consuming, depending on the size of the respondent's house and property. Even then, the gun may not be found. Success is by no means guaranteed, as a 1998 murder/suicide case in Cattaraugus County illustrates. The court ordered Dahl Pearson to stay away from his wife and son and to surrender his firearms. (Pearson did not have a handgun license or apparently any handguns. However, he did own twenty to thirty rifles and shotguns.)[20] The county sheriff's deputy served the protection order on Pearson and demanded surrender of his guns. Pearson claimed that he had already disposed of them. At the deputy's insistence, Pearson signed a document stating that he no longer possessed any firearms and that he refused to provide any further information. Three months later, on October 4, 1998, Pearson killed his son and himself using a twenty-gauge shotgun.[21]

Preventing Protection-Order Respondents from Acquiring a Gun

Even if the domestic violence offender or protection-order respondent is disarmed, he or she might still attempt to acquire a new gun from an

FFL, from a black-market seller, by borrowing from a friend, or by theft. If the protection-order respondent's name is promptly entered into the statewide criminal record (rap sheet) database or the Protection Order Registry, and if the county clerk checks these databases before approving the necessary amendment to the respondent's firearms license, the firearms-disqualified individual should be blocked from purchasing a handgun from a licensed dealer. (Likewise, county clerks are often notified by the judge who issued the protection order.) No permit or county clerk amendment is needed to purchase a long gun. However, if the judge's protection order is communicated to NICS, the respondent will be blocked from purchasing a long gun from a law-abiding FFL. Still, the firearms-ineligible respondent could easily purchase a gun from a friend or a stranger who is willing to ignore the SAFE Act's universal-background-checking requirement.

Civil Liberties

There is a possibility that the SAFE Act provision disqualifying protection-order respondents from purchasing or possessing a firearm could be found to violate the Second Amendment. In *Voisine v. United States* (2016) the Supreme Court upheld (6–2) the federal law imposing lifetime firearms disqualification for conviction of misdemeanor domestic violence assault.[22] The majority said that to rule otherwise would open a "dangerous loophole" in the federal gun control regime. The majority limited itself to this statutory interpretation issue, declining to opine on whether lifetime forfeiture for a domestic violence misdemeanor violates the Second Amendment. In a vigorous dissent, Justice Clarence Thomas argued that permanent loss of Second Amendment rights for an unintentional assault is unconstitutional (in Maine, where the case arose, domestic violence assault included reckless injury to the victim):

> Under the majority's reading, a single conviction under a state assault statute for recklessly causing an injury to a family member—such as by texting while driving—can now trigger a lifetime ban on gun ownership. . . . We treat no other constitutional right so cavalierly. At oral argument the Government could not identify any other fundamental constitutional right that a person could lose forever by a single conviction for an

infraction punishable by only a fine. . . . In construing the statute before us expansively so that causing a single minor reckless injury or offensive touching can lead someone to lose his right to bear arms forever, the Court continues to "relegat[e] the Second Amendment to a second class right."[23]

The Supreme Court has not ruled on the constitutionality of disarming the subjects of domestic violence protection orders, but several US Circuit Courts of Appeal have held that the federal firearms disqualification for persons subject to a domestic violence protection order violates neither the Second Amendment's right to keep and bear arms, nor the Fifth and Fourteenth Amendments' right to due process of law.[24] However, federal law only renders firearms-disqualified an individual who is subject to a domestic violence protection order "issued after a hearing at which the respondent had an opportunity to participate." Therefore, this federal rule might not apply to some protection orders issued by family courts because hearings in family courts are typically conducted ex parte (with the respondent lacking notice).

Even a protection-order firearms disqualification following a due process hearing might be constitutionally vulnerable on substantive due process grounds—that is, that it lacks a rational basis. That argument would be strongest if the abuse allegation did not involve a gun. In *United States v. Chapman* (2012), the Fourth Circuit said that the "exceedingly narrow" sweep of the federal law constituted a "reasonable fit" between the prohibition on gun possession by domestic violence protection-order subjects and the government's goal of reducing domestic gun violence.[25] The court emphasized that the firearm disqualification was limited to respondents with protection orders currently in force, the West Virginia court's order had a 180-day duration, the respondent was entitled to a hearing for which he received actual notice and an opportunity to participate, and the order prohibited harassment stalking or threatening or engaging in conduct that would place an intimate partner or child in reasonable fear of bodily injury.[26]

A protection order issued after a less-respondent-friendly procedure would present a stronger Second Amendment issue, for example, pursuant to a statute that authorizes seizure of firearms pursuant to an ex parte order based on allegations of threats that did not involve a gun.

Moreover, it is sometimes difficult to determine before a trial which intimate partner or family member is the aggressor and which person has a legitimate need for self-defense options.[27] According to the National Center on Domestic and Sexual Violence's "Practitioner's Guide to Family Court Litigation:"

> Another consequence of bringing a family offense case is the risk of retaliatory or unwanted litigation. Oftentimes the mere filing of a family offense petition incites batterers and encourages them to initiate cases or claims that may not have otherwise pursued. For example, a batterer served with a temporary protection order may retaliate by filing a cross-petition in which he alleges he is the victim and seeks a protection order. While family court policy discourages the issuance of mutual, ex parte protection orders, courts occasionally issue them. In these instances, a victim becomes subject to New York's mandatory arrest law requiring the arrest of a suspect alleged to have violated a protection order. In fact, some batterers intentionally use this statute to have victims arrested on false charges to intimidate them, control them and discourage them from pursuing family court relief. In the criminal context, where parties file cross-complaints, the police will determine who the "primary physical aggressor" was before making an arrest (although such a determination does not prevent officers from arresting both parties).[28]

The duration of the firearms license disqualification should also bear on the constitutionality of a protection order's firearm disqualification. The longer the protection order's duration, the stronger the challenger's constitutional argument. A generation ago, protection orders usually were imposed for a maximum of six months, albeit sometimes with the possibility of one six-month renewal. Today, many protection orders have a two-year or even five-year duration. When the protection order expires, the defendant's or respondent's firearms are not automatically returned; that requires a court order, which, according to gun owners, is often indefinitely delayed.

* * *

Why the SAFE Act's drafters did not include a provision requiring seizure of firearms by police at the scene of a domestic violence disturbance is puzzling. Perhaps the perception was that police already have sufficient authority to accomplish such seizures.

In the spring of 2018, New York enacted a new law, disqualifying a wider group of domestic violence abusers from firearms possession. At the signing ceremony, Governor Cuomo said, "With this legislation, we can sever the undeniable connection between domestic abuse and deadly gun violence, and continue to build upon the strongest gun laws in the nation."[29] The 2018 law (1) expanded the range of misdemeanor convictions that trigger disarmament, including menacing and assault, and created a procedure for criminal court judges to report those convictions to DCJS, (2) included language to prevent those who are subject to arrest warrants from obtaining or renewing a handgun license, and (3) included language to assure that, upon conviction for a serious offense or a protection order that includes gun surrender, surrender orders are applied by law enforcement to all of the offenders' firearms, not just handguns.

Prior to the SAFE Act, New York State judges had a discretion under certain circumstances to include a disarmament order with a protection order. Although there was no evidence to suggest that judges were ordering disarmament in too few domestic violence cases, the SAFE Act drafters made disarmament orders mandatory in more circumstances. We can safely assume that, prior to the SAFE Act, judges routinely ordered disarmament in egregious cases, that is, those involving threats with a firearm. The SAFE Act amendment assured that gun-surrender orders are issued in a greater percentage of cases. The Act expanded the pool of gun-surrender orders to be executed, although the pre–SAFE Act number already far exceeded police capacity. It is useful to remember that in the majority of New York State counties, there are zero to one domestic violence homicides annually. No county outside of New York City has more than five. And about a quarter of all these domestic and intimate homicides involve a gun.

Advocates for victims of domestic violence say that the real obstacle to disarming domestic abusers is not inadequate substantive law but inadequate implementation.[30] The state's information systems do not make it easy to find out if a protection-order respondent has a license that should be revoked. County clerks and licensing officers are not always notified about protection orders against "their licensees." After revocation, the police still face the daunting challenge of effectuating the surrender of all firearms. A list of the licensee's handguns should be available at the county clerk's office, but there is no record of rifles and shotguns,

The problem is not inadequate law but insufficient police resources. There are simply not enough police to investigate the vast pool of protection-order respondents subject to disarmament orders. Ironically, the police would be more effective in carrying out disarmament orders if they could focus on the most high-risk protection-order defendants and respondents rather than on all such respondents and defendants. If there is no way to prioritize respondents and defendants with regard to homicidal risk, courts and police are left with an insurmountable task.

There are approximately 135–140 domestic homicides per year in a state that produces three hundred thousand domestic violence protection orders. About 60 percent of domestic homicides are intimate-partner homicides. Of the intimate-partner homicides, about one-third are perpetrated with a gun. All told, there were twenty-five intimate partners murdered with guns in 2016. Reducing the annual total of intimate-partner gun homicides each year by attempting to disarm three hundred thousand domestic abusers is something like finding a needle in a haystack.

The effort to disarm domestic abusers is severely undermined if those who are disarmed can easily acquire new firearms. Even in New York State, it is easy for an individual whose name has been added to the Protection Order Registry to obtain a gun. There is a good chance that NICS would not identify a prospective rifle or shotgun purchaser as firearms-ineligible on account of a disqualifying protection order. More importantly, it remains easy for an individual subject to a protection order to acquire a gun on the secondary or black market or in the primary market by means of a straw purchaser. Moreover, two-thirds of intimate-partner homicide victims are killed by means other than a firearm. This means that anti-domestic-violence strategies other than gun control should be high priorities.

8

Recertifying Handgun Licensees

Under New York State law, drivers, cosmetologists, waxers
and barbers all must renew their licenses every few years,
yet handgun owners get a lifetime pass. It's absurd that New
York State is more interested in the mental health of the person who waxes your eyebrows than someone who owns a
gun.
—State Senator Eric Schneiderman, Apr. 23, 2009[1]

I can tell you that there is a general feeling that people do not
want to [re]certify either online or early. Anecdotally, most
of what I am hearing from people is that they plan on re-
filing at the latest possible date by certified mail unless the
law is overturned or repealed first.
—Stephen Aldstadt (president of the New York State Shooter's Committee on Political Education), January 21, 2015[2]

Practically all US states require firearm licenses, at least to carry a concealed weapon in public. The majority of states have "shall issue" laws
that provide for a presumptive right to issuance of a carry license. These
states invariably require license renewal every few (typically five) years.

New York is a restrictive handgun-licensing state for both premises
and carry licenses. The onus is on the applicant to show good character
and, for a carry permit, special need as well. However, before passage of
the SAFE Act, New York did not require license renewal or recertification. A state handgun license was valid indefinitely, except in New York
City, which required license renewal every three years for both long guns
and handguns, and in Nassau, Suffolk, and Westchester Counties, which
required handgun license renewal every five years. A handgun licensee
who was convicted of a felony or a domestic violence misdemeanor
or who became firearms-ineligible for any other reason was subject to

license revocation. Revocation did not occur automatically; it required action by the firearms-licensing official in the county where that license was issued. Since state law already required that such persons have their licenses revoked, the SAFE Act's drafters were probably concerned that disqualifying events were not reliably resulting in revocation. Consequently, the Act required every person whose handgun license was issued prior to the effective date of the Act (January 15, 2013) to apply to the State Police for renewal ("recertification") by January 31, 2018, and, if renewed, every five years thereafter.[3] Individuals who are issued licenses after January 15, 2013, must apply for recertification five years from the date their license was issued.

While the benefits of handgun-license recertification are difficult to assess, the costs are considerable. The State Police face an enormous administrative challenge in processing hundreds of thousands of recertification applications. For county clerks, the task of determining whether nonapplicants have moved out of state, have died, or need to have their licenses revoked amounts to a substantial administrative burden.

Brief Review of the New York State Firearm-Licensing System

The New York State Sullivan Act of 1911 provides that county licensing officers may issue a handgun "premises" license to an applicant who has no statutory disqualifications and demonstrates "good moral character," based on at least four personal references.[4] A concealed-carry license may be issued to an applicant who, in addition to good character, demonstrates "proper cause" (special need to carry a gun). The licensing officer relies on the county sheriff's and county clerk's investigation and recommendation. The sheriff has access to state-level databases of persons disqualified on account of their criminal record or mental illness. The county clerks maintain county handgun-licensing records. A county clerk's office has staff or, in some of the bigger counties, units responsible for handgun licensing. The county clerk's office is responsible for issuing new handgun-license applications; processing licenses for amendments, acquisitions, disposals, for transfers; and for maintaining handgun-license files.

A handgun licensee is authorized to possess only those handguns, identified by manufacturer, model, and serial number, listed on their license. An unlimited number of handguns can be listed. Before a licensee acquires a handgun from a licensed dealer, the licensee must file an amendment to his or her license with the county clerk and obtain a permit to purchase. A copy of the permit to purchase must then be shown to the licensed dealer. Prior to the SAFE Act, a handgun purchaser did not have to show any documents to a nonlicensed seller. The SAFE Act requires all sales to be processed through a licensed dealer. Because the clerk is supposed to send a copy of the amendment to the State Police within ten days, the State Police should have up-to-date information on the handguns possessed by every licensee.

New York law states that a license is revocable if the licensee becomes subject to a statutory disqualification.[5] Nevertheless, despite the apparently mandatory language, license revocation does not occur automatically. The county licensing officer must determine whether the license should be suspended or revoked. This requires notice to the licensee and an opportunity for the licensee to show cause as to why his or her license should not be revoked; a hearing is not obligatory. Upon revocation, the gun owner is required immediately to surrender *all firearms*, including long guns. The sheriff or police may or may not be successful in seizing the revoked licensee's firearms for the reasons discussed in chapters 6 and 7. The county sheriff or local police chief must notify the county firearms officer and State Police about surrendered firearms in their possession. Possession of a firearm by a revoked licensee is punishable as a class E felony.[6]

Recertification Provisions

The Act's recertification provisions require handgun licensees to apply to the State Police for license renewal every five years. Those persons with licenses issued prior to January 15, 2013 (the effective date of the SAFE Act), must apply no later than January 31, 2018, and thereafter every five years. Those licensed after January 15, 2013, must apply for recertification five years from the date of issuance. (Recertification does not apply to handgun licensees in New York City and Nassau, Suffolk, and Westchester Counties, where county-level recertification is already required.)

The SAFE Act specified that the application for recertification to be devised by the State Police must "request the license holder's name, date of birth, gender, race, residential address, Social Security number, firearms possessed, email address at the option of the license holder and an affirmation that the licensee is not subject to a statutory firearms disqualification." Applicants do not have to submit new character references. The Act also provides for background checking, "limited to determining whether the [federal law disqualifications] apply or whether a registrant has been convicted of a serious offense . . . or whether a report has been issued pursuant to section 9.46" (the SAFE Act's provision mandating mental health professionals report on patients deemed to be a danger to themselves or others). The Act's recertification provisions do not mention being subject to a domestic violence restraining order as a disqualification. Surprisingly, as we shall see, recertification has been implemented without any background checking.[7]

The SAFE Act's drafters were not the first to identify the state's lack of a recertification procedure as a regulatory weakness. Democratic Party senators and assembly members had several times unsuccessfully introduced bills to require quinquennial handgun-license recertification. The most prominent effort occurred in 2009 following the massacre at the American Civic Association Immigration Center in Binghamton (thirteen dead, four seriously wounded). The shooter had held a handgun license since 1997. Then–state senator (later state attorney general) Eric Schneiderman and Assemblywoman Amy Paulin insisted that the Binghamton shooting demonstrated the need to change the state's "dangerous lifetime permit system."[8] Clearly Schneiderman and Paulin regarded the purpose of recertification to be identification and disarmament of disqualified licensees. However, even if the Binghamton shooter's license had been subject to recertification review between the date of issue and the massacre, there was nothing disqualifying on his record. The media reported that police had arrested, cited, or had minor contact with the perpetrator at least five times since 1990. About ten years prior to the massacre, the New York State Police had investigated him following a tip that he had a crack-cocaine habit and planned to rob a bank. Nothing came of it. He obtained a handgun license in 1997.[9]

Computerization of State Handgun License Records

A key component of the SAFE Act recertification initiative is the creation of an up-to-date, digitized State Police handgun-licensee database.

The State Police regard creation of a "pristine handgun-licensee database," purged of licensees who have died, moved out of state, or had their licenses revoked, as an important end in itself. The Act requires the State Police to create a "Statewide License and Record Database," capable of communicating with the firearms-disqualification databases held by the Division of Criminal Justice Services, the Office of Mental Health, and the Office of Court Administration, in order to identify licensees who should be revoked.[10] State Police officials believe that an additional advantage is that an up-to-date licensee database could more reliably alert police on their way to a residence to the possible presence of a person with a handgun.

Using earmarked funds from the state's 2013 budget, the State Police digitized their paper licensee records. They also requested that counties submit new licensee information electronically and share electronic records from prior years if they had them. (Some county clerks balked at these requests, insisting that if the State Police wished to use a county's electronic records, the state should reimburse county funds previously expended on digitizing their handgun-license records.)

Implementing Recertification

The SAFE Act did not specify what handgun recertification would involve. License renewal, like licensing itself, comes in many different forms, ranging from stringent testing and vetting (medical licenses) to no vetting at all (fishing). Consider driver's license renewal, often held up as a model for firearms licensing. In New York, an initial driver's license is issued by the State Department of Motor Vehicles, which has an office in every county in the state, only after the applicant passes a written test on basic road rules and a short driving competency test. Once issued, a driver's license is valid for eight years and can be renewed online. The renewal applicant need only fill in current residential information, give proof of a vision test, and pay a fee. Dangerous drivers are not removed from the road at the license renewal stage but upon conviction of certain crimes, traffic violations, or failure to possess automobile insurance.

We assumed that since the SAFE Act stated that recertification for handgun licensees is limited to determining whether the federal law disqualifications apply, whether a licensee has been convicted of a serious offense or whether the licensee has been reported as a danger to self or others, *at least that much background checking* would be required. Our assumption was incorrect. According to the State Police Counsel's Office, the State Police are not conducting background checks on recertification applicants. Rather, the applicant's affirmation on the application form that he or she is not subject to disqualification is accepted as truthful and sufficient for recertification. The goal of recertification appears to have shifted from assuring revocation of disqualified licensees to establishment of a licensee database purged of licensees who are deceased, no longer living in New York, or no longer interested in having a license. According to the State Police spokesman "This is essentially a record-keeping exercise. . . . We don't know how accurate our pistol permit records are because they go back decades."[11] Clearly, the SAFE Act's drafters intended recertification to be more than just a "record-keeping exercise."

Preparing for Recertification

Shortly after the SAFE Act's enactment, the governor appointed a SAFE Act committee composed of representatives from the governor's office, the Office of Mental Health, the Sheriffs' Association, the New York State Association of County Clerks, and the Office of Court Administration to work out the details of SAFE Act implementation, including the recertification scheme. The State Police initially proposed sending out recertification applications in five tranches over the period 2013–2018 in order to avoid being inundated by applications around the January 2018 deadline. If a large number of licensees waited until the last minute to submit applications, the backlog might take years to clear. (SAFE Act opponents hoped that exactly this would happen, triggering further criticism of the Act's recertification scheme.) Staggered recertification deadlines, beginning in say January 2015, would have placed less strain on the State Police but would have required amending the Act. Alternatively, the State Police could have encouraged, or perhaps incentivized, licensees to apply early.

In fall 2013, the SAFE Act committee ceased meeting regularly. Persons close to the committee speculate that the governor, surprised by the extent of local governments' and gun owners' opposition to the SAFE Act, did not want to implement recertification prior to the 2014 gubernatorial election. Perhaps the same concern delayed recertification until after the 2016 presidential election. Ultimately, recertification did not become operational until March 2017, more than four years after the SAFE Act's passage.

Gun Owners' Opposition to Recertification

For gun owners, the seeds of opposition to recertification may have been planted in 2010, when the media publicized the identity of over a million handgun licensees. Although New York law states that "the name and address of any person to whom an application for any license has been granted shall be a public record," up until the early 1990s, the State Police handgun-licensee records were held in hard copy and therefore not disclosable in bulk. The State Police and county clerks only disclosed the identity of firearms licensees in response to Freedom of Information Law (FOIL) requests for information about specific individuals. However, licensee records have progressively been digitized, and in 2010 a website called Who's Packing NY posted the names and addresses of 1.3 million handgun licensees, on the basis of information disclosed by the State Police in response to a bulk FOIL request.[12] Gun owners reacted angrily, claiming that criminals would target licensees' homes to steal guns and that anti-gun neighbors would shun licensees.[13]

The media, advocates for open government, and some gun control proponents argue that New York residents have legitimate safety concerns in knowing which members of their communities are licensed to own and to carry a handgun. Some people might use such knowledge to inform where they choose to live and to avoid particular neighbors' homes. Moreover, given information about other types of license holders (lawyers, doctors) is in the public domain, they argue that the identity of handgun-license holders should also be available.

The New York Senate passed a Republican-sponsored bill to keep the names and addresses of handgun licensees confidential (except in cases where a FOIL request was made with respect to a named individual), but it stalled in the Assembly. Several subsequent legislative attempts also failed.[14]

The controversy over disclosing the names of handgun licensees re-ignited on December 23, 2012 (nine days after Sandy Hook), when the *Journal News* published the names of 33,614 Westchester County and Rockland County handgun licensees (obtained via a FOIL request), along with a map showing the licensees' residential addresses.[15] Putnam County refused a similar newspaper FOIL request but was ordered by a state Supreme Court judge to disclose the handgun licensees' names. Putnam County Clerk Dennis Sant opposed the request: "I could not live with myself if one Putnam pistol permit holder was put in harm's way, for the sole purpose of selling newspapers." Judge Robert Neary held that the while "these provisions address legitimate issues of privacy and safety held by pistol license holders, . . . they also unequivocally di-rect the public disclosure of names and addresses of license holders who did not choose to seek an exception."[16] Then *Gawker* posted the names of 22,688 New York City firearms licensees.[17]

Gun owners claimed that these public disclosures not only violated their privacy interests but were also meant to cast indirect blame for the Sandy Hook massacre and to insinuate that licensed handgun own-ers posed a threat of future gun crime or mass shootings.[18] The NRA called the disclosures a "gun thief shopping list."[19] Even some nonli-censees criticized disclosure on the ground that it made them more vul-nerable to crime since would-be burglars would opt to break into their homes rather than those of handgun licensees.[20] (A June 2013 *Journal News* follow-up story reported that the feared burglary spree had not materialized.)[21]

The SAFE Act's drafters, apparently sensitive to these protests, in-cluded in the Act a 120-day moratorium on public access to handgun-licensee information. During this period, licensees could file a "New York State Firearms License Request for Public Records Exemption."[22] The requester had to base the request on at least one of four grounds:

1. The applicant's life or safety is endangered because the applicant is an active or retired police, peace, probation, parole, or correc-tions officer; a protected person under a currently valid order of protection; a witness in a criminal proceeding involving a crimi-nal charge; participating or previously participated as a juror in a criminal proceeding; or is or was a member of a grand jury.

2. The applicant is the spouse, domestic partner, or household member of a protected person.
3. The applicant has reason to believe his or her life or safety may be endangered by disclosure due to reasons stated by the applicant.
4. The applicant has reason to believe he or she may be subject to unwarranted harassment upon disclosure.[23]

This is tantamount to nondisclosure upon request, since any handgun licensee could claim reason to believe that disclosure of his or her handgun license would result in "unwarranted harassment."

Some pro-gun politicians claimed victory. Praising the opt-out provision, Putnam County's Republican senator said, "We have won a big battle against [the *Journal News*'] unwarranted invasion of privacy" and have "put an end to this public safety nightmare."[24] Putnam County Assemblyman Steve Katz said that the "only bright spot in the gun control legislation is that the *Journal News* will never again be able to endanger the law-abiding gun owners of Putnam County and our state with a malicious FOIL request."[25] The county's executive claimed that the opt-out provision vindicated his opposition to handgun-licensee disclosure: "The Governor and the state legislature saw the logic and recognized the merit of our stand and as a result, state laws were changed. . . . The text of this law reaffirms our position that the importance of protecting an individual's privacy far exceeds any unfettered 'right to know.'"[26]

Some gun owners' anger and sense of victimization was not fully assuaged, expressing doubts that the State Police and other government agencies would keep licensee information confidential. Subsequently, Republicans introduced legislation in both chambers to change the "opt-out" presumption from disclosure to nondisclosure. In other words, the Republicans preferred that a licensee's status not be disclosed unless he or she filed a disclosure request. As of summer 2018, that bill had not been enacted.

The Counties Resist

More surprising than gun owners' opposition to recertification was county clerks' opposition. County clerks complained that, although they are the linchpins of New York's handgun-licensing regime, they were not consulted during the SAFE Act drafting process or in the design of the recertification procedure. They also complained about a lack of communication from state officials about the state's progress with rolling out the recertification scheme and about the role it contemplated clerks would play in implementing it. Rensselaer County Clerk Frank Merola articulated the view of many of his colleagues when he said, "It took [the State Police] almost four years from the day the SAFE Act was passed to implement the most important segment of the Act, and when they do it, there is little notice, and little communication with the officials who have the most day to day contact with these license holders."[27] The New York State Association of County Clerks passed a resolution criticizing recertification as an "unfunded mandate on county taxpayers" and demanded that the state bear the costs of the program.[28] Between December 2013 and January 2014, forty-four counties passed resolutions prohibiting state agencies from using county seals on any correspondence concerning the SAFE Act and, in particular, on any materials related to recertification. For example, Cayuga County passed a resolution in January 2014 stating:

> WHEREAS, in recent discussions the State has indicated an interest in using the Seal of the Cayuga County and the names of the Offices of the Cayuga County Sheriff and Cayuga County Clerk in pistol permit recertification notices; and
>
> WHEREAS, the County Sheriff and Clerk have voiced their strong objection to this request and suggestion; now therefore be it
>
> RESOLVED, that the Cayuga County Legislature denies the State of New York permission to use the name, seal of the county, letterhead or address for purposes of correspondence with legal and registered gun owners regarding permit recertification or for any purpose associated with the SAFE Act.[29]

While the resolutions have expressive significance, counties do not have legal authority to prohibit state agencies in this way.

Recertification Is Launched: January 2017

It took the state four years to launch recertification. On January 3, 2017, the State Police announced that recertification applications could be downloaded from the State Police's website and that completed applications could be submitted electronically.[30] Licensees could also obtain and submit printed application forms by mail. The applicant must provide license details (the date when and county location where the license was issued), their identifying information (driver's license number; social security number), and demographic characteristics (race, height, weight, eye and hair color), as well as identifying information for each handgun (manufacturer, model, caliber, serial number). Recertification is free of charge.

Implementation Challenges for State Police

The SAFE Act's handgun-licensee recertification program poses extraordinary challenges for both the State Police and county clerks. Until the SAFE Act, the State Police did not play a major role in implementing handgun licensing. It is essentially a law enforcement agency, not a regulatory agency. For those who are interested in analogizing the driver licensing system to the handgun licensing system, consider that the Department of Motor Vehicles is a state-level agency in charge of all initial licensing, all renewals, and all revocations. It has offices in every county.

There may be as many as two million persons to whom a New York handgun license has ever been issued. State Police officials have told us (off the record) that they expect that at least 500,000 persons may submit applications. By the recertification deadline (January 31, 2018), the State Police had received 290,000 recertification applications. However, applications continued to be accepted; they totaled 345,000 by the first week of June 2018. The State Police will not disclose how many individuals are assigned to process the recertification applications, but let us assume that there are twelve full-time staffers (as we have been told off the record). If these staffers spent thirty-five hours per week doing nothing but processing applications, and if it takes just ten minutes to check over the form, record the information, and notify the necessary parties, it would take forty weeks to complete 100,000 applications and four years to process 500,000. If some applications require further attention, vetting would take even longer. Additionally, people who were issued their initial handgun licenses after January 15, 2013, will be due to submit recertification applications, adding to the workload.

The State Police decided that recertification, at least for now, does *not* include background checking; rather, it relies on the applicant's word that he or she is not statutorily disqualified from holding a license. Not surprisingly, practically every application for recertification is approved. The only reason an application will be rejected is an error in filling out the form. Seventy percent of recertification applicants apply online and receive an immediate approval unless there is an error on the form. However, notification to hard-copy applicants takes approximately four months.

Investigating and Revoking Nonapplicants

If and when the State Police do clear the avalanche of recertification applications, they will need to determine which licensees have not applied for recertification ("nonapplicants"). If the 1.3 million licensee names disclosed in 2010 represent a ballpark figure for the number of current licensees, then recent application figures imply that nearly a million licensees have failed to recertify. These will include persons who are deceased, no longer living in the state, or no longer interested in having a license, as well as those who intentionally or inadvertently failed to apply. Some nonapplicants can be purged from the licensee database by cross-checking death records. The State Police can assume that persons whose licenses were issued before a certain date, say, January 1, 1940, are dead. (Of course, that could have been done in the absence of a recertification procedure.) To determine whether a presumably living licensee is still a state resident, the State Police could cross-check drivers' licenses. If a nonapplicant licensee can be traced to a residential address, the relevant county clerk will have to be notified in order to initiate the license revocation process. If the nonapplicant cannot be traced to a residence through their driver's license and other databases, the State Police may assume that the person is dead or living out of state.

The State Police argue that it is not their responsibility and that they lack resources to determine whether nonapplicants are still alive, still reside in-state, and still own the handguns listed on their licenses. They insist that this is the responsibility of the county clerks. The county clerks strongly disagree, calling recertification a wholly state initiative. As of summer 2018, this dispute remains unresolved. The process of accounting for and vetting nonapplicants has not begun.

It is true that the clerks have statutory responsibility for revoking licenses whether on account of a licensee not submitting a recertification application or other statutory disqualification. But the State Police have responsibility for creating and maintaining the handgun-licensee database. Arguably, they could purge the names of persons born before a certain date or listed in state death records.

If anyone is tasked with determining whether a presumptively living licensee still resides in the county, it is the county clerk. Yet the clerks' resources are far from adequate. A former president of the New York State Association of County Clerks told us that "no one will track down licensees who have moved to another county." According to Oneida County's assistant licensing officer:

> I, along with other counties, I believe, would be pretty confident to say that we're not going to have the ability to handle the revocations if as many people don't recertify as I think they're going to. . . . There's just shy of 29,000 registered gun owners in Oneida County. I think there might be as many as 10,000 who don't recertify. Even if there was 1,000 who don't recertify, that's 1,000 revocations that (an Oneida County Court judge) has to issue and 1,000 residences that law enforcement has to go to and if they all only have one gun—that's 1,000 guns.[31]

The county sheriffs complain that they lack resources to investigate and disarm rejected applicants and nonapplicants. The Saratoga County sheriff said, "I will not commit resources by taking deputies off the street to enforce this SAFE Act provision when our deputies have important work to do keeping our communities a safe place."[32] Local police agencies will bear the greatest responsibility for assuring that revoked licensees are disarmed. This is likely to be a huge job, requiring contact (probably home visits) with revoked licensees to seize their guns or confirm that the guns have been properly disposed of. Guns turned over to the local police have to be properly tagged and secured—no modest task, especially for a small police department.

* * *

The SAFE Act's drafters apparently assumed that failure to bring license-disqualifying events to the attention of county officials is a significant problem. Even if that empirical assumption were true, it would have been easier and cheaper to improve the flow of information about disqualifying events (e.g., convictions, mental health reports, and domestic violence protection orders) to the county firearms licensing officers than to vet and process more than a million applicants and nonapplicants. Moreover, even if the SAFE Act's drafters were right about the problem, quinquennial recertification is not an effective solution, since the licensee's disqualification could arise during the five years between recertification. Consider that when a driver is convicted of a violation, the Department of Motor Vehicles is immediately notified, and if the defendant's record warrants, the license is immediately revoked. Revocation does not await vetting pursuant to a five-year renewal cycle.

The State Police decided that recertification, at least for now, does *not* include background checking; rather, it relies on the applicant's word that he or she is not statutorily disqualified. Not surprisingly, practically every application for recertification is approved. There is no reason, other than insufficient staff and the need to respond to applicants expeditiously, not to check the recertification applicant's name against the disqualifying databases. Indeed, we believe that the SAFE Act's drafters included the recertification provision for that very reason—that is, to ensure that a county clerk is notified that a licensee had become firearms-ineligible.

The only remaining purpose of recertification is to create an up-to-date licensee database. We do not see what law enforcement advantages accrue from the deletion of deceased and out-of-state-residents from the database. State Police officials claim that it will be useful to local police officers, answering a call for assistance, to know that the alleged troublemaker is a handgun licensee. This assumes that the responding police have a name and supplemental identification information to check against the State Police's licensee database; that probably is rarely the case. The troublemaker may be an intruder or visitor. (Moreover, individuals who own rifles or shotguns, but not handguns, are not included in the database.) Perhaps the State Police database will be searchable by address as well, but we have been unable to confirm that that is or will be possible. In any event, police report that gun-crime arrestees are rarely licensees. Police should never assume that there will be no gun present at a crime-in-progress destination.

An online statewide license and record database would have real value if it were linked to the databases of firearms-disqualifiable persons. Such a system would be similar, except for the role of county officials, to the driver's license system.

Putting aside whether law enforcement would benefit from having a pristine handgun-licensee database, producing such a database is far from assured. The State Police will have to identify people holding licenses who do not submit recertification applications. And either or both the State Police and the county clerks will have to investigate whether these nonapplicants still live in the state. Revocation procedures will have to be initiated against those who do.

Implementation of the SAFE Act's recertification provisions holds a number of lessons for other states. First, the purpose of recertification needs to be carefully thought through, because that should dictate what background checking, if any, is required. If the goal is to create a double check that ensures that persons with revocable events on their record are denied firearm licenses, the recertification process has to include a search of those records. In New York, this appears to be reliably done at the time of the initial licensing decision. It would only need to be done again if there is a lack of confidence that a subsequent disqualification will be promptly communicated to the county licensing officer. If such a lack of confidence exists, it ought to be addressed by improving communication between the court or administrative agency that records the disqualifying event and the county licensing officer. If there are serious flaws in that communication, a background check every five years is not an effective strategy for spotting firearms licensees whose licenses should be revoked.

New York's experience also raises a question about the proper allocation of licensing responsibility between the counties and the state. A firearms regulatory system, decentralized to the county level, makes sense in a diverse state where gun problems and gun culture differ substantially from county to county. Just as "one size fits all" does not make sense for the country as a whole, it does not make sense for a large, diverse state. Once the decision is made to implement firearms licensing at the county level, it also makes sense to implement license recertification at the county level. In retrospect, since the counties are responsible for issuing, amending, and revoking handgun licenses, it would have made more sense to have required handgun licensees to apply directly to the county clerk for recertification. Of course, this would have placed a burden on the county clerks, but the system that New York implemented burdens them anyway. In addition, unnecessarily antagonizing the clerks could undermine the efficacy of current and future state firearms regulation.

Regulating Ammunition Sales and Purchasers

Responsible dealers can act as a line of defense against the
planning, and stockpiling of a potential mass killer.
—US Rep. Carolyn McCarthy (D-NY), July 2012[1]

[Banning online ammunition sales would] turn back the
clock to the days when ammunition was only available in
person at licensed stores, driving up prices and making less
popular cartridges nearly unobtainable for . . . lawful gun
owners. The effect . . . on competitive shooters, who buy ammunition by the case lot for consistent accuracy and shoot
tens of thousands of rounds each year in practice, would be
especially devastating.
—National Rifle Association's Institute for Legislative
Action, August 2012[2]

The SAFE Act's ammunition-control provisions aim to prevent dangerous persons from acquiring firearm ammunition by background
checking purchasers. In addition, the Act seeks to monitor sales by registering ammunition sellers and mandating to the State Police they report
all sales, so that the amount of ammunition acquired by every purchaser
can be tracked. The goal is to prevent mass shootings by identifying
and investigating high-volume ammunition purchasers.[3] Gun control
advocates hailed these provisions as "groundbreaking."[4] However, implementation problems have proved insurmountable. This chapter explains
why the State Police never implemented the Act's ammunition controls.

Federal Ammunition Control

The 1968 Gun Control Act (GCA) made it a crime for federally licensed
dealers (FFLs) knowingly to sell ammunition to persons who are under

the age of eighteen, have ever been convicted of or are under indictment for any federal or state felony, are fugitives from justice, are addicts or unlawful users of illegal drugs, have ever been adjudicated as mentally defective, or have ever been committed to a mental institution.[5] Likewise, the Act prohibited possession of ammunition by such persons. However, while the GCA prohibited using the US postal system to transport ammunition,[6] it did not make it unlawful to sell ammunition to a resident of an ammunition-restrictive state or to ship ammunition across state lines via common carriers such as UPS (provided that the sender alerts the carrier that there is ammunition in the package and the package is labeled accordingly). Commercial airline passengers may carry ammunition in checked luggage, as long as it is securely packed.

Ammunition is commonly sold in bait-and-tackle shops, gas stations, and general stores. As long as these vendors do not sell firearms, they do not need an FFL license and need not keep any records of their sales. FFLs who sold ammunition were previously required to record to whom they sold ammunition and the quantity, caliber, and manufacturer of the purchased ammunition. The original purpose of this recording requirement is unclear. If it was predicated on the belief that cartridges or shell casings found at a crime scene, like guns, could be used to trace the retail seller and then the purchaser, that belief was erroneous. While guns can be traced via their serial numbers, cartridges do not have serial numbers. As Rex D. Davis, then director of the Bureau of Alcohol, Tobacco, and Firearms (ATF), explained to a Senate subcommittee in 1975, "[ATF is] on record to the extent that the sale of ammunition has not proven to be a very effective enforcement tool. Obviously they have no serial numbers or other identifying features beyond the fact of a brand name of the producer of the ammunition; a box of ammunition or an individual shell cannot be associated with the purchaser. . . . So, we have had a very limited number of cases in which a suspect was identified or the evidence against him was fortified through ammunition records."[7]

In 1986, then ATF director Stephen Higgins proposed eliminating FFLs' ammunition record-keeping obligation on the ground that "the Bureau and the [Treasury] Department have recognized that the current record-keeping requirements for ammunition have no substantial law enforcement value. In addition, their elimination would remove an unnecessary recordkeeping burden from licensees."[8] Congress agreed.

The 1986 Firearm Owners Protection Act (FOPA) eliminated the ammunition record-keeping requirement.[9]

FOPA made it illegal for *anyone* (not just FFLs) knowingly to transfer ammunition to any fugitive, person convicted of a felony, unlawful drug user or addict, person ever adjudicated as mentally defective or involuntarily committed, undocumented alien, alien admitted to the US under a nonimmigrant visa, person dishonorably discharged from the military, person who has renounced his or her US citizenship, person subject to a restraining order for threatening an intimate partner or who has been convicted of a misdemeanor crime of domestic violence, or person under indictment for a crime punishable by more than two years' imprisonment. The Act also made it a felony for members of these disqualified categories to possess ammunition.[10] Despite these categories of ammunition-ineligibility, federal law does not require FFLs to submit ammunition purchasers' identity information to NICS for background checking.

The 1994 Youth Handgun Safety Act made it illegal to knowingly transfer handguns and "ammunition suitable for use only in a handgun" to persons under the age of eighteen and made it illegal for juveniles to possess such ammunition.[11] This makes little sense because most ammunition that can be fired by a handgun can also be fired by some rifles.[12] Consequently, Walmart, one of the largest US ammunition retailers, instructs its cashiers to ask youthful-looking purchasers how they intend to use the ammunition. If the customer says that the ammunition is for a handgun, the cashier must not complete the sale. If the purchaser says he or she plans to use the ammunition in a rifle, the cashier completes the sale. This does not accomplish much, because a rejected purchaser can try again with the proper answer later that day at a different Walmart or even at the same store.

Since the mid-1990s, Democratic Party US senators have proposed, but never managed to pass, other strategies for limiting ammunition sales. In 1993, Senator Daniel Patrick Moynihan of New York introduced a bill that would have increased the sales tax on most handgun ammunition exponentially from 11 percent to *1,000 percent*.[13] Two years later, he reintroduced the bill, this time with a 10,000 percent tax on hollow-point ammunition.[14] This hypertax was meant to prohibit Black Talon cartridges, which, according to the manufacturer, expand "to expose razor-sharp reinforced jacket petals."[15] His bill would also have imposed an annual $10,000 tax on handgun-ammunition manufacturers and importers. Moynihan probably introduced these bills with no expectation of passage in order to call attention to the potential benefits of regulating ammunition.

In 1994, then Rep. Charles Schumer of New York unsuccessfully tried to limit to one thousand rounds the number of cartridges a person (other than a licensed dealer) could possess.[16] His bill also sought to increase taxes on ammunition by a modest (compared to Moynihan's bill) 50 percent. It would also have outlawed "non-sporting" handgun ammunition.[17] Moreover, Schumer's bill required ammunition-purchaser background checks and prohibited common carriers from transporting ammunition.[18] These bills, like Moynihan's, attracted little congressional support.

When it was disclosed that James Holmes, the perpetrator of the July 2012 Aurora, Colorado, massacre, possessed thousands of rounds of ammunition that had been purchased online and delivered by FedEx, gun control advocates renewed their calls for ammunition controls.[19] The 2015 Stop Online Ammunition Sales bill, sponsored by New Jersey's Senator Frank Lautenberg and New York's Representative Carolyn McCarthy required ammunition vendors to be federally licensed. Ammunition purchases would have to be transacted in person. Vendors would have to verify a purchaser's identity, maintain sales records, and report to state or local police sales of more than one thousand rounds to the same purchaser during any five consecutive business days.[20] No report would be required if the purchaser waited a week between one-thousand-round purchases or made several one-thousand-round purchases from different sellers, even on the same day. The bill contained no requirement (much less strategy) for aggregating an individual's multiple purchases from one or more sellers. The bill did not achieve a floor vote.

After the December, 14, 2012, Sandy Hook Elementary School massacre, Senator Richard Blumenthal of Connecticut introduced a bill to extend NICS background checking to ammunition purchasers from FFLs. His bill would also have reinstated ammunition seller record-keeping and reporting requirements (repealed by FOPA in 1986), including for sales of more than one thousand rounds. The bill did not include a strategy for aggregating an individual's multiple purchases from the same or different sellers.[21] It too died in the Republican-controlled Senate

Judiciary Committee. In 2015, Representative Bonnie Watson Coleman of New Jersey reintroduced the Lautenberg-McCarthy bill, with the same unsuccessful result.[22] Congressional action, at least while Republicans control the Senate or House, is highly unlikely. Even if a bill were to pass both houses, President Trump would almost certainly not sign it.

A few other state jurisdictions have tried to regulate ammunition sales. Connecticut, Illinois, Massachusetts, New Jersey, and the District of Columbia require ammunition purchasers and possessors to be licensed. Those jurisdictions, plus California, Maryland, Minnesota, and Washington, also regulate ammunition sellers. Eighteen states prohibit ammunition sales to certain ineligible categories, including juveniles. In 2013, the California Court of Appeals affirmed a decision striking down California's attempt to require all purchases of "handgun ammunition" to be registered. The court said the term "handgun ammunition" was unconstitutionally vague.[23] Three years later, California voters passed a referendum requiring licenses for ammunition sellers, background checks for ammunition purchasers, and prohibiting the transportation of ammunition into California from out of state.

New York's Pre–SAFE Act Regulation of Ammunition

Prior to passage of the SAFE Act, the only New York State statute regulating ammunition sales, passed in 1969, was connected to a bill regulating fireworks, not guns. It provided that "dealers in firearms" could only sell "ammunition designed exclusively for use in a pistol or revolver" to purchasers holding a valid handgun license.[24] That law did not apply to non-FFL ammunition sellers and did not apply to ammunition that could be used in rifles as well as handguns. Not surprisingly, it appears to have been hardly ever enforced. Prior to 2013, it was also a crime under New York law to possess "armor piercing ammunition" with intent to use it unlawfully and to possess explosive-tipped cartridges.[25]

The SAFE Act's Regulation of Ammunition Sellers

The SAFE Act requires persons and entities "engage[d] in the business of purchasing, selling or keeping ammunition" to be either federally registered as FFLs or registered (by January 15, 2014) with the State Police as "sellers of ammunition" (RSA).[26] Individuals who have been convicted of, or involuntarily committed, a felony offense, will not be approved as sellers of ammunition. If an individual fails to register by the deadline and sells ammunition, a first offense is a violation (with a maximum $1,000 fine), and a subsequent offense is a class A misdemeanor.[27]

To complete an ammunition sale, an FFL or RSA would have to confirm the purchaser's identity by means of a photo ID and then initiate a purchaser background check by sending the purchaser's identity information to the State Police along with information about the quantity, caliber, manufacturer, and serial number of the purchased ammunition.[28] This scheme assigned the State Police an ammunition-purchaser background-checking role similar to the FBI's (via NICS) firearm background-checking role.

The SAFE Act's requirement that an ammunition seller verify the purchaser's identity in effect makes it unlawful for a New York resident to receive ammunition directly from an out-of-state seller.[29] New Yorkers who wish to purchase ammunition from an out-of-state seller must have it shipped to a New York FFL or RSA, who must run a background check on the purchaser before handing over the ammunition.

Protest

Owners and managers of gun clubs and shooting ranges, of which there are at least 240 in New York State, criticized the SAFE Act's in-person requirement for ammunition transfers. Accustomed to purchasing ammunition in bulk at a discount from wholesalers or directly from manufacturers, they anticipated that compliance would be expensive and burdensome. Addressing these concerns, the superintendent of State Police issued an "Open Letter" in 2014 exempting businesses and organizations that sell ammunition for use on premises from the in-person ammunition-purchase requirement. "This [exception] may be of particular interest to shooting ranges, hunting clubs, and youth safety and education programs . . . [allowing] those groups to continue to receive discounted ammunition directly from the manufacturer."[30] Since the State Police superintendent lacks authority to amend legislation, this letter technically constituted a promise that the State Police would not enforce the ammunition provisions against clubs and shooting ranges.

Clubs and ranges that give or sell ammunition at cost price to their members may apply for registration as "ammunition keepers" rather than "sellers."[31] The applicant organization must explain (1) why it distributes ammunition on its premises and (2) how it intends to safely store and distribute ammunition.[32] A person who acquires ammunition from a "keeper of ammunition," whether or not he or she intends to use the ammunition on the keeper's premises, does not have to undergo a background check. Thus, a person who knows he cannot pass a background check could circumvent the SAFE Act's restrictions by acquiring ammunition from one or more shooting ranges. Shooting ranges and clubs are not obliged to monitor their patrons or to ensure that patrons do not take ammunition off the premises. (In addition, an ammunition purchaser who cannot pass a background check could recruit a straw purchaser or locate a black-market seller.)

Ammunition-Purchaser Background Checking

The SAFE Act's drafters expected NICS to execute background checks on ammunition purchasers just as it conducts background checks on firearms purchasers.[33] NICS, however, refused to take on this responsibility, which is not surprising since NICS is not authorized to conduct background checks on *ammunition* purchasers. Therefore, to effectuate the SAFE Act's goal of subjecting ammunition purchasers to background checks, New York would have to establish its own databases of ineligible purchasers and its own system by which ammunition vendors could initiate a real-time background check. The State Police would have to check the eligibility of the prospective purchaser against state databases of ammunition-ineligible persons. If the State Police found no disqualification, it would inform the ammunition vendor that the sale could be completed and send the vendor an identification number to record the sale.[34]

Reporting and Monitoring Ammunition Sales

The SAFE Act requires an ammunition seller to keep a record of the details of each transaction in a record book kept available for police inspection (although not a public record).[35] The seller would also be required to send the State Police information about the purchaser, quantity of ammunition purchased, and identifying markings, if any, on the ammunition. The State Police would populate a database with this information, but entries would have to be deleted after one year.[36] A first failure to record an ammunition sale properly is a violation; subsequent offenses are class B misdemeanors.[37]

The drafters intended the State Police to have the necessary information to identify high-volume purchasers, who could then be investigated (as possible mass shooters). Implementation of this scheme requires an information system that keeps track of all ammunition purchases by the same individual, whether from the same or multiple vendors. That objective is seriously frustrated by the SAFE Act's provision requiring deletion of information about purchases older than one year, which prevents the State Police from identifying, as a large-quantity purchaser, someone whose suspicious stockpile was amassed in two purchases thirteen months apart.

(Perhaps the state could have drawn on its experience with the federal NPLEx (National Precursor Log Exchange), a real-time electronic logging system used by pharmacies and law enforcement agencies to track sales of over-the-counter cold and allergy medications that can be used to make methamphetamine. That system makes it possible to monitor drug purchasers in the same way the SAFE Act envisioned monitoring ammunition sales. A "stop sale" feature will identify a purchaser who has exceeded a predetermined quota. NPLEx cannot detect straw purchasers.)

Even if the SAFE Act's system worked the way the Act's drafters envisioned, the assumption that criminals and mass murderers necessarily purchase large quantities of ammunition is unfounded. Armed robbers and other criminals do not require large quantities of ammunition. In fact, most gun crimes do not involve any shots being fired: when shots are fired, it is rarely more than a few.[38] Even rampage killers do not fire a huge number of bullets. James Holmes, despite having purchased 6,000 rounds in the months before the Aurora, Colorado, shooting, actually fired 76 rounds.[39] The perpetrator of the June 2016 Orlando, Florida, nightclub massacre, the most deadly mass shooting in American history, fired approximately 250 rounds.[40] In the two mass murders that occurred in New York in the past twenty-five years, the perpetrators each fired fewer than 200 rounds: the Long Island Railroad shooter emptied two 15-round magazines, while carrying 160 bullets;[41] the Binghamton shooter fired 99 rounds.[42]

Assuming that the state was able to track and aggregate every individual's in-state ammunition purchases, how many rounds over what period of time should be regarded as suspicious? Overwhelmingly, large-quantity ammunition purchasers are target shooters, who not uncommonly fire several hundred, even a thousand, rounds in a couple of hours. It would be impossible to investigate every gun owner who purchased over one hundred rounds in a twelve-month period. Ammunition is typically sold in fifty-cartridge boxes for handguns and twenty-cartridge boxes for rifles. Would, for example, the purchase of a dozen boxes on a single or multiple occasions within a specified time frame, say one year, warrant investigation? The lower the investigatory threshold, the more people to investigate and the more cursory each investigation would be. The criminally minded would soon catch on and endeavor to keep their purchases small and under the radar.

Presumably, a law enforcement officer, armed with information that John Doe's ammunition purchase(s) had exceeded the high-volume threshold, would attempt to interview Doe in person or perhaps by phone. Doe would not likely confess criminal intent. Most likely, he would claim to be a target shooter. On the basis only of information about a lawful but large-quantity ammunition purchase, the police would not have probable cause to believe that a crime was being committed or planned. Under New York's strict regulation of police questioning, a large ammunition purchase might not even justify a personal inquiry. The police could try to interview the uncooperative individual's neighbors and coworkers or even surveil him, but such investigations would be unrealistic in most cases for reasons of cost and manpower.

Prohibiting Receipt of Ammunition from Out-of-State Vendors

The SAFE Act prohibits New York State residents from receiving ammunition directly from out-of-state vendors. However, a New Yorker can purchase ammunition from an out-of-state supplier by having the ammunition shipped to an FFL or RSA registered in New York. That intermediary is required to initiate a background check on the purchaser, who must appear in person. Alternatively, individuals could themselves register as a seller of ammunition and directly receive ammunition shipments from out-of-state suppliers.

The SAFE Act's requirements for ammunition purchasers can be easily circumvented. Federal law does not prohibit a vendor from shipping ammunition across state lines, even to a recipient whose own state does not authorize receipt of ammunition from out of state. Alternatively, a New York resident, desirous of purchasing ammunition without a background check, could travel to any state (practically every state) where there are no controls on ammunition sales and purchase an unlimited quantity of ammunition. The SAFE Act does not make it an offense to possess ammunition purchased out of state; nor could such a law be easily enforced.

Attack on the Constitutionality of the Ammunition Provisions

The New York State Rifle and Pistol Association (NYSRPA), the New York State Amateur Trapshooting Association (NYSATA), and several other plaintiffs challenged the constitutionality of the SAFE Act's in-person ammunition-purchasing requirement.[43] The plaintiffs argued that prohibiting New Yorkers from purchasing ammunition from out-of-state vendors violated the due process clause of the US Constitution's Fourteenth Amendment as well as the "dormant commerce clause." The latter forbids states from discriminating against, or unduly burdening, interstate commerce.

Chief Judge William Skretny (US District Court for the Northern District of New York) employed a two-part test to evaluate the constitutionality of the SAFE Act's ammunition provisions: (1) If the challenged regulation discriminates against or unduly burdens interstate commerce, the state must justify it by demonstrating a compelling interest; and (2) if the challenged regulation imposes only an incidental burden on interstate commerce, the plaintiff must demonstrate that the burden is clearly excessive in relation to a legitimate state interest. Skretny concluded that the in-person ammunition-purchase requirement does not unconstitutionally discriminate against out-of-state sellers because those sellers can establish retail outlets in New York or coordinate with a state intermediary:

> The SAFE Act applies restrictions evenhandedly between in-state and out-of-state arms and ammunition dealers. It does not create a "monopoly" for New York dealers, as Plaintiffs argue; instead . . . it eliminates the direct sale of ammunition to New Yorkers no matter the seller's place of business. . . . Even assuming that the only way an out-of-state dealer could legally sell ammunition to New York consumers is to establish a brick-and-mortar outlet in New York, so too must in-state sellers. And, even if it is costly and burdensome for out-of-state dealers to establish brick-and-mortar outlets in New York, that is insufficient to establish a discriminatory effect.[44]

Skretny found the burden on interstate commerce "incidental" and not clearly excessive, given the state's legitimate interest in assuring that an ammunition seller confirms a buyer's identity and initiates a background check. His ruling was not appealed.[45]

In response to the SAFE Act's requirement that ammunition purchases be transacted in person, online retailers now provide information on how consumers can connect with FFLs and RSAs in nearly every New York county, who are willing to serve as intermediaries.[46] Most FFLs and RSAs charge between $10 and $20 per transaction, but some charge as much as $70 per transaction or 15 percent of the purchase price.[47] Many ammunition sellers have said that they would not act as an intermediary. Perhaps this means that ammunition purchasers, ignoring the SAFE Act, are doing business directly with out-of-state sellers. Or perhaps New York purchasers have shifted their patronage to New York vendors. Some New York sellers claim that their ammunition sales have increased.

Ammunition Regulation Collapses

The SAFE Act set January 15, 2014, as the operational date for the ammunition background-checking regime. However, on October 25, 2013, the State Police announced that they needed more time to develop an information system that would enable ammunition vendors to transmit purchasers' identity information to the State Police (in order for the State Police to search relevant databases of ammunition-ineligible persons, and to notify the ammunition seller whether to complete the sale). NICS firearm background checks usually take about ninety seconds, but the State Police were unable to design a system, at a reasonable cost, that would take less than thirty minutes. Another problem was that many bait-and-tackle shops (registered sellers of ammunition) did not have a computer terminal or, if they did, not one that would support rapid information exchange with the State Police. State officials considered it infeasible politically and fiscally to require every ammunition seller to purchase computer hardware or software and for the state to provide equipment and training to every ammunition seller.[48]

With Governor Cuomo's approval, in July 2015, the State Police decided to suspend temporarily their effort to create an online ammunition background-checking and reporting system.[49] Meanwhile, the New York State Senate passed a bill, cosponsored by twenty-four Republicans and two Democrats, to repeal the SAFE Act's ammunition background-checking and reporting provisions.[50] However, the bill died in the Assembly.

On July 10, 2015, the New York State director of operations and the Senate's Republican majority leader signed a memorandum of understanding "Regarding the Statewide License and Record Database Utilization for Eligibility to Purchase Ammunition." The memorandum stated that the ammunition-purchaser database "[could] not be established and/or function in the manner originally intended at this time" due to "lack of adequate technology."[51] The parties agreed that "no expenditures of state monies shall be allocated for the purposes of purchasing and installing software, programming and interface required to transmit any record for the purpose of performing an eligibility check" for the database's future development without bilateral agreement.[52] Governor Cuomo's counsel said:

There have been concerns raised that the State should not implement the database prematurely as it could cause unmanageable disruption in retail establishments and could cause undue delays. We agree. In fact, over the last two years the Superintendent of State Police has clearly said no system would be implemented until it is ready. . . . Members of the Republican Senate have indicated that, despite those prior statements, they continue to be questioned by the public and want to answer definitively that we are aware of the concerns and will act responsibly. The MOU issued by the Director of Operations simply restates that point. . . . To be clear, the memorandum reiterates the administration's intention to implement a functional database when it is ready and reinforces that the system cannot be launched prematurely. The memorandum can in no way supersede the law as passed by the legislature and further, there is nothing in the memorandum that is inconsistent with the letter, spirit or intent of the law.[53]

SAFE Act critics celebrated the memorandum of understanding. According to Republican Senator James Seward, it constituted "a clear victory for Second Amendment rights" and a "banner day for law-abiding gun owners in New York." Republican Assemblyman Bill Nojay said, "All this does is state something that we've known to be true for the last two years, which is that they don't have the technology to do the database." Republican Senator Joe Griffo called the agreement "a major accomplishment in confronting one of the most troubling provisions of this misguided law," adding, "I am relieved that this database has been stopped before it ever had a chance to start." An NRA lobbyist praised it as "a step in the right direction to restore a degree of sanity after the SAFE Act's over-the-top demonization of lawful New York gun owners."[54]

Some disappointed Democratic senators excoriated the memorandum of understanding as an unconstitutional subversion of the SAFE Act. Senate Democratic Minority Leader Andrew Stewart-Cousins's spokesperson sarcastically commented, "This two-way agreement is outrageous. I'm looking forward to the MOUs on the minimum wage, paid family leave, . . . and the numerous other things that the Senate Republicans are blocking." Deputy Senate Minority Leader Michael N. Gianris argued, "The notion that one house of the Legislature [Senate] will have greater powers than another and that the governor, with one house only, can agree to change state law, turns our democracy on its head." Assembly Speaker Carl E. Heasties criticized the memorandum as "an ill-advised end run around the legislature and the SAFE Act."[55] The memorandum of understanding left in place the Act's requirement that ammunition sales be transacted in person.

* * *

In the face of significant logistical and fiscal obstacles, New York has been unwilling or unable to implement the SAFE Act's ammunition-control provisions, other than the in-person purchase requirement. There is no prospect of ammunition-purchaser background checking or of a system to report and monitor large-quantity ammunition sales. While the Cuomo administration remains publicly committed to eventually implementing the SAFE Act's ammunition background-checking scheme, there is no suggestion of near-term funding to develop the state's necessary software and to make available the necessary hardware.

Ammunition background checking would be easier to implement if ammunition vendors were required to have computer hardware and software capable of communicating in real time with the State Police. Even if that could be accomplished politically, which is unlikely, the effectiveness of ammunition background checking would hardly be guaranteed. Ineligible purchasers could enlist a family member or friend to purchase ammunition for them. They could purchase ammunition in a state that has no controls, or on the black market. They could also make their own ammunition with readily available and inexpensive devices that enable a shooter to make large quantities of ammunition at below retail cost.[56] In short, keeping ammunition out of the hands of prospective criminals and rampage shooters poses huge implementation and enforcement challenges that the state has not begun to address.

Looking toward the future, any strategy for monitoring ammunition purchases would have to include a system for keeping track of each individual's total ammunition purchases. That strategy would require a supplementary prohibition on purchasing ammunition directly in another state, but there is no strategy for enforcing such a prohibition. A federal law prohibiting sale of ammunition to out-of-state residents would be a small first step, but there is no federal capacity to enforce such a law.

The prospect of preventing rampage shootings by denying perpetrators access to large quantities of ammunition is dubious. A rampage shooter would not need more than, say, 250 rounds of ammunition at the most. It would be impossible to investigate every person whose purchases exceed that modest quantity every year or even on a single day. Nor is it clear what "investigate" in this context would mean. New York State has *never* had a mass shooting in which a perpetrator used that much ammunition. Thus, preventing a future mass shooting by "monitoring" ammunition sales is unlikely to be effective.

10

New and Enhanced Punishments

New York has enacted some of the toughest, most sensible gun safety laws in the country, and with today's charges, we are sending a message that these laws will be vigorously enforced.
—New York Attorney General Eric Schneiderman, June 21, 2016 (announcing charges against Kordell Jackson)[1]

There is nothing that the state of New York has done in the SAFE Act that will make anybody in the state any safer. The laws that were on the books prior to it were more than adequate to keep guns out of the hands of criminals as long as the district attorneys and the police forces of New York State wanted to pursue enforcing those laws.
—Tom King, president of the New York State Rifle and Pistol Association, March 6, 2016[2]

Criminal law plays an important role in every gun control regime. In New York, there are dozens of pre– and post–SAFE Act gun crime offenses and sentence enhancements. Use of a gun in the commission of another crime (assault, rape, robbery, carjacking) is typically defined as a separate or aggravated form of the underlying criminal conduct and punished more severely than commission of the predicate offense without a firearm. In addition, criminal laws back up sale, record-keeping, purchase, and possession regulations. For example, more than a century ago, the Sullivan Law made it a crime to possess a firearm without a license; this remains New York's most frequently prosecuted regulatory gun crime, though it is often used as an additional charge when the top count is murder, armed robbery, or aggravated assault.

One of the main challenges when it comes to enforcing regulatory gun offenses, for which there is no underlying predicate offense, is the

absence of a specialized regulatory agency and of a specialized law enforcement agency in charge of enforcing the regulatory regime. The
State Police licenses sellers, registers assault weapon owners, maintains
a handgun-licensee database, and recertifies handgun licensees every
five years, but it is not funded or staffed to enforce criminal laws aimed
at regulatory noncompliance. The State Police is fundamentally a criminal law enforcement agency; its firearm regulatory role is a subsidiary
function carried out by a very small unit. While that unit implements
certain regulatory functions and issues some regulations, it is not staffed
to effectively enforce the regulatory regime. Instead, enforcement falls
to local police and county sheriff departments. But arresting, much less
prosecuting, otherwise law-abiding citizens for violating firearms regulations is not a high priority in upstate counties. The New York City
Police Department's specialized firearms unit, which focuses on gun
trafficking, is the exception.

Advocacy groups lobby lawmakers, not law enforcers. They have
little, if any, influence over police's and prosecutors' priorities, strategies, and tactics. The prominent gun control researcher Anthony Braga
observed in a 2015 journal article on the impact of gun control in Massachusetts, one of the nation's strongest gun control states, that "a highly
problematic gap between having strong gun laws in place and actually
enforcing their provisions exists in Massachusetts. This lack of enforcement seems to contribute to the relatively large number of crime guns
directly or indirectly originating from Massachusetts FFLs over time."[3]
This observation also holds true for New York's SAFE Act.

SAFE Act Offenses Reinforcing Regulatory Gun Controls

Every new SAFE Act gun regulation is backed up by a criminal law prohibiting and establishing a maximum punishment for noncompliance.
Compliance suffers if these laws go unenforced. Nevertheless, for practical and political reasons, enforcement has been minimal.

Criminal Possession and Weapon Disposal

Straw purchasing (using a firearms-eligible person to purchase a firearm on behalf of a firearms-ineligible person) is an easy way for a

firearms-ineligible individual to acquire a gun. New York's omnibus 2000 gun control law criminalized straw purchasing as a class A misdemeanor, punishable by a maximum one year jail term. The SAFE Act promoted straw purchasing to a class D felony, punishable by a maximum seven-year prison term, perhaps on account of William Spengler Jr.'s, assassination of two first responders in Webster, a town outside Rochester on December 24, 2012.[4] Spengler, who could not pass a background check on account of a prior manslaughter conviction, paid his neighbor $1,000 to purchase for him a Bushmaster semiautomatic rifle and a shotgun. A New York State judge sentenced the neighbor to sixteen months for lying on the state's purchase form. A federal judge sentenced her to eight years (to run concurrently) for (1) lying on the federal purchase form, (2) transferring guns to a person she knew previously to have been convicted of a felony, and (3) possessing guns herself despite being ineligible on account of drug (marijuana) use. The families of the murdered firefighters (represented by the Brady Campaign to Prevent Gun Violence) sued the owner of the store from which the neighbor purchased the guns, claiming that the store's staff should have known that she was a straw purchaser.[5] The plaintiffs alleged that the store failed to follow protocols established by the National Shooting Sports Foundation, specifically recommending questions for retailers to ask a suspicious purchaser ("Don't Lie for the Other Guy"). The case is still pending as of summer 2019.

The SAFE Act's felony straw-purchasing offense has rarely been enforced. In the three-plus years from March 2013 to July 2016, there were only ten arrests statewide for criminal purchase of a weapon for another person and nine arrests for criminal disposal (transfer) of a weapon.

Private Sales

Universal background checking is one of the SAFE Act's most important provisions. To discourage noncompliance, the SAFE Act makes transfer of a firearm, rifle, or shotgun without an FFL's involvement a class A misdemeanor punishable by a up to one year in jail.[6] Realistically, noncompliant sales between willing buyers and sellers rarely come to light. From March 2013 to July 15, 2016, there were zero arrests in New York for violating this provision. Since universal background checking is at the top of the national gun control agenda, this enforcement statistic should cause proponents of universal background checking to focus on implementation and enforcement.

Failure to Report a Lost or Stolen Firearm

Prior to the SAFE Act, failure to report a lost or stolen firearm within twenty-four hours of discovering the loss was classified as a violation punishable by a maximum $100 fine. For whatever reason, the SAFE Act upgraded nonreporting to a class A misdemeanor, punishable by up to one year in jail.[7] Lawful gun owners are likely to report a lost or stolen gun for insurance purposes, if for no other reason. (A substantial percentage of reported gun thefts probably involve the theft of other property as well.) Statewide, more than two thousand firearms are reported lost or stolen each year.[8] An unlicensed gun owner whose gun is lost or stolen would be unlikely to report it to the police since that would be admitting to the crime of illegal gun possession. Between March 2013 and July 2016, there were just nine arrests statewide for this offense. The strategic value to the police of knowing that a resident's gun or ammunition has been lost or stolen is not clear. Perhaps gun owners, knowing that they could be prosecuted for failing to report a lost or stolen gun, are more likely to secure their guns. However, there is no punishment for storing a firearm carelessly as long as the gun owner reports the loss.

The SAFE Act extended the reporting obligation to lost or stolen ammunition. Although the Act specified no minimum number of cartridges, the drafters must have had in mind theft or loss of a significant quantity, not just a few cartridges. It is also hard to see what use police could make of information about lost or missing cartridges regardless of the quality.

Failures to Register as an Ammunition Seller

The SAFE Act's provisions for ammunition-purchaser background checking and sales monitoring were never implemented due to technological obstacles and resource limitations. Nevertheless, ammunition sellers who do not already hold a federal firearms license still have to register with the State Police. A first failure-to-register offense is graded as a noncriminal violation, subject to a $1,000 fine; a subsequent offense is a class A misdemeanor, punishable by up to a year in jail.[9] From January 15, 2014 (the date this provision became effective), until July 2016, there were eleven arrests statewide.

The Act's ammunition provisions make first-time failure to maintain a record of an ammunition transfer a violation (punishable by a $500 fine) and each subsequent offense a class B misdemeanor (carrying a maximum penalty of three months in jail).[10]

Criminal Possession of a Firearm

Unlicensed possession of a handgun has been an offense since the passage of the 1911 Sullivan Act. It backs up the state's handgun-licensing system, and it is routinely used as a subsidiary charge when a handgun-crime perpetrator is unlicensed. The SAFE Act upgraded criminal possession of a firearm from a class A misdemeanor to a class E felony. The offense applies to (1) unlicensed possession of any firearm and (2) knowing failure to register an assault weapon that was lawfully possessed before the SAFE Act's registration requirement became effective. Between January 2013 and July 2016, there were 7,828 arrests statewide for criminal possession of a firearm. Eighty-eight percent of those arrests occurred in New York City, where there are relatively few licensed gun owners and the vast majority of gun crimes are committed by unlicensed perpetrators. That the entire rest of the state accounted for just 12 percent of arrests for this offense, despite licensed gun ownership being much more common, is perhaps attributable to it being much easier to get a license outside New York City or perhaps to less vigorous enforcement, or probably to both.

Assault Weapon Offenses

New York State's 2000 omnibus gun control law, paralleling the 1994 federal assault weapons ban, criminalized possession of a post-1994 center-fire semiautomatic that accepts a detachable magazine and has two military-like features. The New York Penal Law retains that offense, but the SAFE Act criminalizes semiautomatics with just one military-like feature, that is, guns that were previously legal under the 2000 law.

Assault weapon owners can keep assault weapons that were legal prior to the SAFE Act if they registered them with the State Police by April 15, 2014. Alternatively, without registering, they could keep their prohibited gun by permanently removing the military-like features. For example, they could "remove the bayonet lug by cutting or grinding, grind off the barrel threads, or remove the foregrip so that it cannot be readily reattached."[11] The only other legal options are to sell the prohibited weapon to an FFL in the state or to transfer it to someone in another state.

The SAFE Act makes it a crime to knowingly fail to register an assault weapon as well as a crime to knowingly possess an unregistered assault weapon. (It is hard to see how a person who violates one would not also violate the other.) The first offense (a class A misdemeanor) applies to a person who, having lawfully possessed an assault weapon prior to the SAFE Act, knowingly failed to register it within sixty days of the Act's enactment.[12] While tens of thousands of state assault weapons owners (perhaps as many as 95 percent) did not register, between April 15, 2013, and July 2016, there were only eleven arrests statewide for knowingly failing to register an assault weapon.

Police will rarely encounter someone carrying a gun that might qualify as a prohibited assault weapon because most of these weapons (with the important exception of "machine pistols" such as the Tech 9 and Mac 10), not being concealable, are rarely carried in plain view. Even if the police were to spot such a weapon, perhaps in a car, they will not necessarily have probable cause to believe that the weapon is not registered. Between April 15, 2013, and July 2016, there were fifty-eight arrests statewide for unlawful possession of an unregistered assault weapon. All but twelve of those arrests occurred in New York City, where it is especially unlikely that a person would openly carry an assault weapon. Unfortunately, we do not know how many of these arrests were connected to an arrest for another crime.

The SAFE Act prohibits the sale or transfer of assault weapons and large-capacity magazines. It classifies this offense as a class A misdemeanor, punishable by up to one year in jail.[13] The prosecutor must prove that the defendant *knew* that the gun in his or her possession was a prohibited assault weapon. Gun owners claim to be uncertain about which semiautomatic models are prohibited and whether various modifications render a prohibited assault weapon legal. Between March 2013 and July 2016, there were just four arrests statewide for unlawful sale or transfer of an assault weapon.

The Kordell Jackson Case

After the SAFE Act went into effect, Kordell Jackson, an anti–SAFE Act activist, sold more than one hundred assault weapons with kits that, according to the manufacturer, can be used to change a semiautomatic's detachable magazine receptor into a fixed magazine that cannot be removed without a tool.[14] To reload a semiautomatic fitted with such a kit, it is necessary to use a "bullet button" or other "tool" to release the empty magazine. According to the kit manufacturer, "[It] is an upgrade to your current mag lock or factory magazine catch we've developed so you don't have to register your AR Rifle or Pistol as an 'Assault Weapon.' . . . Easy to remove if traveling to a 'Free State'; Avoid top-loading by creating a fixed magazine rifle that can also be released by using the included quick-release rear takedown pin. . . . No tools required to detach magazine once included quick rear take-down pin is pulled!"[15] New York State courts still have not ruled on whether an otherwise-prohibited assault weapon modified to eject a spent magazine by depressing a button with an implement, such as a bullet, are prohibited. (A January 2017 California statute explicitly included in the definition of "unlawful assault weapon" a semiautomatic fitted with a magazine detachable by means of a bullet button.)[16]

While the Erie County prosecutor declined to prosecute Jackson, New York State Attorney General Eric Schneiderman charged Jackson with multiple felony counts of sale of an assault weapon (criminal sale of a firearm in both the first and second degree) and with two felony counts of disposal and transport of an assault weapon.[17] According to Schneiderman, "With today's charges, we are sending a message that these laws will be vigorously enforced. . . . Weapons of war have no place on the streets of America and, in New York, we're doing something about it."[18]

Before trial, Jackson's lawyers argued that the SAFE Act's assault weapon provision is so vaguely worded that it "makes potentially every law-abiding citizen a criminal." According to his defense lawyer at the time, "There are a lot of issues with interpretation, at least with our interpretation, that make it almost impossible for any citizen to comply with the law and that's probably a product of how fast it was pushed through [the legislature] without any vetting in the legislature, and mistakes were made."[19] Schneiderman, rejecting this argument, accused Jackson and his supporters of "feigning ignorance": "They [gun owners] said, 'well we're confused by the SAFE Act,' but then witnesses were able to report that they knew in great detail what the SAFE Act required, what features of guns had to be changed before they could be sold."[20] Facing a twenty-five-year sentence, Jackson ultimately pled guilty to a class D felony and received a two-year jail sentence.

Unlawful Possession of Large-Capacity Magazines

New York State's omnibus 2000 gun control law made it an offense to possess a large-capacity magazine manufactured before 1994 (the date of the federal ban on large-capacity magazines). "Large capacity" was defined as greater than ten-round capacity. As described earlier, the SAFE Act reduced the permitted maximum capacity to seven rounds but was quickly amended in response to gun owners' insistence that there were no such magazines that would fit many of the most popular semiautomatics. The Cuomo administration then imposed a seven-round loading limit. A federal court struck down that policy as irrational.

The SAFE Act technically did not grandfather preexisting large-capacity magazines but provided a reduced penalty for a person who lawfully possessed a pre-1994 large-capacity magazine before the SAFE Act's enactment. It also provided a one-year grace period, during which large-capacity magazines could be permanently modified, surrendered to police, or transferred to a New York State firearms dealer or to an out-of-state person. After January 15, 2014, a person who knowingly possesses a magazine of greater than ten-round capacity that was manufactured before September 1994 commits a class A misdemeanor.[21] This provision seemingly provides a plausible defense to anyone apprehended with a large-capacity magazine because magazines are not stamped with a date of manufacture. Moreover, reasonable belief that the magazine is lawful, paired with surrender or disposal within thirty days of notification by police, protects a person from being prosecuted at all. Between

March 2013 and July 2016, there were sixty-four arrests statewide for this misdemeanor offense.

A possessor of a large-capacity magazine who is apprehended with a prohibited magazine acquired after passage of the SAFE Act can be charged with criminal possession of a weapon in the third degree, a class D felony punishable by up to seven years' imprisonment.[22] It would be hard to prove when a large-capacity magazine was acquired and even harder to prove that the possessor of the magazine knew when it was manufactured. There are no data on the number of arrests and prosecutions for this felony offense because third-degree criminal possession of a weapon includes a number of different gun crimes, which the Division of Criminal Justice Services' reporting does not differentiate between.

Safe Storage

A 1996 New York Department of Health survey found that 18 percent of 2,267 respondents reported that their household contained a firearm; of those, 38 percent admitted unsafe storage (either failing to lock all their firearms or failing to store ammunition separately in a locked place).[23] Another recent study, published in April 2018, found that more than half of gun owners do not securely store all their guns.[24]

The SAFE Act created a new criminal offense applicable to a gun owner who resides with an individual whom the owner knows or has reason to know is prohibited from possessing a firearm under federal law. Gun owners to whom this law applies must lock their gun(s) securely either in a locked container or with a locking device attached to the gun whenever the gun is not in their "immediate possession or control."[25]

A gun owner who resides with a person who is disqualified from possessing a firearm on account of a misdemeanor conviction for domestic violence is required to secure his or her gun if the coresident's conviction occurred within the previous five years. Violation is a class A misdemeanor, punishable by up to one year in jail. In other words, a battered woman could be convicted for failing to secure her gun because she lives with a man who has previously been convicted of domestic assault on her.

A person who shares a residence full of other actual and potential weapons (for example, knives, scissors, bats) might consider easy access to his or her gun necessary for self-defense against a potential assault by the firearms-ineligible resident. Because "immediate control" is not defined, that firearms-eligible person might plausibly claim to believe that a gun kept in the nightstand drawer of the shared bedroom is under his or her "immediate control." This is one of several reasons why the SAFE Act's safe-storage provision is unenforceable. Police do not have authority to enter homes to confirm that firearms are properly stored. Even if they had such authority, they would have neither time nor resources to check whether licensed gun owners are keeping guns secure at all times. Moreover, even if police could somehow inspect, probably pursuant to a scheduled visit, how a licensee's guns are stored, it could certainly not be assumed that the gun would remain similarly stored after inspection.[26] Finally, the gun owner would have a strong constitutional argument that the Supreme Court's Second Amendment decisions guarantee access to a gun at home that can be immediately deployed for self-defense.

Between March 2013 and July 2016, there were thirteen arrests statewide for violation of the SAFE Act's safe-storage provision. The only reported case involved Vittorio Ciraco, who was on probation for criminal contempt and domestic violence convictions. When his handgun license was revoked, Ciraco told his probation officer that he planned to transfer his handgun to his father, with whom he lived. The court rejected the proposed transfer because Ciraco's father kept his firearms in a locked glass case that could easily be broken into. The court's decision was not surprising considering Ciraco's convictions. A challenge to the safe-storage provision from a licensed gun owner who claims to need immediate access to his or her gun for self-defense would be stronger and might produce a different result.

New Criminal Offenses and Sentence Enhancements for Gun Crimes

Historically, New York State Senate Republicans have favored tougher criminal and sentencing laws, whereas Assembly Democrats have generally opposed creating new criminal offenses and enhancing sentences, on the ground that they fuel mass incarceration. However, the SAFE

Act's Democratic drafting team viewed a number of new offenses and sentence enhancements as an acceptable price to pay for Senate Majority Leader Dean Skelos's support for the SAFE Act's regulatory provisions.[27]

Murder of a "First Responder"

In the early hours of Christmas Eve 2012 in West Webster, New York (near Rochester), sixty-two-year-old William Spengler Jr., who previously served eighteen years for a first-degree manslaughter conviction, deliberately set fire to his house and car, called the fire department, and ambushed the responding firefighters, killing two and injuring two others before killing himself.

Prior to the SAFE Act, state law treated murder of a police, corrections, or peace officer, but not a firefighter or other emergency responder, as first-degree ("aggravated") murder, carrying a mandatory life sentence without the possibility of parole.[28] Had Spengler lived, under pre–SAFE Act law, he would have been prosecuted for two counts of second-degree murder and two counts of attempted second-degree murder, each count punishable by a maximum sentence of life in prison, with a minimum period of fifteen to twenty-five years, *with the possibility of parole.*[29] The SAFE Act's "Webster Provision" made murder of a "first responder" (firefighter, emergency medical technician, ambulance driver, paramedic, physician, or registered nurse involved in a first-response team or any other individual who, in the course of official duties, performs emergency response activities) in performance of his or her duty prosecutable as aggravated or first-degree murder. The former is punishable by a mandatory life sentence without parole and the latter by a maximum term of life imprisonment and a minimum of not less than twenty years.[30]

Governor Cuomo chose to sign the SAFE Act in Rochester, nearby to Webster. At the signing ceremony, he said, "[The SAFE Act] is appropriate . . . [because] just weeks ago a gunman senselessly murdered two first responders as they responded to a fire in Webster."[31] Assembly Majority Leader Joseph Morelle commented, "After the murder of two brave firefights in Webster and 20 innocent children in Newtown, New Yorkers demanded action on gun safety. We have responded with what I strongly believe is common sense legislation that reduces the likelihood of such tragedies."[32] The State Sheriffs' Association praised the Webster provision: "First responders need this protection, evidenced all too often by attacks on them when they attempt to provide help, and in special recognition of the terrible attacks in Webster, NY and attacks on first responders in Jefferson County."[33] No one has ever been charged under the largely symbolic Webster provision.

Aggravated Criminal Possession of a Weapon

The SAFE Act created an offense "aggravated criminal possession of a weapon," defined as criminally possessing a weapon in the second degree while committing a drug-trafficking or violent felony offense arising out of the same criminal transaction.[34] In effect, this is an example, of recriminalizing already-criminal conduct for expressive effect.

Criminal possession of a weapon in the second degree is defined as possessing (1) a machine gun or disguised gun with intent to use the weapon unlawfully against another person, (2) five or more firearms, or (3) any loaded firearm with the intent to use it unlawfully against another person.[35] A drug-trafficking felony is defined as any of the following offenses: (1) use of a child to commit a controlled-substance offense; (2) criminal sale of a controlled substance in the first through fourth degrees; (3) criminal sale of a controlled substance in or near school grounds; (4) unlawful manufacture of methamphetamine in the first or second degree; and (5) operating as a major trafficker.[36] The new felony offense and criminal possession of a weapon in the second degree are class C felonies (carrying a fifteen-year maximum). "Violent felony" covers a long list of crimes against the person, including assault in the first and second degrees, burglary in the first and second degrees, arson in the second degree, and kidnapping in the second degree.[37]

Aggravated criminal possession is punishable by a five-year minimum sentence, compared to the pre–SAFE Act's three-and-a-half-year minimum. However, the SAFE Act's offense is limited in two respects. First, some violent crimes, such as assault, robbery, and burglary, already incorporate use of a weapon in their definition. Indeed, prior to the SAFE Act, if an armed robbery was charged as second-degree robbery plus criminal possession of a weapon in the second degree, the maximum sentence was twenty-five years' imprisonment, a higher maximum than what is available for the SAFE Act's aggravated criminal possession of a weapon.

Second, unless the defendant is a "major drug trafficker," the prosecutor must prove that the defendant used a gun in the course of a drug *sale* or immediately thereafter. This offense can be deployed against a "major drug trafficker defendant who is apprehended in possession of both guns and drugs."[38] From March 2013 to July 2016, there were eighty-six state-wide arrests for aggravated criminal possession of a weapon, seventy-eight (91 percent) occurring in New York City.[39] For example, in July 2015, eighteen-year-old Nicholas Barranco and an unnamed seventeen-year-old boy were arrested on charges of aggravated criminal possession of a weapon after committing a series of drive-by paintball-gun shootings in Staten Island. From inside their SUV, Barranco and his friend shot five randomly targeted pedestrians in several incidents.[40]

Criminal Possession

The SAFE Act added two offenses covering use of an unloaded firearm to commit (1) a drug-trafficking felony or (2) a violent felony offense.[41] Between March 2013 and July 2016, there were seventy-nine arrests state-wide for these two subsections of third-degree criminal possession of a firearm: ten while committing a drug-trafficking felony (four of these in New York City), and sixty-nine while committing a violent felony offense (twenty-three in New York City). One could persuasively argue that *reducing* rather than increasing punishment for using an unloaded gun would have made a greater contribution to public safety. Why not incentivize criminals to use unloaded guns?

The "Community Gun"

Proponents of the SAFE Act's new "community gun" offense claim that it was needed to deal with gang members who hide guns in public or semipublic places—mailboxes, garbage cans, behind hallway radiators, in wheel wells, or in a park—where fellow gang members can retrieve them when needed. (They also argue that community guns pose a threat to children who could find them and injure themselves or others.) Manhattan District Attorney Cyrus Vance Jr. explained to reporters, "[Gang members] don't want to keep the weapons on them, but want to have access to them. It poses challenges in terms of prosecution, to the police on the street. It puts the weapon in the hands of a larger number of people. . . . We are always confronted with a changing crime dynamic. I think the community gun circumstance is an adaptation to effective prosecution and police action. It's designed to try to insulate themselves [gang members] from being caught with weapons on their person."[42]

Prior to the SAFE Act, in order to charge co-gun-possessors, who are neither accomplices nor co-conspirators in a shooting, prosecutors would have had to prove criminal facilitation, accomplice liability, or conspiracy to commit the homicide. Those crimes would have required proving that the defendants made the gun available to the shooter believing that he or she intended to commit murder. That burden would not be satisfied by proof that the defendants hid the gun where the shooter or his or her associates could retrieve it. In effect, the SAFE Act's new community-gun offense reduces the burden of proof and requires proof only of complicity in someone else's gun possession.

The community-gun offense is traceable to a high-profile September 2010 gang murder in New York City.[43] Shanell Crute and her boyfriend set out to buy marijuana when they were confronted by five gang members. When an argument ensued, one of the men shouted, "Get the Waka Flocka," the street name for their shared "community gun." Two gang members ran off to retrieve the gun from a stairwell in a nearby apartment building. One of the men used the gun to kill Crute with nine shots to the head and chest.

Another case cited by District Attorney Vance involved Afrika Owes, who carried a gun for her boyfriend, Jaquan Laynes, the leader of a violent Harlem street gang. He was convicted of first-degree drug-trafficking conspiracy and sentenced to twenty years to life. Owes was charged with carrying a nine-millimeter pistol for use by Laynes and his gang colleagues. Under pre–SAFE Act law, Owes could have been prosecuted for criminal facilitation in the second degree, a class C felony punishable by up to fifteen years' imprisonment. However, she was sentenced as a youthful offender to a term of one year of judicial supervision, during which time she had to stay out of trouble or risk being sentenced to up to four years in prison.[44] It is hard to see this case as an example of inadequate substantive criminal or sentencing law. Giving a break to youthful offenders with potential for rehabilitation is a firmly established policy with wide support.

The SAFE Act's community-gun provision expanded the definition of criminal facilitation by making it a crime to "make available, sell, exchange, give or dispose of a community gun, which in fact, aids a person to commit a crime."[45] At least one of the persons sharing the gun must be ineligible to possess a gun. Upon conviction, the sentence depends on the grade of the crime committed with the shared gun and the age of the principal offender. The official commentary to New York's Penal Law opined that if the SAFE Act's drafters intended to eliminate the mental element of "criminal facilitation," they should have created a strict liability facilitation offense. In other words, they should have made it a crime to provide a community gun to someone who is not licensed, regardless of whether the prosecutor can prove that the defendant believed it probable that he or she was rendering aid to a person who intended to commit a crime. That would apply to the situation in which a gang member makes a gun generally accessible to fellow gang members but does not hand over, or specifically direct retrieval of, the gun for the purpose of perpetrating a particular crime.

Thus, the SAFE Act's expanded definition of criminal facilitation to include possession of a community gun adds little, if anything, to the prosecutor's quiver. The prosecutor still must prove that the defendant "believe[d] it probable" that he or she was rendering aid to a person who intended to commit a specific crime. The prosecutor shouldered that same burden under the pre–SAFE Act law. The SAFE Act provision does not cover any conduct that is not already criminal.[46]

There are no available statistics for arrests or prosecutions for criminal facilitation committed by making a community gun available, but prosecutors whom we interviewed believe that there have been few, if any, because of the difficulty of proving that a person who was not in possession of a gun knowingly made that gun available to a person whom he or she believed was going to use it to commit a specific crime. Indeed, if all that could be proven, the defendant could be convicted as an accomplice or co-conspirator.

Aggravated Enterprise Corruption

The SAFE Act includes a new "aggravated enterprise corruption" offense, graded as a class A-1 felony, punishable by a minimum of fifteen to twenty-five years in prison and a maximum of life imprisonment.[47] Prior to the SAFE Act, the Penal Law's "enterprise corruption" offense required proof that the defendant (1) intentionally participated in the affairs of an enterprise by participating in a pattern of criminal activity, (2) acquired or maintained an interest in or control over an enterprise by means of a pattern of criminal activity, or (3) acquired an interest in an enterprise with money derived from a pattern of racketeering activity. The offense was a class B felony carrying a maximum twenty-five-year prison sentence.[48]

Like pre–SAFE Act enterprise corruption, the SAFE Act's aggravated enterprise corruption offense targets individuals who take an interest in or operate an enterprise via a "pattern of criminal activity" (defined as three or more specified criminal acts). The difference between the two offenses is the seriousness of the predicate offenses. The SAFE Act's aggravated enterprise corruption offense requires the prosecutor to prove that (1) the defendant committed two or more acts graded as class B or higher felonies and (2) at least two armed felonies; or one armed felony and one criminal purchase or disposal of a weapon (purchasing a firearm for another, knowing that it would be unlawful for the other person to possess the firearm); or one class B violent felony and two acts of criminal purchase or disposal of a weapon. Aggravated enterprise corruption could be used to prosecute gang members who repeatedly engage in firearms violence and/or trafficking. Pre–SAFE Act defendants who met those criteria would also have faced decades of incarceration.

From March 2013 to July 2016, there have been only two arrests statewide for this offense. The first case involved a 657-count indictment against five defendants for transporting weapons including AK-47s and nine-millimeter handguns aboard Delta Airlines commercial flights from Atlanta to New York City.[49] The Brooklyn district attorney charged four of the defendants with enterprise corruption and three with an additional count of aggravated enterprise corruption.[50] The lead defendant, a former Delta employee, carried backpacks and bags filled with guns and ammunition on seventeen commercial flights between Atlanta and New York. According to the Brooklyn district attorney's press release, "The indictment charges that the firearms trafficking enterprise had an ascertainable structure that was distinct from the pattern of criminal activity in that each participant had a specialized role within the enterprise. The enterprise was comprised of buyers, distributors, sellers and security access coordinators, all of whom contributed to the possession and sale of illegal firearms in Brooklyn."[51]

Mandatory Surrender of License and Firearms at Sentencing

Prior to the SAFE Act, a criminal court judge could revoke a defendant's handgun license upon conviction of a felony or other "serious offense." "Serious offense" includes a long list of crimes, among them illegally using, carrying, or possessing a pistol or other dangerous weapon; making or possessing burglar's instruments; buying or receiving stolen property; unlawful entry of a building; and aiding an escape from prison.[52] The SAFE Act amended the license-revocation-upon-conviction provision, so that a license is automatically revoked at the time the licensee becomes license-ineligible.[53] Upon revocation, the gun owner must surrender all his or her firearms to a law enforcement agency.[54] This change seems marginal at most.

Recklessly Injuring a Child by Discharge of a Firearm

Several SAFE Act offenses aim to punish and prevent accidental gun injuries. Each year, statewide, on average, 210 individuals under nineteen years of age are treated at a hospital for an unintentional firearm injury; 75 are injured severely enough to require hospital admission; 2 die.[55] (Many, probably most, of these unintentional injuries are self-inflicted.)

Prior to the SAFE Act, a person responsible for negligently killing someone with a gun (or, for that matter, with another type of weapon or with no weapon) could be prosecuted for criminally negligent homicide. An injury short of death could be prosecuted as third-degree assault (a class A misdemeanor, punishable by up to one year in jail); the prosecutor must prove that the defendant "recklessly caus[ed] physical injury to another person; or with criminal negligence, caus[ed] physical injury to another person by means of a deadly weapon or dangerous instrument."[56] Second-degree assault (a class D felony, carrying a seven-year maximum prison term) required proof that the defendant recklessly caused *serious* physical harm to another person "by means of a deadly weapon or dangerous instrument."[57] Another possible charge was reckless endangerment in the second degree (a class A misdemeanor, punishable by up to one year in prison), which required proof of reckless conduct creating a substantial risk of serious physical injury to another person.[58]

The SAFE Act added a new offense: recklessly causing physical injury to a child under eighteen by intentional discharge of a rifle, shotgun, or firearm, graded as a class D felony punishable by a seven-year maximum prison term.[59] In effect, this offense increases the maximum punishment for a defendant who *intentionally* fires a gun but *unintentionally* injures an under-eighteen-year-old victim. It eases the prosecution's burden with respect to the seriousness of the injury that must be proved. However, it still requires proof that the defendant intentionally fired the gun; that is, causing a gun to discharge by dropping or mishandling does not suffice.

Between March 2013 and July 2016, there were eight arrests statewide for this offense. Either such incidents are extremely rare or prosecutors are disinclined to file charges or prefer to use pre–SAFE Act offenses.

Criminal Possession of a Weapon on School Bus or Grounds

Prior to the SAFE Act, criminal possession of a firearm on a school bus or on school, college, or university grounds was classified as a class A misdemeanor, punishable by a maximum one-year jail term.[60] (It was also a federal felony.)[61] The SAFE Act promoted the offense to a class E felony, punishable by a maximum four-year prison term.[62] It is no defense that the gun is properly licensed or not loaded. (However, a school can exempt its security personnel.)

Between March 2013 and July 2016, there were 207 arrests statewide for this offense (65 percent in New York City). Because this provision applies to possession of knives and other weapons, a significant percentage of arrests may be for knife possession. Indeed, during this period, the New York City Police Department conducted a vigorous initiative to apprehend students carrying gravity knives.

* * *

At the time of the Sandy Hook massacre, New York did not suffer from inadequate substantive criminal law or criminal sentences

TABLE 10.1. New York City and New York State SAFE Act Arrests and Arraignments, March 2013–July 2016

Crime	Provision number	New York City total	Rest of state	New York State total
Second-degree assault—recklessly injure a child by discharge of a firearm	PL 120.05(04-a)	4	4	8
Aggravated murder—victim is a firefighter, emergency medical technician, paramedic, doctor, or nurse	PL 125.26(1)(a) (ii-a)	0	0	0
First-degree murder—victim is a firefighter, emergency medical technician, paramedic, doctor, or nurse	PL 125.27(1)(a) (ii-a)	0	0	0
Criminal possession of a weapon on school grounds (class E felony)[a]	PL 265.01-a	136	71	207
Criminal possession of a firearm	PL 265.01-b	503	375	878
Criminal possession of a firearm— possess a firearm (class E felony)[b]	PL 265.01-b(1)	6,870	958	7,828
Criminal possession of a firearm— unregistered assault weapon	PL 265.01-b(2)	46	12	58
Third-degree criminal possession of a weapon—while committing a drug trafficking felony (class D felony)	PL 265.02(09)	4	6	10
Third-degree criminal possession of a weapon—while committing a violent felony offense (class D felony)	PL 265.02(10)	23	46	69
Aggravated criminal possession of a weapon (class C felony)	PL 265.19	78	8	86
Unlawful transfer of an assault weapon (class A misdemeanor)	PL 265.00(22h)	0	4	4
Failure to register lawful (prior to SAFE Act) assault weapon (class A misdemeanor)	PL 400.00(16-a)	0	11	11
Unlawful possession of a large capacity ammunition feeding device (class A misdemeanor)	PL 265.36	6	58	64
Unlawful possession of certain ammunition feeding devices (category and class vary)	PL 265.37	17	71	88
Private sale of firearm— failure to obtain a background check (class A misdemeanor, non-finger-printable)	GB 898	0	0	0

TABLE 10.1. (*cont.*)

Crime	Provision number	New York City total	Rest of state	New York State total
Seller of ammunition—fails to register or fails to keep records (category and class vary)	PL 400.03(8)	0	0	0
Criminal purchase or disposal of a weapon—ineligible purchase (class D felony)	PL 265.17(1)	0	84	84
Criminal purchase or disposal of a weapon—buy for another (class D felony)	PL 265.17(2)	0	10	10
Criminal purchase or disposal of a weapon—dispose to another (class D felony)	PL 265.17(3)	0	9	9
Safe storage of rifles, shotguns, and firearms (class A misdemeanor)	PL 265.45	0	134	13
Report of theft or loss of a firearm, rifle, or shotgun (class A misdemeanor)	PL 400.10(01)(a)	0	9	9
Aggravated enterprise corruption (class A-1 felony)	PL 460.22	2	0	2

[a]Replaces PL 265.01 (03)—fourth-degree criminal possession of a weapon (class A misdemeanor).
[b]Fourth-degree criminal possession of a weapon (class A misdemeanor) remains in effect.

for perpetrators of gun crimes. Gun crimes carried heavy maximum (and often minimum) punishments, supplemented by repeat-offender sentencing enhancements. Defendants were routinely charged with multiple counts of the same offense or with overlapping offenses arising from the same criminal conduct. Nevertheless, it is always good politics to propose tougher laws to deter and punish violent criminals. Even when every species of gun crime has already been covered by tough substantive criminal and sentencing law, politicians happily pass more laws applicable to the same conduct. Police and prosecutors have no reason to object because the more severe the punishment facing the defendant, the greater the prosecutor's plea-bargaining leverage.

While we can be sure that police and prosecutors will vigorously enforce the criminal law against individuals who commit gun crimes, enforcement of regulatory controls against otherwise-law-abiding gun owners who fail to comply with those controls is a different matter. As the data presented in this chapter attest, regulatory firearms offenses are hardly enforced at all, at least as measured by arrests. There are two main reasons. First, police rarely encounter regulatory violators in the course of routine policing. Second, police and elected prosecutors have little incentive to expend resources on enforcing firearms regulations against otherwise-law-abiding neighbors and constituents.

Conclusion

The numbers are indisputable. The SAFE Act has enabled
the state to better protect New Yorkers.
—Melissa DeRosa, spokeswoman for Governor Andrew
Cuomo, December 2013[1]

Legislation of this type will have no effect on crime. It is not
intended to. It is designed to convince the public that something is being done. It is irrelevant whether the something
is an improvement. In the search for a response to future
tragedies, it is easier to lash out at an inert device than to
deal with the fundamental societal issues that permit an individual to engage in such an act.
—Shooters Committee on Political Education (SCOPE)[2]

New York State's SAFE Act was by far the most impressive state statutory response to the Sandy Hook Elementary School massacre. The
Act's gun control initiatives represent maximally feasible state-level
gun control. However, we have shown that many of the SAFE Act's
provisions have not been effectively implemented and/or enforced. In
so doing, we have shone a light on a critical, but mostly neglected,
aspect of gun control: implementation and enforcement. If gun control
laws are left unimplemented or unenforced, they amount to little more
than expressive politics. If one takes regulation of weapons and access
to weapons seriously, it is essential to focus from the outset on the fea-
sibility of implementing and enforcing a particular gun control policy.
That exercise, in turn, will affect decisions such as how many gun control policies should be enacted simultaneously or within a short time
frame, which policies should get priority, what kinds of entities (private as well as public) should be assigned what responsibilities, what

additional resources those entities need to fulfill their responsibilities, and how the efficacy of the policy's implementation and enforcement can be assessed.

Political Lessons

New York State gun control advocacy organizations were essentially satisfied with New York's pre–SAFE Act laws; their focus was on federal legislation. At the time of the Sandy Hook massacre, gun violence in New York had diminished remarkably over the previous three decades. The SAFE Act did *not* result from lobbying by gun control groups; rather, it is primarily attributable to Governor Andrew Cuomo. Why did he go all out for a new toughest-in-the-nation gun control law? He may well have believed that more gun controls were needed to make New Yorkers safer. He may well have felt that getting out front on gun control after Sandy Hook would boost his national political ambitions. Perhaps both reasons affected his decision. Once Cuomo made that commitment, there was no doubt that a comprehensive bill would be enacted. Thanks to his high approval numbers, plus Democrats' control of the Assembly and near control of the Senate, Cuomo could obtain passage of practically any gun control law he wanted. His drafting team wanted a "big law" that would overshadow other states' and President Obama's responses to Sandy Hook. To bulk up the SAFE Act, the drafting team included numerous strategies unconnected to preventing mass shootings. The inclusion of at least ten gun control strategies in a single bill presented state, county, and local officials with herculean implementation and enforcement challenges. But it seems unlikely that much, if any, thought was given to the complexities or costs of implementing and enforcing the Act.

The Act was drafted behind closed doors in a thirty-day period between mid-December 2012 and mid-January 2013. Unlike in Washington, DC, where gun control proposals have to be negotiated between Republicans and Democrats in the context of intense lobbying by advocacy groups, the SAFE Act passed without legislative hearings or public input. The bill was introduced into the legislature late at night on January 13 under a message of necessity and signed the following day. While easy to pass, the law has proven very difficult to implement and enforce.

While the governor achieved just the kind of high-visibility victory he sought, gun owners and their advocates were outraged at having been shut out of the legislative process. Cuomo underestimated the extent, depth, and persistence of popular opposition. While gun owners are a minority in New York State, they punch above their weight on account of their intense commitment to gun owners' rights. Thousands rallied in Albany a month after the SAFE Act's passage and again a year later. Tens of thousands of upstate home owners planted "Repeal the SAFE Act" signs on their front lawns. What is more, county and local officials resented the new load of implementation responsibilities the law imposed on them. They also resented their communities holding them partly responsible for the unpopular Act, which it was now their job to administer.

The majority of New York survey respondents tell pollsters that they favor the SAFE Act, but it is likely that most of those who approve it possess scant knowledge about the Act's actual mechanics. By contrast, gun owners are familiar with, and opposed to, all or most of the Act's provisions. They believe that the Act's proponents' primary objective is winning symbolic victories over law-abiding gun owners, not preventing mass shootings and reducing violent crimes, suicides, and accidents. Many believe the Act is a harbinger of future restrictions. This belief, that gun control advocates are never finished passing gun control laws, was reinforced in the 2013–2014 and 2015–2016 legislative sessions, when Democrats introduced more than 110 pro-gun-control bills, including bills requiring that all new guns be subjected to ballistic fingerprinting and fitted with locking devices, that gun purchasers be limited to one gun per month, and that persons convicted of gun crimes be ineligible for student loans.

The SAFE Act energized the gun-owning constituency. Advocacy organizations saw their memberships swell; new pro-gun-owner organizations sprang up. Cuomo's margin of reelection in 2014 was much smaller than in 2010, and Republicans won a Senate majority. These reversals seem to have dampened the governor's enthusiasm for implementing and enforcing the Act. The taskforce formed to supervise implementation stopped meeting; the Act's ammunition provisions were indefinitely suspended. The launch of handgun-licensee recertification was delayed for four years and its scope significantly curtailed. The lesson we draw is that even in a very strong pro-gun-control state such as New York, gun owners still wield significant influence. They can affect election outcomes in some districts. They can bring lawsuits that delay and even frustrate implementation of legislation. And they can, with de facto impunity, refuse to comply with laws that they adamantly oppose.

Gun Control Federalism

Even if a pro-gun-control majority could be mustered in Washington, DC, and could garner presidential support, the federal government does not have the administrative, policing, and adjudicatory infrastructure to enforce gun controls at the grass-roots level. Federal law enforcement is tiny compared to state and local law enforcement. Major expansion of the federal government's role in enforcing firearms regulation is highly unlikely. Historically, there has never been significant support for creating a federal super police agency (gendarme) with front-line law enforcement responsibilities (consider that the FBI, which is responsible for enforcing the federal criminal law across the entire country, has about half the number of agents as the New York City Police Department has uniformed officers.) Furthermore, federal prosecutions amount to less than 10 percent of state and local felony prosecutions and a negligible share of misdemeanor prosecutions.

The Bureau of Alcohol, Tobacco, Firearms, and Explosives (ATF) has fewer than 5,000 agents and support staff. Moreover, it has regulatory responsibilities over alcohol and explosives, as well as firearms. Its firearms regulatory responsibilities alone are daunting. These include licensing and regulatory oversight for hundreds of manufacturers and importers. (In 2015 alone, US companies manufactured 9.36 million firearms; in addition, there were almost 4 million firearm imports.) ATF issues federal licenses to firearms dealers and is responsible for auditing 140,000 licensed dealers. In 2015, ATF conducted 8,700 compliance inspections. At that rate, a licensed dealer could expect to be inspected once every sixteen years. If an inspection reveals a regulatory violation, ATF normally issues a warning letter or holds a warning conference. If dissatisfied with the dealer's responses, ATF can revoke the license. However, fewer than 1 percent of noncompliant dealers have their license revoked.[3] From 2010 to 2014, ATF rejected or revoked, on average, seventy-nine licenses per year.[4] Moreover, license revocation does not necessarily put the revoked licensee out of business; he or she could conceal their business by placing it in the hands of a spouse, relative, or friend with a license.

A May 2003 report from Americans for Gun Safety, a prominent gun control advocacy organization, opined:

> Overall prosecutions for violations of federal gun laws do not in any way reflect the number of federal gun crimes committed. Despite a massive black market in crime guns, the five major federal laws to combat gun trafficking are virtually ignored. Corrupt gun dealers are rarely prosecuted. Federal laws designed to keep guns out of the hands of kids and away from schools are almost never enforced. There is one federal prosecution for every 1,000 stolen firearms. Individuals who lie on the criminal background check form are rarely punished. Although police routinely recover crime guns with obliterated serial numbers, prosecutions are rare. Nearly all federal prosecutions involve those with previous criminal histories in possession of a firearm or for the use of a firearm in a federal crime of violence or drugs.[5]

For better or worse, states and their subdivisions will continue to be almost the exclusive enforcers of gun control laws.

New York politicians and police officials often blame the availability of guns in New York on traffickers who purchase them in states with "lax gun laws" and then sell them in New York. For example, according to a 2016 New York State Attorney General's Office report, 74 percent of the guns used in New York crimes were first sold in one of six "source states."[6] (The study traced the state of first retail sale for fifty thousand firearms recovered by police in New York from 2010 to 2015.) The report claims that the source states do not have "laws fundamental to preventing illegal diversion."[7] However, the federal Brady Law applies in every state; all federally licensed dealers, in every state, must initiate an NICS background check on every gun purchaser. All licensed dealers are subject to federal law that makes it a crime knowingly to sell a gun to a straw purchaser. All licensed dealers are subject to license revocation if they knowingly sell a gun without subjecting the purchaser to an NICS background check or sell a gun despite an NICS instruction not to complete the sale. All states make it a crime knowingly to sell a firearm to a firearms-ineligible person. Perhaps some states' federally licensed dealers are more willing to sell guns to firearms-ineligible people than their New York State counterparts are?[8] Note, however, that the number-one source state for traced New York City crime guns is New York (although all other states combined account for a significant majority of all traced crime guns).

Implementation and Enforcement Lessons

The SAFE Act looks different in practice than on the books. We attribute implementation and enforcement problems to design flaws, decentralized administration, lack of leadership, lack of funding, and high rates of noncompliance. These problems are not impossible to fix, but would, at a minimum, require a major commitment of resources for which to date there has been no political push. Beyond that, several of the SAFE Act's provisions need to be reconceived or discarded altogether.

Design Flaws

The SAFE Act was praised by Governor Cuomo's liberal base, liberal media, and gun control advocacy organizations. Whether the Act would be or could be effectively implemented and enforced was a salient issue. Politicians and gun control advocacy groups tend to view legislation as an end in itself, rather than as a means to an end. Until this book, practically no attention has been paid to how the SAFE Act or any other major state gun control law has been implemented and enforced.

A number of SAFE Act provisions never got off the ground. For example, the seven-round limitation on magazine capacity could not be implemented because seven-round magazines do not exist for most firearm models. The governor's compromise position, allowing ten-round-capacity magazines but prohibiting loading them with more than seven rounds, was mocked by gun owners and struck down by the courts. This kind of design flaw makes gun control proponents look ill informed. It reinforces the cynicism of gun owners who see such gun controls as political gestures.

The SAFE Act's ammunition-control provisions proved unworkable because the state could not procure or develop software capable of linking ammunition sellers to the Division of Criminal Justice's firearms-ineligible databases. The Act's drafters apparently did not give careful consideration to the types of ammunition sellers in New York, many of whom do not have computers capable of communicating with state databases. Further, the purpose of monitoring ammunition sales is unclear. Neither the State Police nor county sheriffs and municipal police have the capacity to investigate people who purchase large quantities of ammunition, even if "high volume" could be defined. Again, to critics, the ammunition-control provisions look like a grand political statement rather than a well-thought-out crime-control initiative.

The SAFE Act required every firearm licensee to apply for license renewal by winter of 2018. Incredibly, after a delay of four years in making applications available, the State Police, presumably in an attempt to cut down the large administrative burden they faced, decided that independently confirming applicants' license eligibility would not be part of the recertification process. Without such vetting, recertification lacks a persuasive purpose.

New York requires licenses for handgun, but not long-gun, ownership. This makes sense if the only concern is to prevent street crime and suicide, which are rarely committed with shotguns or rifles. But it makes little sense if the main concern is mass shootings, which are often committed with long guns. (Rifles and shotguns also are involved in accidents.) Since the SAFE Act was prompted by the Sandy Hook massacre, which was perpetrated with a rifle, the Act's drafters missed an opportunity to extend licensing to all long guns, instead focusing on registering assault weapons, but not their functional equivalents.

Decentralized Administration

The SAFE Act perpetuated and even reinforced the decentralized implementation and administration of New York's gun control regime. New York's 1911 Sullivan Law assigned responsibility for issuing and revoking handgun licenses to county-level licensing officers who are predominantly sitting judges. State law also gives counties authority to add additional gun controls as they see fit. Devolution of authority over gun control policy to the counties permits urban, suburban, and rural counties to tailor license issuance and revocation to their respective gun cultures and crime problems. On the one hand, devolving gun policy to counties makes good sense because New York is a big state with substantial geographical differences in gun culture and gun crime. On the other hand, it means that a license will be easier to obtain and retain in some counties than in others. The migration of guns and gun owners from laxer to stricter counties is facilitated by the law that, with the important exception of New York City, treats a carry license issued in one county as valid in every other county. (Interestingly, though more New York City crime guns are traced to a first sale in New York State rather than to any other single state, we are not aware of any gun control advocates, lawmakers, or political commentators who attribute New York City gun crime to more lax upstate gun policies.)

Lack of Leadership

No person or agency is in charge of implementing and enforcing the SAFE Act or New York State's regulation of firearms more generally. Implementation and enforcement responsibilities are spread across a number of state agencies (State Police, Division of Criminal Justice Services, Office of Mental Health, Office of Court Administration), county decision makers (licensing officers, directors of community services, sheriffs), and local police.

New York does not have a designated state agency responsible for designing, implementing, enforcing, and evaluating the firearm regulatory matrix. The county firearms-licensing officers are responsible for issuing and revoking handgun licenses. The SAFE Act assigned the State Police responsibility for creating databases and information systems, registering assault weapon owners, monitoring ammunition purchases, facilitating ammunition-purchaser background checks, and carrying out handgun-licensee recertification. But the State Police, at its core, is a law enforcement agency whose five thousand uniformed troopers work to deter, prevent, and solve crimes on highways and in unincorporated villages. Its Pistol/Revolver License Bureau is not central to the agency's organization, operations, or identity, nor is that unit appropriately staffed or funded to implement and evaluate the complex statewide gun control regime. A state committed to thoroughly regulating firearms manufacture, sale, possession, and use would do well to make those functions the responsibility of a dedicated state agency. (One thinks of the Department of Motor Vehicles, which has wide-ranging authority over regulation of vehicles and drivers, although of course enforcement is often left to state, county, and local police agencies.)

Inadequate Resources

The lack of significant budgetary support for the implementation of the SAFE Act is a recipe for failure. The 2013 New York budget gave the State Police a small supplement to cover SAFE Act–related expenses. Other state agencies tasked with SAFE Act implementation—the Division of Criminal Justice Services and Office of Mental Health—received no additional funds. Likewise, county mental health officials, county clerks, and county sheriffs received no state financial assistance to cover the cost of carrying out their SAFE Act–related responsibilities. For them, the SAFE Act is an unfunded state mandate that is administratively burdensome and a source of constituents' resentment and anger.

In order to avoid the risk that politicians pass expressive laws that are not effectively implemented, they should be required to affix to their gun control bills realistic implementation cost assessments approved by apolitical bureaucrats or independent entities.

High Rate of Noncompliance

Effective regulation requires compliance by the regulated. Compliance can sometimes be achieved by threat, such as when the regulator threatens to delicense a manufacturer. But the state cannot credibly threaten gun sellers and purchasers with punishment for failing to register their assault weapons, failure to destroy their large-capacity magazines, or failure to process private gun sales through federally licensed dealers. There is little chance that such noncompliance will be detected and, if it is, that significant punishment will be imposed.

The State Police have been unwilling to release any specific information about the rate of compliance with the handgun-licensee recertification provisions. However, it is likely that, for reasons of administrative burden and cost, identifying and revoking the licenses of nonapplicants will never be comprehensively undertaken.

We do not know the extent to which people who are rendered firearms-ineligible on account of being diagnosed as mentally ill and dangerous or subject to a domestic violence protection order will abandon their intention to acquire a firearm or surrender guns they already possess. Members of both groups, like all firearms-ineligible persons, can easily acquire a gun on the primary market by means of a straw purchaser, on the secondary market by purchasing from a willing private seller, or on the black market from a seller specializing in selling guns to ineligible persons.

Punishing otherwise-law-abiding persons for noncompliance with gun regulations poses other dilemmas. Light punishment will probably have little effect on compliance, while police, prosecutors, courts, and juries may resist imposing heavy punishments for regulatory violations.

Specific Lessons

Assault Weapons Ban

In 2000, New York prohibited semiautomatic rifles, shotguns, and pistols with two or more military-like features, thereby providing a safe harbor for semiautomatics with one military-like feature. (The two-feature definition was based on the federal assault weapons ban.) In December of 2012, the month of the Sandy Hook massacre, there was no evidence that semiautomatics with one military-like feature endangered the public—that is, that these one-military-feature semiautomatics were turning up in crime, suicide, or multiple murders. If semiautomatics with one military-like feature are actually more dangerous than other semiautomatics are, the SAFE Act drafters should have omitted the registration option and sought to remove them from civilian hands, perhaps by offering a generous buyback. Gun owners and their advocates fear that the registration database will, in the future, probably after a mass shooting in New York or elsewhere, lead to confiscation of these firearms—hence their unwillingness to register.

Even if a high rate of registration compliance could be achieved, how would assault weapon registration make a massacre less likely or less deadly? It is not plausible that a would-be massacre perpetrator would be deterred because his or her weapon of choice was registered, particularly given that the vast majority commit suicide or are killed or captured at the scene. The most persuasive justification for assault weapon registration is that, combined with the prohibition of transferring registered assault weapons to any New York resident, these weapons will become extinct in New York when all current registrants die.

The SAFE Act's assault weapons ban is not readily enforceable. Admittedly, if police are alerted that a gun store is selling illegal assault weapons, the seller can be arrested and the store shut down. But there is no obvious way to enforce the law against individual owners. Police are unlikely to see such a weapon unless they come across it at a crime scene, probably in the hands of its owner. (However, assault weapons are rarely used in crime.)

Putting aside the ease of acquiring assault weapons in other states or on the black market in New York State, would eliminating all registered one-military-feature assault weapons reduce the risk of high-casualty mass shootings? Even if a would-be perpetrator of a mass shooting could not legally acquire an assault weapon, he or she could easily acquire a semiautomatic that is functionally equivalent to a banned assault weapon.

Obviously, there has to be an "upper limit" on the kind of weaponry available to civilians. Prohibition of civilian possession of shoulder-fired missiles, tanks, and military ordnance is not controversial. Stringent regulation of automatic-fire weapons (machine guns) does not draw serious opposition.[9] What is controversial is banning a class of semiautomatic firearms largely on the basis of their appearance. If some semiautomatics are to be prohibited, it should be on account of exceptional dangerousness, not on account of cosmetic features such as a bayonet mount or a folding stock. Determining what makes some semiautomatics more dangerous than others is an important question that is often overlooked in the gun control debate. Ammunition caliber is one obvious possible answer. Rate of fire is another possible answer. Machine guns are banned on account of rate of fire. In 2019, New York banned "bump stocks" which permit semiautomatics to fire like automatics. Semiautomatics that fire faster than a certain rate should also be banned. Identifying the acceptable rate of fire is beyond our expertise. Some commentators have recommended banning all semiautomatics, apparently because they fire at a faster rate than bolt action, slide action, and other nonsemiautomatic weapons. That recommendation is more logical than banning some semiautomatics on the basis of appearance.

The Ban on Large-Capacity Magazines

At the time of the Sandy Hook massacre, New York already banned detachable magazines with greater than ten-round capacity, albeit with a grandfathering provision based on manufacture date that made enforcement impossible. The SAFE Act's drafters, wishing to establish the nation's lowest magazine-capacity limit, reduced permitted magazine capacity to seven rounds and eliminated grandfathering. That no seven-round magazines existed for the most popular firearm models made the SAFE Act vulnerable to the charge that it was for political effect, and not a crime-control measure. Governor Cuomo, having no effective answer to the criticism, agreed to reinstate the ten-round-capacity limitation but without grandfathering of larger magazines and with the proviso that a ten-round magazine not be loaded with more than seven rounds; that is, the magazine-capacity limit was replaced by a magazine-loading limit. The idea that criminals, much less mass shooters, would limit their ten-round magazine to seven cartridges reinforced gun owners' cynicism about the governor's motives and stimulated further protests. Eventually, federal courts struck down the seven-round loading limit as irrational.

The upshot is that ten-round detachable magazines can be sold in New York and loaded to their full ten-round capacity. But what happens to the tens of thousands of larger-capacity magazines held by New Yorkers? Many existing owners are disinclined to destroy or surrender them because they believe that eventually the prohibition will be repealed or amended. The chance of apprehension is negligible, and if a person apprehended with a large-capacity magazine is a first offender, the punishment is an administrative violation.

Limiting magazine capacity is a sound policy idea. Since ten rounds is the standard capacity for detachable magazines, it is a reasonable policy choice and should be sufficient for self-defense purposes. If mass shooters have to make do with ten-round magazines (a big if), some potential victims may escape to safety. A federal law prohibiting magazines with capacity of more than ten rounds would be highly desirable. Short of that, New York and other strong gun control states need a federal law that prohibits sellers in states where large-capacity magazines are legal from selling or shipping them to residents of states where they are illegal. Admittedly, such a law would be very hard to enforce. There are not enough ATF agents to deter or apprehend scofflaw sellers.

Universal Background Checking

The SAFE Act's universal-background-checking initiative is an important experiment. The federal Brady Law's use of purchaser background checking to keep dangerous persons from acquiring firearms is seriously flawed because it requires (and authorizes) background checking only for individuals who purchase guns from licensed dealers. It leaves the secondary market completely unregulated. An ineligible gun purchaser need only look for a gun-for-sale advertisement on a bulletin board, in a newspaper, or online, then make contact with the seller. There is no background checking of the purchaser and no record of the sale.

New York's version of universal purchaser background checking is among the nation's strongest. A New Yorker who seeks to purchase a handgun on the secondary market (that is, from a private seller) has to bring the gun to a licensed dealer and show him or her an updated license from the county clerk or licensing officer. (The scheme would be even stronger if licensing applied to long-gun owners.) However, an ineligible person who could not find a private seller willing to ignore the SAFE Act could recruit a straw purchaser, perhaps a spouse, intimate partner, or friend with a clean record. He or she could tell that straw purchaser what gun to buy. He or she could even go gun shopping with the straw purchaser, identify the desired gun, and send the straw purchaser back alone to consummate the purchase. A straw purchaser who is denied service at one store could try other stores.

A person asked to serve as a straw purchaser might hesitate, considering what might happen if the beneficial purchaser uses the gun to commit a crime and the crime gun is recovered and traced back to the straw purchaser. The police would ask the straw purchaser what happened to the gun, and if the excuse is that it was lost or stolen, they would also ask why the recorded owner (the straw purchaser) did not report the loss to state authorities. This might deter some persons from acting as straw purchasers, but it is likely that many will not consider this risk or, having considered it, will ignore it. For one thing, unless the straw purchaser acquires the gun from an FFL or brings it to an FFL for a background check, there will be no way of identifying the straw purchaser. A criminally minded beneficial purchaser would surely tell the straw purchaser to acquire the gun from the secondary or black market and not to fill out any paperwork. In that case, the chance that the straw purchaser would ever be apprehended is slight and, if apprehended, that he or she could be proven to have made the purchase and disposition even slighter. A strong registration system anchored by a database that keeps track of the ownership of every gun would, in principle, reduce the frequency of straw purchasing. But in practice, that would require a great deal of compliance on the part of gun owners, which, in turn, would require credible enforcement. This would not be easy or cheap to accomplish.

New York's universal background checking law does not have to be "implemented." It requires only that private (secondary-market) sellers comply and that enough licensed dealers agree to process private sales. We found that there seem to be sufficient numbers of licensed dealers who are prepared to take on this role, but the question is the extent to which private sellers are complying with the law. Prospective purchasers who know or suspect that they cannot pass a background check can approach one private seller after another until they find one who is willing to transfer the gun without taking it to a licensed dealer. Eighteen months before passage of the SAFE Act, a sting operation by New York City Mayor Michael Bloomberg's office found that 62 percent of people advertising a gun for sale online agreed to complete the sale after the faux purchaser explained that he could not pass a background check.[10] Moreover, after the SAFE Act's passage, NICS reported a very small percentage of purchaser background checks emanating from private sales, indicating a high rate of noncompliance.

Disarming Persons Assessed to be Mentally Ill and Dangerous

Mental illness is not a risk factor for gun crime, but it is a risk factor for mass shootings and suicide. Most mass-shooting perpetrators had a history of severe psychological problems. In some cases, the perpetrator was directed to treatment but did not follow up, or the treatment was terminated prematurely. Critiquing the delivery of mental health services is beyond the scope of this project. Increasing and improving mental health services is an obvious recommendation. Of course, there will be questions as to the potential and limitations of mental health treatment for preventing mass shootings, just as there are questions as to the potential and limitations of firearm regulation for preventing mass shootings.

The SAFE Act casts a very wide net in seeking to keep guns out of the hands of people alleged to be mentally ill and dangerous. It mandates that mental health professionals report to county officials the names of patients believed to present a significant risk of serious injury to self or others. Hospital personnel have reported more than eighty thousand patients. The Office of Mental Health enters the reported names into a firearms-ineligible database. No mass shootings have occurred in New York State since passage of the SAFE Act, but only two had occurred in the twenty-five years before the SAFE Act. With numbers this small, it is difficult to assess the efficacy of this law.

Successfully implementing this strategy of disarming dangerous mentally ill persons requires more than reporting; it requires preventing reported persons from acquiring guns and getting reported persons who possess guns to surrender them. Since county clerks can search the database of New Yorkers disqualified from firearm possession on account of mental illness, a patient reported by a mental health professional should not be able to obtain the county clerk's permission to purchase a new handgun from a licensed dealer. However, since no license is needed to purchase a long gun, and NICS does not have access to the database of § 9.46-reported patients, a disqualified person will not be blocked from purchasing a shotgun or rifle. This regulatory loophole could be closed by extending firearm licensing to long guns or by making the SAFE Act's mental health reporting database available to NICS. (There is disagreement about whether that change would require federal legislation.)

Persuading persons reported as mentally ill and dangerous to surrender their guns is an even greater challenge. The Division of Criminal Justice Services (DCJS) is supposed to "periodically" check its database of handgun licensees against the SAFE Act's mental health reporting database. If there is a match, the relevant county clerk should be notified to initiate license-revocation and gun-surrender procedures. The system would be more efficient if DCJS had authority to revoke the license. Still, the licensee would have to be notified, and local police would have to carry out or confirm the gun(s) surrender. As long as the revoked licensee is not in prison or in hospital, the person could of course retrieve a hidden gun or acquire another.

A bigger problem is that DCJS has no way of knowing whether a person reported as potentially dangerous on account of mental illness is an *unlicensed* gun owner. There is no database of unlicensed gun possessors. Police do not have the capacity to interrogate, much less thoroughly search the premises of, every § 9.46-reported person. However, a good first step would be to require DCJS to notify every § 9.46-reported person that he or she is the subject of a SAFE Act mental health report and must surrender all guns. There would have to be some kind of immunity for unlicensed gun possessors who surrender their guns.

The SAFE Act's provisions on disarming persons who are mentally ill and dangerous are closely linked to the Sandy Hook massacre. However, the goal should be to prevent such persons from getting their hands on a gun in the first place. This is much easier said than done. Some mass murderers, such as the Sandy Hook shooter, stole guns belonging to another family member.[11] This ought to call attention to one of the most promising gun controls: smart guns that will fire only for the individual or individuals for whom they are programmed. The SAFE Act did not address smart-gun technology. A federal law imposing a smart-gun requirement on manufacturers and importers is obviously preferable to leaving the matter to each state. Otherwise, if New York enacted such a law, there would still be hundreds of thousands, perhaps millions, of nonsmart guns in the state, supplemented by new nonsmart guns trafficked from out of state.

Disarming Subjects of Domestic Violence Protection Orders

The SAFE Act made it mandatory for criminal and family court judges to revoke or suspend a protection-order respondent's firearm license in the event that the judge finds "substantial risk that the respondent may use or threaten to use a firearm unlawfully." Although prior to the SAFE Act there were no data indicating that judges were failing to issue firearm-surrender orders in appropriate circumstances, the SAFE Act provision will lead to surrender orders being issued in a greater percentage of cases. Judges do not lose all discretion because, in every case, they have to determine whether the respondent poses a "substantial risk."

Ironically, expanding the number of persons subject to a domestic violence firearm-surrender orders might not save lives. New York judges issue more than three hundred thousand protection orders annually. Increasing the percentage of these orders that are accompanied by firearm-surrender orders will spread finite police resources over a greater number of cases. If more low-risk respondents have to be visited, investigated, and disarmed, that means less time and attention for high-risk cases. An overwhelmed system will not serve the interests of those who are in serious danger. Maybe, prior to the SAFE Act, judges were better at identifying the respondents who merit police attention than the SAFE Act drafters assumed. This is an empirical question for which data do not exist.

Ordering disarmament and accomplishing it are two different things. Accomplishing disarmament requires (1) getting respondents to surrender all their guns and (2) preventing respondents from acquiring another gun. The most belligerent and dangerous respondents will be least likely to comply. They might tell the enquiring police officer that they do not to have a gun, might surrender some but not all their guns, or might surrender their guns but acquire another one.

Taking guns out of the hands of domestic violence abusers no doubt makes victims somewhat safer but by no means ensures their protection. Of seventy-eight intimate (spouse, intimate-partner) homicides in New York in 2016, twenty-five were committed with a gun. There were more domestic knife fatalities than gun fatalities.

Regulating Ammunition Sales and Monitoring Purchasers

The SAFE Act's ambitious ammunition-regulation provisions might be aimed at preventing would-be criminals or suicidal persons from obtaining *any* ammunition, but more likely the drafters' intent was to prevent a potential rampage shooter from acquiring a "large quantity" of ammunition. Ammunition purchasers must acquire ammunition in person from a seller registered with the State Police. Ammunition sellers must (1) verify a purchaser's identity and initiate a background check and (2) report information about each sale to the State Police.[12] The State Police must keep track of every purchaser's total ammunition purchases (but only for one year) and investigate high-volume purchasers. The reporting exemption for shooting ranges and gun clubs creates an opportunity for a shooter to acquire unreported ammunition. Ammunition could also easily be purchased out of state; no federal law bars selling ammunition to an out-of-state resident.

Either the SAFE Act's drafters did not realize that NICS would not be available to check the firearms-eligibility of ammunition purchasers, or they did realize it but decided to ignore the problem. After the SAFE Act's passage, it became clear that New York would have to create a database of ammunition-ineligible persons and an information system that would provide registered ammunition sellers with real-time access to that database. This background-checking regime for ammunition purchasers would essentially have duplicated background checking for long-gun owners and tripled background checking for handgun owners. Handgun purchasers would be background checked when they (1) apply for a handgun license, (2) purchase a gun from a licensed dealer or a private seller (under the SAFE Act's universal background checking), and (3) purchase ammunition. Long-gun purchasers would be background checked when they (1) purchase a gun and (2) purchase ammunition. State officials gave up on implementing ammunition-purchaser background checking when the establishment of a database of ammunition-ineligible persons proved infeasible, at least at a cost that they were willing to shoulder.

Ammunition-seller registration and reporting could have been accomplished without technological innovation. Ammunition sellers could have been required to register with the State Police and to send (by fax, snail mail, email) to the State Police daily, weekly, or monthly reports on every sale. These reports could include purchasers' names and other identity information as well as the type and amount of ammunition purchased. The State Police would have had to aggregate each individual's ammunition purchases from all registered state ammunition sellers each year. (It is not clear whether the drafters envisioned calendar-year aggregation or aggregation for each purchaser for a year beginning on the day of first ammunition purchase.) In any event, this part of the SAFE Act's ammunition regulations was also abandoned. So the SAFE Act's ammunition-control strategies are a dead letter.

If New York someday implements a system capable of tracking each New Yorker's ammunition purchases, state officials would have to decide what quantity of ammunition purchased over what period of time should trigger what kind of investigation. A prospective mass shooter does not need an exceptionally large quantity of ammunition, certainly no more than a couple of hundred cartridges. Perhaps tens of thousands of New Yorkers, including most target shooters, purchase that much ammunition annually. Furthermore, it is hardly clear what kind of "investigation" of purchasers of large quantities of ammunition (however defined) would be conducted, or who would conduct it. Certainly, a large quantity of ammunition purchased over a year would not establish probable cause to believe that a crime had been committed or was contemplated. It would not by itself provide probable cause for a search warrant. The State Police or a local police department might call the large-quantity purchaser and ask, "What's with all the ammunition?" The purchaser might say, "Target shooting" or "None of your business." What then?

Our conclusion is that the SAFE Act's ammunition-purchaser provisions serve no achievable purpose. It is probably fortunate that they were judged infeasible because a significant attempt to implement and enforce them would have placed yet more administrative burden on the already-overburdened State Police, perhaps detracting from efforts to implement and enforce other SAFE Act provisions.

Handgun-Licensee Recertification

The SAFE Act's drafters intended handgun-licensee recertification as a strategy for confirming that a handgun licensee had not become firearms-ineligible at some point after obtaining a license, or had become ineligible and not been revoked due to an administrative snafu. However, because of the crushing administrative burden of vetting up to a million recertification applications, the State Police decided that recertification should go forward without any background checking. Thus, a license-recertification applicant who claims to be firearms-eligible is automatically recertified. (The State Police say that they will begin background checking at the next five-year recertification point; that is dubious because in spring 2023, hundreds of thousands, possibly more than a million, applications will have to be processed, producing the same crushing administrative burden.)

The State Police have spun the extraordinary decision to go forward with recertification without background checking applicants by shifting the rationale for recertification from background checking to producing a "pristine" licensee database. We have been told several times that the State Police's master database of New York handgun licensees still includes Eleanor Roosevelt's name. If the State Police want to eliminate the names of deceased licensees, it would be easy to remove the names of licensees born or licensed before a certain date.

Identifying and revoking the licenses of those people who failed to apply for renewal will be another massive administrative challenge that we doubt will ever be seriously attempted. Here is how it would have to work: After all recertification applications have been processed, the State Police would need to identify, according to their master licensee database, those handgun licensees who did not apply for recertification. This would probably produce a list of several hundred thousand names, perhaps the majority of whom are deceased. Because county firearms-licensing officials rather than the State Police have legal authority to revoke handgun licenses and because revocation requires notification and an opportunity to be heard, county officials will need to investigate whether each nonregistrant is deceased, moved out of state, moved to another county, or has a valid excuse for not submitting an application (or is the victim of a recertification-processing clerical error). Revocation procedures for those who do not voluntarily renounce their licenses will have to be initiated. This would impose on county officials an administrative burden that they are neither willing nor capable of assuming. In short, New York's recertification scheme, while consuming large resources, has little payoff.

New Criminal Offenses and Sentence Enhancements

The SAFE Act added numerous new criminal-offense provisions to back up new regulatory controls. For example, it is an offense to fail to register an assault weapon and an offense to transfer a gun without taking it and the transferee to a licensed dealer to initiate an NICS background check. However, in upstate counties where gun ownership is common, police chiefs, sheriffs, and prosecutors are reluctant to bring charges against otherwise-law-abiding residents for failing to comply with gun regulations. One district attorney candidly told us that he would not pursue charges against any SAFE Act regulatory offense unless it involved underlying criminal activity such as drug trafficking or domestic violence.

Enforcement of gun regulations is not easy. Regulatory violations are not likely to be detected by police on patrol or in response to 911 calls. Proactive policing, including stings and undercover operations, which are time-consuming, resource intensive, and beyond the capacity of most local police departments, will be necessary. Even a large police department is unlikely to assign high priority to apprehending unregistered possessors of assault weapons and large-capacity magazines who have not engaged in other criminal activity. It will be an even lower priority to identify casual gun sellers who fail to route their sales through a licensed dealer. Statewide, there have been very few arrests for violating the SAFE Act's regulatory provisions; it is not possible to say how many of those were stand-alone arrests unrelated to predicate criminal activity.

* * *

Effective gun control needs to go far beyond passing symbolically satisfying laws that cannot or will not be implemented and enforced. We need to focus on which agencies at which levels of government are best placed to carry out particular implementation and enforcement functions. We need to be realistic about how much regulation we can implement and enforce and at what cost. And we need to recognize that regulating access to firearms is not the only, or necessarily the most effective, way to reduce lethal violence. With the important exception of mass shootings, lethal violence has declined dramatically over the past three decades. No scholar to our knowledge attributes this decline primarily to better gun controls. We should not be mesmerized by calls for "commonsense gun control." We need a kind of Gun Control 2.0 that focuses on regulations that are implementable, are enforceable, and have a plausible likelihood of reducing firearm injuries.

ACKNOWLEDGMENTS

Over the course of several years, we interviewed scores of people involved with different aspects of the SAFE Act. Big thanks go to Alex Crohn, Seth Agata, James Coughlin, Joseph Fucito, Kim Halayko, Elizabeth Larkin, Paul Piperato, Alex Wilson, and Christopher Ryan. And thanks too to the many officials and former officials who spoke to us on condition of anonymity.

We benefited from interviews with a number of NGO personnel who were knowledgeable about issues covered by the SAFE Act. Among them, we want especially to thank Richard Aborn, Liberty Aldrich, Amy Barasch, and Maureen Curtis.

We are grateful to dozens of federally licensed gun dealers who agreed to be interviewed regarding their willingness to broker private gun sales pursuant to the SAFE Act's universal-background-checking provision.

Among gun owners' rights advocates and SAFE Act critics, we received helpful comments from Steve Aldstadt, Michael Benard, Paul V. Ciminelli, Tom King, and Bill Nojay.

We benefited from comments and advice from academic colleagues and friends, including David Garland, Roy Germano, David T. Hardy, Judge Martin Marcus, John Monahan, Andrew Schaffer, Jeffrey Swanson, and Frank Zimring.

We could not have completed this research without the wonderful assistance from research assistants who dug up data, set up interviews, prepared memos, critiqued drafts, and generally provided assistance at every step of the way. Sincere thanks to Amitav Chakraborty, Gregory Crane, Andrew Debbins, Alex Haberman, Erik Herron, Jason Kaplan, Lucy Kissel, Nurit Lavie, Paige Jill Mankin, and Vedad Tabich.

The NYU School of Law, its dean, Trevor Morrison, and its superb reference librarian, Jay Shuman, could not have been more generous and supportive. Faculty assistant Veronica Cruz assisted us in a dozen different ways.

NOTES

INTRODUCTION

1. Office of the Child Advocate, State of Connecticut, *Shooting at the Sandy Hook Elementary School* (November 21, 2014), www.ct.gov.
2. Jake Tapper, Devin Dwyer, and Manny Bruce, *President Obama Launches Gun Violence TaskForce*, ABC News (December 19, 2012).
3. James B. Jacobs & Zoe Fuhr, *The Potential and Limitations of Background Checking for Gun Purchasers*, 7 Wake Forest J.L. & Pol'y 487 (2017).
4. Rick Unger, *Here Are the 23 Executive Orders on Gun Safety Signed by the President Today*, Forbes (January 16, 2013), www.forbes.com.
5. *See State Laws Enacted in the Year after Newtown*, New York Times (December 10, 2013), www.nytimes.com.
6. The Brady Campaign's Scorecard grades are based on thirty separate policies falling under nine subheadings: Background Checks and Access to Firearms; Other Regulation of Sales and Transfers; Gun Owner Accountability; Firearms in Public Places; Classes of Weapons and Ammunition/Magazines; Consumer and Child Safety; Investigating Gun Crimes; Local Authority to Regulate; and Other. See Brady Campaign to Prevent Gun Violence & Giffords Law Center to Prevent Gun Violence, *2013 State Scorecard: Why Gun Laws Matter*, www .bradycampaign.org.
7. Phil Cook, *Homicide and Suicide Rates Associated with Implementation of the Brady Handgun Violence Prevention Act*, 284 JAMA 585 (2000).

CHAPTER 1. THE POLITICS OF THE SAFE ACT

1. Jessica Alaimo, *N.Y. Gun Law Mandates Magazines That Don't Exist*, USA Today (March 1, 2013), www.usatoday.com.
2. Editorial, *New York Leads on Gun Control*, New York Times (January 16, 2013), www.nytimes.com.
3. New York State Governor's Office, *Statement from Governor Andrew M. Cuomo on Shooting at Sandy Hook Elementary School* (December 14, 2012), www.governor .ny.gov.
4. CNN, *Transcript of Press Conference with Andrew Cuomo, Secretary of Department of Housing and Urban Development, and Ed Shultz, President and CEO of Smith & Wesson* (March 17, 2000), http://transcripts.cnn.com. The NRA and other gun owners' rights groups excoriated Smith & Wesson for settling the case and organized a boycott of the company's products. Clinton's successor,

President George W. Bush, had no interest in enforcing the settlement, which in any event became irrelevant after Congress passed the Protection of Lawful Commerce in Arms Act of 2005, providing tort immunity for firearms manufacturers: *see* Protection of Lawful Commerce in Arms Act of 2005, codified at 15 U.S.C. sec. 7901–7903.

5. Michael Shnayerson, *The Contender: Andrew Cuomo, a Biography* 373 (2015).

6. David Ariosto, *Governor Signs Nation's First Gun-Control Bill since Newtown*, CNN (January 28, 2013), http://edition.cnn.com.

7. Kenneth Lovett, *Gov. Cuomo Eyeing an All-Out Assault on GOP If It Continues to Hold Up His Plan to Institute the Nation's Toughest Gun-Control Laws*, New York Daily News (January 7, 2013), www.nydailynews.com.

8. Press Release, New York State Senate, *Senator Skelos Unveils Tough Plan to Crack Down on Illegal Guns and Criminals Who Use Guns* (January 5, 2013), www.nysenate.gov.

9. Andrew Cuomo, *Governor Andrew M. Cuomo's 2013 State of the State Address* (January 9, 2013), www.governor.ny.gov.

10. The New York Court of Appeals held in *Maybee v. State of New York*, 4 N.Y.3d 415, 796 N.Y.S.2d 18 (2005), that as long as the governor provides some factual statements, the governor's conclusion that a message of necessity is required may not be challenged. This applies even if "the facts" are nothing more than the bill's contents. Chief Judge Judith Kaye observed in her concurrence that messages of necessity, which were meant to be an exception, had become the "practice of government" and that to "put in doubt legislation enacted on such messages would lead to great unsettlement."

11. New York State Legislative Annual—2013, 1; New York State Senate, *Senate Bill S2230*, www.nysenate.gov.

12. S.2230/A.2388 (2013–2014).

13. Casey Selier, *New Gun Law Offers Reply to Mass Killings*, Albany Times Union (January 16, 2013), www.timesunion.com.

14. Press Release, Office of the Governor, *Governor Cuomo Signs NY SAFE Act in Rochester* (January 16, 2013), www.governor.ny.gov (emphasis added).

15. Thomas Kaplan, *Cuomo's Gun Law Plays Well Downstate but Alienates Upstate*, New York Times (October 24, 2014), www.nytimes.com.

16. Editorial, *The States Confront Gun Violence*, New York Times (January 17, 2013), www.nytimes.com.

17. Editorial, *Long-Overdue Action on Guns*, Journal News (January 17, 2013).

18. Press Release, Office of the Mayor, *Statement of Mayor Michael R. Bloomberg on Passage of NY SAFE Act* (January 15, 2013), http://www1.nyc.gov.

19. Press Release, Office of the New York State Comptroller, *New York State Comptroller Thomas P. DiNapoli on Passage of Historic Gun Legislation* (January 15, 2013), www.osc.state.ny.us.

20. Press Release, Office of the Governor, *Governor Cuomo Signs NY SAFE Act in Rochester* (January 16, 2013), www.governor.ny.gov.

21. Thomas Kaplan, *Sweeping Limits on Guns Become Law in New York*, New York Times (January 15, 2013), www.nytimes.com.
22. Barbara Mantel, *Should Lawmakers Tighten Firearm Restriction?*, CQ Researcher (March 8, 2013), http://library.cqpress.com.
23. Rashed Mian, *NY Gun Control Bill Approved by Legislature*, Long Island Press (January 15, 2013), www.longislandpress.com; Casey Seiler, *New Gun Law Offers Reply to Mass Killings*, Albany Times Union (January 16, 2013), www.timesunion.com.
24. Press Release, Office of Christopher S. Friend, Assembly member, New York State Assembly, *Albany Lacks Transparency Once Again* (January 16, 2013), http://nyassembly.gov.
25. Press Release, Office of Steven F. McLaughlin, Assembly member, New York State Assembly *McLaughlin: Moscow Would Be Proud Of New York* (January 16, 2013), http://assembly.state.ny.us.
26. Colin Campbell, *Cuomo Defends Gun Control Plan in Feisty Debate with Dicker*, New York Observer (January 17, 2013), http://observer.com.
27. Kyle Hughes, *Petitions to Repeal the NY SAFE Act Collect Thousands of Signatures on Senator Websites*, New Haven Register (January 29, 2013), www.nhregister.com.
28. Ian Benjamin, *Hundreds Attend Forum to Voice SAFE Act Opposition*, Troy (NY) Record (April 1, 2013), www.troyrecord.com.
29. Kyle Hughes, *Petitions to Repeal the NY SAFE Act Collect Thousands of Signatures on Senator Websites*, New Haven Register (January 29, 2013), www.nhregister.com.
30. Mary Lou Lang-Byrd, *Protesters Shred Safe Act Registration Cards*, Washington Free Beacon (April 16, 2014), http://freebeacon.com; Associated Press, *Gun-Rights Protesters Burn Assault Weapons Registration Forms at NY Rally*, Syracuse.com (March 17, 2014), www.syracuse.com.
31. Mikael Thalen, *New York Residents Set Fire to Gun Registration Forms*, InfoWars (March 17, 2014), www.infowars.com.
32. A list of county and local resolutions opposing the SAFE Act can be found at NY SAFE Resolutions, *Resolutions*, www.nysaferesolutions.com (last visited December 18, 2018).
33. Res. 2013082 (Dutchess County, March 21, 2013), www.co.dutchess.ny.us.
34. New York State Sheriffs' Association, *New York State Sheriffs' Association Response to NY SAFE Act* (January 24, 2013), www.nyscc.com.
35. *Id.*
36. Versions introduced in 2013–2014 legislative session: S6616/A8666, an act to amend the county law, in relation to use of official seals. Versions introduced in 2015–2016 legislative session: S3897A/A3569A.
37. New York State Conference of Local Mental Hygiene Directors, *Testimony to the Joint Budget Committee on Mental Hygiene Regarding the 2013–2014 Executive Budget Proposal* (February 27, 2013), www.nysenate.gov.
38. Dave Urbanski, *New York Gov. Andrew Cuomo: Some Conservatives "Have No Place in the State of New York,"* The Blaze (January 18, 2014), www.theblaze.com.

39. Tom Precious, *Anti-SAFE Act Rally Draws Thousands, Including Speakers Trump and Paladino*, Buffalo News (April 1, 2014), www.buffalonews.com/; Rick Karlin, *Albany Anti–NY Safe Act Rally Draws Trump, Astorino and Paladino*, Albany Times Union (April 2, 2014), www.timesunion.com.

40. *Astorino Calls SAFE Act "A Disaster,"* State of Politics (blog), Spectrum News (January 2014), www.nystateofpolitics.com.

41. Robert Harding, *Sienna Poll: Most New Yorkers Support the SAFE Act, but Majority of Upstate Voters Do Not*, Eye on NY (blog), auburnpub.com (May 26, 2015), https://auburnpub.com.

42. Skelos was convicted in December 2015 of eight counts of bribery, extortion, and corruption. In May 2016, a federal judge sentenced him to five years in prison. In submissions seeking leniency in sentencing, Skelos's lawyer referred to the SAFE Act as one of his client's "notable legislative achievements," which he had supported "without fear or favor of the potential political consequences." Jon Campbell, *Skelos Points to SAFE Act in Bid to Avoid Prison*, Poughkeepsie Journal (March 24, 2016), www.poughkeepsiejournal.com. Assembly Speaker Sheldon Silver was also convicted of (unrelated) corruption charges and sentenced to twelve years in prison. The Second Circuit Court of Appeals overturned the conviction in summer 2017 on grounds of a faulty jury instruction. At retrial, Silver was convicted again.

43. Press Release, New York State Rifle and Pistol Association, *Statement on the Election of John Flanagan as Senate Majority Leaders* (May 11, 2015), www.nysrpa.org.

44. NY SAFE Resolutions, *County Seal / Logo / Name Resolutions*, www.nysaferesolutions.com (last visited December 18, 2018).

45. The resolution of the Erie County Legislature expresses opposition to state agencies using county seals on SAFE Act enforcement documents. Res. 51 RE: Denying the State the Use of the County Seal or Name on Any Document Enforcing the SAFE Act (Erie County, March 13, 2013), www2.erie.gov. All counties that have passed such a resolution are listed by NY SAFE Resolutions, *County / Logo / Name Resolutions*, www.nysaferesolutions.com.

46. *Schultz v. N.Y. Executive*, 108 A.D.3d 856, 969 N.Y.S.2d 195 (3d Dep't 2013).

47. *Schultz v. N.Y. Executive*, Verified Complaint-Petition at 42.

48. See *Schultz v. N.Y. Executive*, 23 N.Y.3d 1010, 992 N.Y.S.2d 771 (2014) (Index no. 1232-13), *aff'd Schultz v. State Executive*, 134 A.D.3d 52, 19 N.Y.S. 3d 92 (3d Dep't 2015).

49. See, e.g., *Mongielo v. Cuomo*, 40 Misc. 3d 362, 968 N.Y.S.2d 828 (N.Y. Sup. Ct. Albany County 2013); *Kampfer v. Cuomo*, 939 F. Supp. 2d 188 (N.D.N.Y. 2014).

50. See *New York State Rifle and Pistol Ass'n v. Cuomo*, 990 F. Supp. 2d 349 (2d Cir. 2015).

CHAPTER 2. WAS THE SAFE ACT NECESSARY?

1. Giffords Law Center to Prevent Gun Violence, *Victory in the Courts: New York's New Gun Law Largely Upheld by Federal District Judge* (January 7, 2014), http://smartgunlaws.org.

2. Thomas Kaplan, *Sweeping Limits on Guns Become Law in New York*, New York Times (January 15, 2013), www.nytimes.com.

3. Jameson Fleming, *New York Ranked Third Lowest in Gun Deaths: See Gun Death Rates for All Fifty States*, Syracuse.com (January 29, 2015), www.syracuse.com; New York State Governor's Office, *Governor Cuomo Announces Lowest Crime Rates in Two Decades* (September 25, 2014), www.governor.ny.gov.

4. Franklin E. Zimring, *The City That Became Safe: New York's Lessons for Urban Crime and Its Control* (2012).

5. Five individual plaintiffs applied for carry licenses; four of the five did not allege a "special need" for self-protection. After their applications were denied, Alan Gura, who had successfully represented Dick Anthony Heller and Otis McDonald in the Supreme Court, brought a federal lawsuit arguing that New York States could not constitutionally require license applicants to demonstrate a special need to carry a concealed handgun. The District Court disagreed, holding that *Heller* recognized a right to possess a firearm *at home*. The Second Circuit US Court of Appeals affirmed in *Kachalsky v. County of Westchester*, 701 F.3d 81, 100 (2nd Cir. 2012). The US Supreme Court denied the plaintiffs' petition for a writ of certiorari.

6. N.Y. Pen. Law § 400.00(2)(f). Licenses are also available to "have, possess, collect and carry antique pistols": *Id.* at § 400.00(2)(g).

7. Matthew Bridge, *Exit, Pursued by a "Bear"? New York City's Handgun Laws in the Wake of Heller and McDonald*, 46 Colum. J.L. & Soc. Probs. 145, 184 (2012).

8. *Kachalsky v. County of Westchester*, 701 F.3d 81, 92 (2nd Cir. 2012).

9. *O'Brien v. Keegan* 87 N.Y.2d 436, 439–440 (1996).

10. Emily S. Rueb, *How Tough Is It? Buying a Gun in Oregon vs. New York City*, New York Times (October 9, 2015), www.nytimes.com.

11. Bureau of Alcohol, Tobacco, Firearms, and Explosives, *Report of Active Firearms Licenses—License Type by State Statistics* (October 2017), www.atf.gov.

12. Richard Perez-Pena, *Pataki Signs the Nation's Strictest Gun Controls*, New York Times (August 10, 2000), www.nytimes.com.

13. N.Y. Gen. Bus. Law §§ 895–897 (Art. 39-DD).

14. *Scope et al. v. Pataki et al.*, 386 F. Supp. 2d. 184 (2005).

15. N.Y. Gen. Bus. Law § 396-ee.

16. N.Y. Const. Art. IX, § 2(c); and N.Y. Munc. Home Rule Law § 10(1)(ii)(a)(12).

17. Jackie Hilly, *New York Gun Laws: An Advocate's View*, 14 Gov't., L. & Pol'y J. 6, 16 (2012).

18. Adam Winkler, *GUNFIGHT: The Battle Over the Right to Bear Arms in America* (2011).

19. Federal Bureau of Investigation, *NICS Firearm Checks: Month/Year by State* (2017), www.fbi.gov.

20. See Gun Show Trader, *New York Gun Shows*, https://gunshowtrader.com (last visited December 18, 2018).

21. US Department of Justice, Office of Juvenile Justice and Delinquency Prevention, *Promising Strategies to Reduce Gun Violence* (February 1999), www.ojjdp.gov.

22. Jacob Bernstein, *New York's Gun Culture*, New York (September 27, 2004), http://nymag.com.
23. New York State Department of Environmental Conservation, *Hunting*, www.dec.ny.gov (last visited December 18, 2018).
24. Range Listings, *Shooting Ranges in New York* (last visited April 5, 2017), http://rangelistings.com.
25. New York State Rifle and Pistol Association, home page, www.nysrpa.org (last visited December 18, 2018).
26. Shooters Committee on Political Education, *About S.C.O.P.E.*, http://scopeny.org (last visited December 18, 2018).

CHAPTER 3. ASSAULT WEAPONS BAN AND REGISTRATION

1. Katie Pavlick, *Obama and Biden Bitterly Clinging to Assault Weapons Ban*, Townhall (March 21, 2013), http://townhall.com.
2. Fredric Dicker, *Hit Us with Your Best Shot, Andy!*, New York Post (January 21, 2013), http://nypost.com.
3. See New York State Senate, *Senate Bill S2230*, www.nysenate.gov. For Governor Cuomo's quote, *see The Safe Act "Emergency": How Cuomo, Past Governors Bypassed Public to Make Laws*, Syracuse.com (March 13, 2013), www.syracuse.com.
4. The SAFE Act's AWB is identical to the Giffords Law Center to Prevent Gun Violence's model assault weapons ban, which was posted in August 2012. See Giffords Law Center to Prevent Gun Violence, *Law Center Releases Model Law to Ban Assault Weapons and Large Capacity Ammunition Magazines* (last updated January 7, 2013), http://smartgunlaws.org.
5. N.Y. Pen. Law § 265.00(22).
6. *See People v. Gray*, IND. 2013-0099 (City of Monroe, Feb. 4, 2014): judge dismissed criminal possession of assault weapon charge because the alleged "adjustable stock" on the defendant's gun only changed the stock's length by three inches, which is insufficient to meet the SAFE Act's definition of "folding or telescoping stock."
7. *New York State Rifle and Pistol Association, Inc. v. Cuomo*, 990 F. Supp. 2d 349 at 400 (W.D.N.Y. Dec. 31, 2013).
8. FBI, *Murder Victims by Weapon* (March 11, 2015), https://ucr.fbi.gov.
9. In contrast, New York City's 1991 assault weapons ban prohibited all possession of assault weapons punishable by up to one year's jail term and/or $5,000 fine.
10. James B. Jacobs & Alexander Haberman, *3D-Printed Firearms, Do-It-Yourself Guns, and the Second Amendment*, 80 Law & Contemp. Probs. 129 (2017).
11. Jeffrey Roth & Christopher Koper, National Institute of Justice, *Impacts of the 1994 Assault Weapons Ban: 1994–1996* 4 (March 1999), www.ncjrs.gov.
12. The New York State Police operates a hotline that provides gun owners with advice with respect to whether a particular firearm model constitutes an assault weapon that must be registered. *See* New York State Governor, *Gun Registration Questionnaire*, http://programs.governor.ny.gov (last visited December 18, 2018).

13. *See* New York State Police, *Assault Weapon(s) Registration*, www.governor.ny.gov (last visited December 18, 2018).

14. N.Y. Pen. Law § 265.01-b.

15. Thomas Friedman, *Up with Extremism*, New York Times (January 6, 2016), www.nytimes.com.

16. Fredric Dicker, *Hit Us with Your Best Shot, Andy!*, New York Post (January 21, 2013), http://nypost.com.

17. *Robinson v. Cuomo*, No. 5118-14 (N.Y. Sup. Ct., Albany County, 2015).

18. Respondent's Answer at Exhibits 1 and 2, *Robinson v. Cuomo*, No. 511-14 (N.Y. Sup. Ct., Albany County, 2015).

19. In New Jersey, an estimated 100,000 to 300,000 assault rifle owners registered 947 assault rifles, rendered 888 inoperable, and turned over 4 to law enforcement personnel. In California, only 10 percent of about 300,000 assault weapon owners registered their weapons. Cleveland and Boston achieved an estimated 1 percent compliance rate. Denver authorities registered 1 percent of 10,000 assault rifles.

20. See Dan Haar, *Untold Thousands Flout Gun Registration Law*, Hartford Courant (February 10, 2014), http://articles.courant.com.

21. Mark Boshnack, *NY Sheriffs: We Won't Enforce Gun Laws, Magazine Limits*, Daily Star (September 7, 2013), www.policeone.com. See also Eric Lutz, *The Right's Latest Tactic on Gun Laws? Just Don't Enforce Them*, Rolling Stone Magazine (May 28, 2019), www.rollingstone.com.

22. Marlena Chertock et al., *"No" Sheriff in Town: Some Lawmen Refuse to Enforce Federal Gun Laws*, NBC News (August 21, 2014), www.nbcnews.com.

23. Mark Boshnack, *NY Sheriffs: We Won't Enforce Gun Laws, Magazine Limits*, Daily Star (September 7, 2013), www.policeone.com.

24. Christian Gomez, *New York Counties Work to Repeal State Gun Control Laws*, New American (March 12, 2013), www.thenewamerican.com.

25. Joel Rose, *Flouting the Law, Some New Yorkers Won't Register Guns*, National Public Radio (July 24, 2015), www.npr.org; Jon Campbell, *SAFE Act Charges Are Rising*, Democrat & Chronicle (March 7, 2016), www.democratandchronicle.com.

26. Jon Campbell, *SAFE Act Charges Up, but Most in NYC*, Lohud (March 6, 2016), www.lohud.com.

27. *See People v. DeBour*, 40 N.Y.2d 210 (1979).

28. David Lohr, *Buffalo Police to Seize Handguns from Recently Deceased Permit Holders*, Huffington Post (November 17, 2014), www.huffingtonpost.com.

29. *District of Columbia v. Heller*, 554 U.S. 570 (2008); *McDonald v. City of Chicago*, 561 U.S. 742 (2010); *New York State Rifle and Pistol Ass'n v. Cuomo*, 990 F. Supp. 2d 349, 360 (W.D.N.Y. 2013).

30. *New York State Rifle and Pistol Ass'n*, 990 F. Supp. 2d at 363.

31. *Id.* at 368.

32. *Id.* at 367.

33. *Id.*

34. *Id.*

35. *Id.* at 368.
36. *Id.* at 369.
37. *Id.* at 377.
38. *Kampfer v. Cuomo*, 993 F. Supp. 2d 188, 190–191 (N.D.N.Y. 2014).
39. Brief of Alabama et al. as *Amici Curiae* in Support of Plaintiffs-Appellants-Cross-Appellees, *Nojay et al. v. Cuomo*, No. 13-46-cv(L) (2d Cir. 2015). State attorneys general from Alabama, Alaska, Arizona, Arkansas, Florida, Georgia, Idaho, Kansas, Kentucky, Louisiana, Michigan, Missouri, Montana, Nebraska, North Dakota, Oklahoma, South Carolina, South Dakota, Texas, Utah, West Virginia, and Wyoming all signed the brief challenging the law. *See* Mary Lou Byrd, *Twenty-Two States Support Lawsuit against Cuomo's SAFE Act*, Free Beacon (May 8, 2014), http://freebeacon.com.
40. Brief of Alabama et al. at 6, No. 13-46-cv (L).
41. *Id.* at 14.
42. *Id.* at 12.
43. Brief for New York State Sheriffs' Ass'n et al. as *Amici Curiae* at 15, *New York State Rifle and Pistol Ass'n, Inc. v. Cuomo*, 990 F. Supp. 2d 349 (W.D.N.Y 2013) (No. 13-cv-00291-WMS), 2013 WL 10767751.
44. *Id.* at 2–3.
45. Brief for National Rifle Ass'n of America as *Amicus Curiae* in Support of Plaintiff's Motion for a Preliminary Injunction at 10, *New York State Rifle and Pistol Ass'n, Inc. v. Cuomo*, 990 F. Supp. 2d 349 (W.D.N.Y. 2013) (No. 13-cv-00291-WMS), 2013 WL 2155770.
46. *Id.* at 12.
47. N.Y. Pen. Law §§ 265.00(22)(c)(viii), 265.02(7), 265.10(2)–(3).
48. Brief for Nat'l Shooting Sports Found. as *Amicus Curiae* in Support of Plaintiff's Motion for Summary Judgment at 8–9, *New York State Rifle and Pistol Ass'n, Inc. v. Cuomo*, 990 F. Supp. 2d 349 (W.D.N.Y. 2013) (No. 13-cv-00291-WMS), 2013 WL 5770868.
49. *Id.*
50. While not argued by the Association, the impact of the SAFE Act in diminishing the value of assault weapon owners' property could give rise to a constitutional challenge under the Fifth Amendment's takings clause (particularly given the lack of notice afforded to owners in the rushed enactment process).
51. Brief of Maryland et al. as *Amici Curiae* in Support of Defendants-Appellees at 16, *Shew v. Malloy*, 994 F. Supp. 2d 234 (D. Conn. 2014) (No. 14-0319-CV), 2014 WL 4275755.
52. Brief for the City of New York as *Amicus Curiae* in Support of Defendants-Appellees-Cross-Appellants at 9, *Nojay et al. v. Cuomo*, No. 13-46-cv(L) (2nd Cir. Aug. 12, 2014).
53. *Id.* at 11–12.
54. Brief of Brady Center to Prevent Gun Violence as *Amicus Curiae* in Support of Appellees at 7, *Nojay et al. v. Cuomo*, No. 13-46-cv(L) (2d Cir. 2014), 2014 WL 4386560.

55. *Id.* at 17.
56. *New York State Rifle and Pistol Ass'n, Inc. v. Cuomo,* 804 F.3d 242, 259–260 (2d Cir 2015).
57. *Id.* at 263.
58. Hearing Protection Act of 2017, H.R. 367, 115th Cong. (2017).
59. *New York State Rifle and Pistol Ass'n,* 804 F.3d at 262.
60. *Id.* at 268.
61. Kenneth Lovett, *Antonin Scalia's Death Halts Lawsuit to Fight Cuomo's Gun Control Law,* New York Daily News (March 7, 2016), www.nydailynews.com.
62. In December 2015, the Supreme Court refused to hear a Second Amendment challenge to a Chicago municipal ordinance banning semiautomatic weapons and large-capacity magazines. *See Friedman v. City of Highland Park, Illinois,* 136 S. Ct. 477 (2015). Justice Thomas, joined by Scalia, dissented from the denial of certiorari.
63. *See also In re Jorge M.,* 23 Cal.4th 866 (2000) (holding that possession of an unregistered assault weapon requires proof that defendant knew or reasonably should have known the characteristics of the weapon bringing it within the registration requirements of the assault weapons ban).
64. Maxim Lott, *Cosmetic Tweaks to AR-15 Thwart NY's Ban on Assault Rifles,* Fox News (February 16, 2014), www.foxnews.com.
65. Mae Ryan, *New York Assault Weapons Ban Circumvented with Simple Modification,* Guardian (April 1, 2014), www.theguardian.com.

CHAPTER 4. THE BAN ON LARGE-CAPACITY MAGAZINES
1. Giffords Law Center to Prevent Gun Violence, *Large Capacity Magazines,* http://smartgunlaws.org (last visited December 22, 2018).
2. Shooters Committee on Political Education, *Position on NYS Bill to Prohibit Large Capacity Magazines,* www.scopeny.org (last visited December 23, 2018).
3. Christopher S. Koper, Department of Justice, *Updated Assessment of the Federal Assault Weapons Ban: Impacts on Gun Markets and Gun Violence, 1994–2003* (June 2004), www.ncjrs.gov.
4. David Kopel, *The History of Firearm Magazines and Magazine Prohibitions,* 78 Alb. L. Rev. 849, 864–868 (2015).
5. Act of July 16, 1959, No. 175, sec. 1, § 224, 1959 Mich. Pub. Acts 249, 250; Firearms Act, ch. 278, sec. 1, § 11-47-2, 1975 R.I. Pub. Laws 738, 738–39, 742 (amended 1989).
6. Kopel, *History of Firearm Magazines,* 850.
7. Act of May 30, 1990, ch. 32, §§ 2C:39-1(y), -3(j), 1990 N.J. Laws 217, 221, 235 (codified at N.J. Stat. Ann. § 2C:39-1(y), -3(j) (West 2014)). See also Kopel, *History of Firearm Magazines,* 867.
8. New York City, N.Y. Code, § 10-306.
9. Act of June 29, 1992, ch. 286, sec. 3. § 134-8, 1992 Haw. Sess. Laws 740, 742 (codified at Haw. Rev. Stat. Ann. § 134-8 (LexisNexis 2014)). In 1993, Canada also instituted a ban on large-capacity magazines following Montreal's Polytechnique

shooting in 1989, in which a gunman armed with a semiautomatic rifle and a thirty-round magazine killed fourteen women. *See* Royal Canadian Mounted Police, *Maximum Permitted Magazine Capacity* (Special Bulletin for Businesses No. 72, last modified May 11, 2015), www.rcmp-grc.gc.ca. There is a five-round capacity limit for magazines designed for use in semiautomatic center-fire rifles and semiautomatic shotguns. Magazines designed for use in handguns are limited to ten rounds.

10. Act of May 26, 1994, ch. 456, § 36H-5, 1994 Md. Laws 2119, 2165 (amended 2013).

11. James B. Jacobs, *Why Ban "Assault Weapons"?*, 37 Cardozo L. Rev. 681 (2015).

12. Kopel, *History of Firearm Magazines*, 872.

13. The Second Circuit cited data estimating fifty million large-capacity magazines in the United States. *New York State Rifle and Pistol Ass'n, Inc. v. Cuomo*, 804 F.3d 242, 264 (2d Cir. 2015). The Fourth Circuit put the number at seventy-five million. *Kolbe v. Hogan*, 813 F.3d 160, 174 (4th Cir. 2016).

14. *Colorado Outfitters Ass'n v. Hickenlooper*, 823 F.3d 573 (2016) (holding that gun owners and sheriffs lacked standing to challenge Colorado's ban on the sale and possession of large-capacity magazines).

15. Michael Shnayerson, *The Contender: Andrew Cuomo, a Biography* 374 (2015).

16. New York State Governor's Office, *Governor's Program Bill #1 Memorandum in Support* 7 (2013), www.governor.ny.gov.

17. N.Y. Pen. Law § 265.00(22)(h).

18. *Id.* at § 265.36.

19. Prior to the SAFE Act, New York's Environmental Conservation Law limited hunters to five rounds in a magazine and one round loaded in the firing chamber. The six-round restriction only applies to center-fire semiautomatic rifles, semiautomatic shotguns, and semiautomatic pistols having eight-inch or longer barrels. This law was not altered by the SAFE Act. Hunters are allowed temporarily to modify magazines to hold five rounds, provided the overall capacity of the magazine does not exceed the ten-round limit: see N.Y. Env. Cons. Law § 11-0931(1)(c).

20. Andrew M. Cuomo, *All Things Possible* 443 (2014).

21. David Fallis, *Data Indicate Drop in High-Capacity Magazines during Federal Gun Ban*, Washington Post (January 10, 2013), www.washingtonpost.com.

22. Second Amendment Foundation, *Second Amendment Foundation Sues New York over "SAFE Act" Magazine Limits*, www.saf.org (last visited December 23, 2018).

23. In 1994, there were an estimated twenty-five million guns (18 percent of all civilian-owned firearms and 21 percent of civilian-owned handguns) in circulation in the United States that accommodated magazines with greater than ten-round capacity. Moreover, 40 percent of the semiautomatic handgun models and a majority of the semiautomatic rifle models manufactured prior to the federal ban were sold with magazines with greater than ten-round capacity.

24. Jessica Alaimo, *N.Y. Gun Law Mandates Magazines That Don't Exist*, USA Today (March 1, 2013), www.usatoday.com.

25. N.Y. Pen. Law §§ 265.37, 265.20(7-f). *See* Jimmy Vielkind, *Gun Law, Tax Policy Part of Budget Talks*, Times Union (March 20, 2013), www.timesunion.com.

26. Jimmy Vielkind, *Cuomo Says Gun Law Was Not Hastily Passed*, Capitol Confidential (blog), Times Union (March 20, 2013), http://blog.timesunion.com.

27. Shooters Committee on Political Education, *Position on NYS Bill*, 2.

28. Murray Weiss, *NY Gun Control Laws Anger Retired Police Who Believe They Should Be Exempted from Some Restrictions*, Huffington Post (January 17, 2013), www.huffingtonpost.com.

29. Jimmy Vielkind, *In Overnight Surprise, Senate Exempts Retired Cops from SAFE Act*, Capitol Confidential (blog), Times Union (June 21, 2013), http://blog.time sunion.com.

30. N.Y. Pen. Law § 265.00(25) extended the exemption to a "qualified retired New York or federal law enforcement officer," defined as an officer separated from service in good standing from a public agency located in New York States, where employed for at least five years as a police officer, peace officer, or federal law enforcement officer (as those terms are defined in the Criminal Procedure Law) and who are not otherwise prohibited from possessing a firearm.

31. Amended Complaint at 24, *New York State Rifle and Pistol Ass'n, Inc., v. Cuomo*, 990 F. Supp. 2d 349 (W.D.N.Y. 2013) (No. 1:13-cv-00291-WMS), 2013 WL 1703504.

32. Brief for Second Amend. Found. et al. as *Amici Curiae* Supporting Appellants, *New York State Rifle and Pistol Ass'n, Inc. v. Cuomo*, 990 F. Supp. 2d 349 (2d Cir. 2014) (No. 14-0036), 2014 WL 5090270.

33. Brief for Nat'l Shooting Sports Found. as *Amicus Curiae* Supporting Plaintiffs' Motion for Summary Judgment, *New York State Rifle and Pistol Ass'n, Inc. v. Cuomo*, 990 F. Supp. 2d 349 (W.D.N.Y. 2013) (No. 13-cv-00291-WMS), 2013 WL 5770868.

34. Brief for New York State Sheriffs' Ass'n et al. as *Amici Curiae* at 21, *New York State Rifle and Pistol Ass'n, Inc. v. Cuomo*, 990 F. Supp. 2d 349 (W.D.N.Y 2013) (No. 13-cv-00291-WMS), 2013 WL 10767751.

35. *New York State Rifle and Pistol Ass'n, Inc., v. Cuomo*, 990 F. Supp. 2d 349, 371 (W.D.N.Y. 2013).

36. *Id.* at 371.

37. *Id.* at 374.

38. *New York State Rifle and Pistol Ass'n*, 990 F. Supp. 2d at 375.

39. *Id.* at 373.

40. *Id.* at 372. Chief Judge Skretny's decision with respect to magazines also resolved a September 2013 lawsuit filed by the Second Amendment Foundation, the Shooters Committee for Political Education (SCOPE), and Long Island Firearms LLC that sought to enjoin the state from enforcing the seven-round cartridge limitation. *See* Stipulation of Dismissal, *Caron v. Cuomo*, No. 1:13-cv-01211 (N.D.N.Y. Apr. 7, 2016).

41. *New York State Rifle and Pistol Ass'n*, 804 F.3d 242.

42. *Id.* at 264. The Ninth Circuit US Court of Appeals unanimously upheld a lower-court ruling dismissing an application for a preliminary injunction against a Sunnyvale, California, ordinance banning large-capacity magazines holding more than ten rounds. *Fyock v. Sunnyvale*, 779 F.3d 991 (9th Cir. 2015).

43. *New York State Rifle and Pistol Ass'n*, 804 F.3d at 264.

44. *Id.* at 266.

45. *Id.* at 264.

46. Harold McNeil, *Chautauqua DA Affirms He Won't Prosecute under "7 Rounds" SAFE Act Provision*, Buffalo News (January 6, 2019), https://buffalonews.com.

47. Andy Greenberg, *Gunsmiths 3D-Print High Capacity Ammo Clips to Thwart Proposed Gun Laws*, Forbes (January 14, 2013), www.forbes.com. Representative Steve Israel of New York's 3rd Congressional District on the north shore of Long Island proposed the renewal of a modernized Undetected Firearms Act that would cover 3D-printed firearms. *See* Undetectable Firearms Modernization Act of 2015, H.R. 2699, 114th Cong. (2015) (as referred to the Subcomm. on Crime, Terrorism, Homeland Sec., and Investigations, July 1, 2015).

48. See James B. Jacobs & Alexander Haberman, *3D-Printed Firearms: Do It Yourself Guns and the Second Amendment*, 80 Law & Contemporary Problems 120 (2017).

49. N.Y. Pen. Law § 265.20(7-f).

50. Jeffrey A. Roth & Christopher S. Koper, National Institute of Justice, US Department of Justice, *Impacts of the 1994 Assault Weapons Ban: 1994–96*, (Research in Brief, March 1999), www.ncjrs.gov.

51. Koper, *Updated Assessment*, 65.

52. *Id.*

53. Baltimore (all guns recovered by the Baltimore Police Department from 1992 to 2000); Milwaukee County (guns recovered during murder investigations from 1991 to 1998); Anchorage (and other parts of Alaska) (guns linked to serious crimes and submitted to state firearm examiners for evidentiary testing from 1987 to 2000); and Louisville, Kentucky (guns and magazines submitted to the Jefferson Regional Forensics Lab from 1996 through 2000). *See id.* at 68.

54. *Id.* at 92. Koper cites other factors that are believed to have contributed to the drop in lethal and injurious gun violence: "changing drug markets, a strong economy, better policing, and higher incarceration rates."

55. *Id.* at 80.

56. *Baltimore Police Are Recovering More Guns Loaded with High-Capacity Magazines, Despite Ban on Sales*, The Trace (March 27, 2017), www.thetrace.org.

CHAPTER 5. UNIVERSAL BACKGROUND CHECKING

1. Everytown for Gun Safety, *Background Checks* (2014), http://everytownresearch.org.

2. Nat'l Rifle Ass'n Inst. for Legis. Action, *Study: Criminals Don't Get Guns from Legal Sources* (September 4, 2015), www.nraila.org (hereinafter *Criminals Don't Get Guns from Legal Sources*).

3. 18 U.S.C. § 922(s).
4. FBI, *National Instant Criminal Background Check System (NICS) Operations* (2014), www.fbi.gov.
5. The 1998 transition to permanent Brady's NICS scheme was fortunately timed. In *Printz v. United States*, 521 U.S. 898 (1997), the United States Supreme Court declared that the CLEO background-checking requirement violated the Tenth Amendment. That decision has significant implications for all federal universal-background-checking options.
6. There have been numerous unsuccessful attempts to enact federal universal background checking: the Gun Violence Prevention Act (1994) ("Brady II"); the Gun Show Accountability Bill (1994); the Manchin-Toomey Amendment (2013); the Public Safety and Second Amendment Rights Protection Act (2015); the Fix Gun Checks Act (2015). For a discussion of these bills, see James B. Jacobs & Zoe Fuhr, *The Potential and Limitations of Universal Background Checking for Gun Purchases*, 7 Wake Forest J.L & Pol'y 537 (2017).
7. Deborah Azrael et al., *The Stock and Flow of U.S. Firearms: Results from the 2015 National Firearms Survey*, 3 Russell Sage Found. J. Soc. Sci. 38, 48–50 (2017).
8. Bureau of Alcohol, Tobacco, Firearms, and Explosives, United States Department of Justice, *How to Become a Federal Firearms Licensee*, www.atf.gov (last visited December 24, 2018).
9. Bureau of Alcohol, Tobacco, Firearms, and Explosives, United States Department of Justice, *Firearms Commerce in the United States: Annual Statistical Update 2015* 8 (March 15, 2016), www.atf.gov.
10. Office of the Inspector General Evaluation and Inspections Division, *Review of ATF's Federal Firearms Licensee Inspection Program* 8–9 (2013), https://oig.justice.gov.
11. Michelle Nichols, *New York City Settles with Last Gun Dealer in Suit*, Reuters (September 24, 2008), www.reuters.com.
12. City of New York, *Gun Sow Undercover: Report on Illegal Sales at Gun Shows* 20 (October 2009), https://everytownresearch.org.
13. Adjudicated as a "mental defective" means "(a) A determination by a court, board, commission, or other lawful authority that a person, as a result of marked subnormal intelligence, or mental illness, incompetency, condition or disease: (1) Is a danger to himself or to others; or (2) Lacks the mental capacity to contract or manage his own affairs. (b) The term shall include—(1) A finding of insanity by a court in a criminal case; and (2) Those persons found incompetent to stand trial or found not guilty by reason of lack of mental responsibility pursuant to articles 50a and 72b of the Uniform Code of Military Justice, 10 U.S.C. 850a, 876b." 27 C.F.R. 478.11.
14. 19 U.S.C. § 922(g)(1)–(9).
15. For example, Seung-Hui Cho, the perpetrator of the Virginia Tech massacre (April, 2007), purchased his firearms legally. So did James Holmes (Aurora, Colorado, movie theater, July 20, 2012) and Omar Mateen (Orlando nightclub, June 2016).

16. FBI, *Terrorist Screening Center*, www.fbi.gov (last visited December 18, 2018).
17. Ban the Box is a civil rights campaign calling to remove a criminal record as a factor in hiring processes, aimed to provide equal opportunity for those who have previously been involved in the criminal justice system and to ease their reentry to society. Alfred Blumstein and Kiminori Nakamura have shown that a previously arrested person who goes three to eight years (depending on the underlying crime) without an additional arrest is no more likely to be arrested for a new crime than are members of the general public: *see* Alfred Blumstein & Kiminori Nakamura, *"Redemption" in an Era of Widespread Criminal Background Checks*, 263 NIJ Journal (2009), www.ncjrs.gov.
18. 18 U.S.C § 922(g)(3); 18 U.S.C. § 802(6). According to DOJ regulations implementing the Brady Law, the "drug user" category applies to any "person who uses a controlled substance and has lost the power of self-control with reference to the use of the controlled substance; and any person who is a current user of a controlled substance in a manner other than as prescribed by a licensed physician." See 27 C.F.R. 478.11. An inference of current use may be drawn from "evidence of a recent use or possession of a controlled substance or a pattern of use or possession that reasonably covers the present time, e.g., a conviction for use or possession of a controlled substance within the past year; multiple arrests for such offenses within the past 5 years if the most recent arrest occurred within the past year; or persons found through a drug test to use a controlled substance unlawfully, provided that the test was administered within the past year." See 27 C.F.R. 478.11. Regarding the relationship between drug use and gun violence, *see* Shima Baradaran, *Drugs and Violence*, 88 S. Cal. L. Rev. 227, 271–288 (2015).
19. Ylan Q. Mui, *Why Americans Are Giving Up Citizenship in Record Numbers*, Washington Post (June 1, 2016), www.washingtonpost.com.
20. Robert Wood, *The New Un-American Record: Renouncing U.S. Citizenship*, Forbes (May 8, 2015), www.forbes.com.
21. Jeffrey Swanson et al., *Mental Illness and Reduction of Gun Violence: Bringing Epidemiologic Research to Policy*, 25 Annals of Epidemiology 366 (2015).
22. FBI, *National Instant Criminal Background Check System (NICS) Operations Report* (2016), www.fbi.gov.
23. Mayors Against Illegal Guns, *Fatal Gaps: How Missing Records in the Federal Background Check System Put Guns in the Hands of Killers* (November 2011), http://everytownresearch.org.
24. *Id.* at 8, 23.
25. *Id.* at 3.
26. *Id.*
27. *Scope, Inc. v. Pataki*, 386 F. Supp. 2d 184, 194–195 (W.D.N.Y 2005).
28. *Id.* at 188.
29. *Id.* at 194.
30. *Id.* at 192.
31. N.Y. Gen. Bus. Law § 898. (Art. 39-DDD)

32. *Id.* at § 898(1).
33. *Id.*
34. See Jacobs & Fuhr, *Potential and Limitations.*
35. New York's categories of ineligibility parallel the federal law, except that persons convicted of misdemeanor crimes of domestic violence are not firearms-disqualified in New York; rather, New York State disqualified persons convicted of "serious offenses" (defined to include misdemeanor stalking, child endangerment, and sexual offense convictions; for the full definition, see N.Y. Pen. Law § 265.00(17)). See *id.* at § 400.00(1).
36. Bureau of Alcohol, Tobacco, and Firearms, *Following the Gun: Enforcing Federal Laws Against Firearm Traffickers* 11 (June 2000), http://everytown.org.
37. N.Y. Pen. Law § 265.17(3).
38. *See* Bureau of Alcohol, Tobacco, Firearms, and Explosives, *2012 Summary: Firearms Reported Lost and Stolen* 6 (June 17, 2013), www.atf.gov.
39. Bureau of Alcohol, Tobacco, Firearms, and Explosives, *Listing of Federal Firearms Licensees (FFLs)—2016* (2016), www.atf.gov (hereinafter *Listing of FFLs*).
40. City of New York, *Point, Click, Fire: An Investigation of Illegal, Online Gun Sales* 3 (December 2011), http://everytownresearch.org.
41. The dark web, using a free Tor browser, gives access to sites that host illegal content, including pirated music and films, child pornography, illegal drugs and firearms, and credit card numbers. A RAND Corporation report details the expanding role of the dark web in facilitating the sale of firearms, ammunition, and explosives. See Giacomo Persi Paoli et al., RAND Corporation, *Behind the Curtain: The Illicit Trade of Firearms, Explosives and Ammunition on the Dark Web* (2017), www.rand.org.
42. California law requires firearms licensees to perform background checks for private firearms transfers as a condition for holding a state license. *See* Cal. Pen. Code §§ 28050, 28065. The licensed dealer may charge a maximum of ten dollars for facilitating a private sale. *See id.* at § 28055(a).
43. N.Y. Gen. Bus. Law § 898(4).
44. *Listing of FFLs.*
45. Brief for Empire State Arms Collectors, Inc. as *Amicus Curiae* Supporting Plaintiffs-Appellants-Cross-Appellees at 27, *Nojay et al. v. Cuomo*, No. 13-46-cv(L) (2d Cir. May 2, 2015).
46. Jessica Alaimo, *Some Gun Dealers Balking at Transfers*, Democrat and Chron. (April 23, 2013). See Brief for Empire State Arms Collectors at 27.
47. Robert W. Hunnicutt, *New York: Dealers Resist Private Background Checks*, Firearm News (April 24, 2013), www.firearmsnews.com.
48. Brief for Empire State Arms Collectors at 28.
49. Nat'l Shooting Sports Found., *Universal Background Checks—Key Facts to Consider* (2013), http://nssf.org.
50. Kate Masters, *Walmart Has Tougher Policies for Background Checks than the U.S. Government Does*, The Trace (May 25, 2016), www.thetrace.org. For Walmart's

ten-point gun-sale policy, see Robert Farago, *WalMart Expands Gun Sales, Still in Bed with MAIG*, Truth About Guns (April 28, 2011), www.thetruthaboutguns.com.

51. Jens Ludwig & Philip J. Cook, *Homicide and Suicide Rates Associated with Implementation of the Brady Handgun Violence Prevention Act*, 284 JAMA 585 (2000).

52. Michael D. Anestis & Joye C. Anestis, *Suicide Rates and State Laws Regulating Access and Exposure to Handguns*, 105 Am. J. Pub. Health 2049, 2049 (2015).

53. Garen Wintemute et al., *Subsequent Criminal Activity among Violent Misdemeanants Who Seek to Purchase Handguns*, 285 JAMA 1019 (2001).

54. *Id.* at 1022.

55. *Id.* at 1020.

56. Daniel Webster et al., *Effects of the Repeal of Missouri's Handgun Purchaser Licensing Law on Homicides*, 91 J. Urb. Health 293 (2014).

57. Clayton E. Cramer, *Background Checks and Murder Rates* (April 11, 2013), http://ssrn.com.

58. *Id.*

59. *Id. See also St. Louis Gangs Series*, St. Louis Pub. Radio (August 18–20, 2008), http://stlpublicradio.org.

60. James D. Wright & Peter H. Rossi, *Armed and Considered Dangerous* (2d ed. 2008); Philip J. Cook et al., *Sources of Guns to Dangerous People: What We Learn by Asking Them*, 79 Prev. Med. 28 (2015).

61. Cramer, *Background Checks and Murder Rates*, 4.

62. *Id.* at 5.

63. Franklin E. Zimring, *The City That Became Safe: New York's Lessons for Urban Crime and Its Control*, 143–144 (2012).

64. Jeffrey W. Swanson et al., *Implementation and Effectiveness of Connecticut's Risk-Based Gun Removal Law: Does It Prevent Suicides?*, 80 Law & Contemp. Probs. 179, 183, 204 (2017).

65. *See* Ctr. for Disease Control & Prevention, WISQARS, *Fatal Injury Reports, National and Regional 1999–2015*, https://webappa.cdc.gov.

66. Gary Kleck, *Targeting Guns: Firearms and Their Control* 87 (1997); Cook et al., *Sources of Guns to Dangerous People*; Philip J. Cook et al., *Some Sources of Crime Guns in Chicago: Dirty Dealers, Straw Purchasers and Traffickers* 104(4) J. Crim. L. & Criminology 717 (2015).

CHAPTER 6. DISARMING THE MENTALLY ILL

1. *District of Columbia v. Heller*, 554 U.S. 570, 626–627 (2008).

2. Consortium for Risk-Based Firearm Policy, *Guns, Public Health and Mental Illness: An Evidence-Based Approach for State Policy* (December 2, 2013), www.jhsph.edu.

3. 18 U.S.C. §§ 922(d)(4), 922(g)(4). Federal law imposes the same firearm restrictions on other categories of firearms-disqualification, including convicted felons, § 922(g)(1), and fugitives, § 922(g)(2).

4. Megan Testa & Sarah G. West, *Civil Commitment in the United States*, Psychiatry (Edgemont) 30, 33 (2010): "The number of psychiatric in-patients declined precipitously from a high of more than 550,000 in 1950 to 30,000 by the 1990s."

5. Firearm Owner's Protection Act of 1986, Pub. L. No. 99-308, 100 State. 449 (1986).

6. 18 U.S.C. § 925.

7. 151 Cong. Rec. H4161 (2005) (Congresswoman Carolyn McCarthy observing that "thirty-three States have not automated or do not share mental health records that could disqualify certain individuals from buying a gun.")

8. Section 104 of the NICS Improvement Amendments Act of 2007 provides that the attorney general may withhold a portion of the funds that would otherwise be allocated to a state under section 505 of the Omnibus Crime Control and Safe Streets Act of 1968, if the state provides less than a set percentage of the records required to be provided by sections 102 and 103 of the Act. Withheld funds are reallocated to states that meet those requirements. *Id.*

9. US Gov't Accountability Off., GAO-12-684, *Gun Control: Sharing Promising Practices and Assessing Incentives Could Better Position Justice to Assist States in Providing Records for Background Checks* 9 (2012).

10. *Id.* at 34.

11. Fix NICS Act of 2017 § 5.

12. Jeffrey W. Swanson et al., *Implementation and Effectiveness of Connecticut's Risk-Based Gun Removal Law: Does It Prevent Suicides?*, 80 Law & Contemp. Probs. 179, 182 (2017).

13. Tom McGhee, *Theater Shooting Victim's Wife Sues Holmes' Psychiatrist*, Denver Post (January 15, 2013), www.denverpost.com.

14. Sarah Garrecht Gassen & Timothy Williams, *Before Attack, Parents of Gunman Tried to Address Son's Strange Behavior*, New York Times (March 27, 2013), www.nytimes.com.

15. Joe Johns & Stacey Samuel, *Would Background Checks Have Stopped Recent Mass Shootings? Probably Not*, CNN (April 10, 2013), www.cnn.com.

16. Office of the Federal Register, *Implementation of the NICS Improvement Amendment Act 2007: A Rule by the Social Security Administration* (December 19, 2016), www.federalregister.gov.

17. American Civil Liberties Union, *ACLU Vote Recommendation on Social Security NICS Rule & Fair Pay and SAFE Workplaces EO* (February 1, 2017), www.aclu.org.

18. H.J. Res. 40—Providing for Congressional Disapproval under Chap 8 of title 5, United States Code, of the Rule Submitted by the Social Security Administration relating to Implementation of the NICS Improvement Amendments Act of 2007 (115th Congress, 2017–2018).

19. N.Y. Mental Hyg. Law § 9.46.

20. *Id.* at § 41.13. The law does not specify qualifications for a director. If a DCS is not a physician, he or she must designate a physician to "conduct examinations on behalf of such director." *Id.* at § 41.09. However, no patient examination is authorized for a § 9.46 report.

21. *Id.* at § 9.01.
22. *Id.* at § 9.46(d).
23. Anemona Hartocollis, *Mental Health Issues Put 34,500 on New York's No-Guns List*, New York Times (October 19, 2014), www.nytimes.com.
24. The University of Colorado psychiatrist who treated the Aurora shooter, James Holmes, was sued by one victim's widow for failing to place Holmes under a seventy-two-hour psychiatric hold. *See* Tom McGhee, *Theater Shooting Victim's Wife Sues Holmes' Psychiatrist*, Denver Post (January 15, 2013), www.denverpost.com.
25. *Id.*; N.Y. Mental Hyg. Law §§ 9.46(b), 33.13(c)(12), 33.13(c)(15); N.Y. Exec. Law § 837(19).
26. Hartocollis, *Mental Health Issues*.
27. NYS Office of Mental Health & NYS Office for People with Developmental Disabilities, *New York SAFE Act Guidance Document*, http://nics.ny.gov.
28. On occasion, due to mistaken identity, guns have been seized from the wrong person. *See* Elizabeth Doran, *Deputies Confiscate a CNY Veteran's Guns. They Were Wrong. What Happened?*, Syracuse.com (July 31, 2017), www.syracuse.com.
29. Testimony of Beth Haroules, on behalf of the New York Civil Liberties Union before the Senate Standing Committee on Mental Health and Developmental Disabilities, concerning the implementation and impact of the mental health requirements in the NY SAFE Act (May 31, 2013), available at www.youtube.com.
30. John Monahan et al., *Rethinking Risk Assessment: The MacArthur Study of Mental Disorder and Violence* (2001); Alex Yablon, *Mental Health Experts Warn of Flaw in NRA-Supported Gun Background Check Bill*, The Trace (August 10, 2015), www.thetrace.org; Henry J. Steadman et al., *Gun Violence and Victimization of Strangers by Persons with a Mental Illness: Data From the MacArthur Violence Risk Assessment Study*, Psychiatric Services 1238, 1240 (2015).
31. "The National Institute of Mental Health's Epidemiological Catchment Area (ECA) study's results implied that even if the elevated risk of violence for people with mental illness were reduced to the average risk posed by persons without mental illness, an estimated 96% of the violence that currently occurs in the general population would continue to occur." Jeffrey Swanson et al., *Mental Illness and Reduction of Gun Violence and Suicide: Bringing Epidemiologic Research to Policy*, 25 Annals of Epidemiology 366, 371 (2015).
32. Consortium for Risk-Based Firearm Policy, *Guns, Public Health and Mental Illness*; John Monahan, *A Jurisprudence of Risk Assessment: Forecasting Harm among Prisoners, Predators and Patients*, 92 Va. L. Rev. 391 (2006); Jennifer L. Skeem & John Monahan, *Current Directions in Violence Risk Assessment*, 20 Curr. Dir. Psychol. Sci. 38 (2011); Swanson et al., *Mental Illness and Reduction of Gun Violence and Suicide. See also* Monahan et al., *Rethinking Risk Assessment.*
33. Wendy Brennan, Executive Director, NAMI-NYC Metro, remarks at NYU Langone Medical Center, *New York State's SAFE Act: What Does It Mean for Medical Health Providers and Their Patients?* (May 1, 2013), www.naminycmetro.org.

34. Jeffrey W. Swanson et al., *Implementation and Effectiveness of Connecticut's Risk-Based Gun Removal Law: Does It Prevent Suicides?*, 80 Law & Contemp. Probs. 179, 186–187 (2017).

35. Consortium for Risk-Based Firearm Policy, *Guns, Public Health and Mental Illness*.

36. *See* Hartocollis, *Mental Health Issues*; Paloma Capanna, *More than 85,000 Secret Reports Made by Doctors to the NYS Police*, Law-Policy.com (March 16, 2017), http://law-policy.com.

37. Alison Knopf, *Guns and Mental Illness: NY SAFE Act*, Behav. Healthcare (January 30, 2013), www.behavioral.net.

38. Testimony of Jed Wolkenbreit on behalf of the NYS Conference of Local Mental Hygiene Directors before the Senate Standing Committee on Mental Health and Developmental Disabilities, concerning the implementation and impact of the mental health requirements in the New York SAFE Act, at 2 (May 31, 2013), www.clmhd.org.

39. *See* RAND Center for Military Health and Policy Research, *Invisible Wounds of War: Psychological and Cognitive Injuries, Their Consequences, and Services to Assist Recovery* (2008), www.rand.org.

40. Paul Adams, *Will Gun Laws Hurt the Mentally Ill?*, BBC News (March 29, 2013), www.bbc.com.

41. Curtis Skinner, *VA Says No to SAFE Act*, New York World (March 11, 2013), www.thenewyorkworld.com.

42. *Id.*

43. Testimony of Glenn Martin on behalf of the New York State Psychiatric Association, Inc., before the Senate Standing Committee on Mental Health and Developmental Disabilities, concerning the implementation and impact of the mental health requirements in the New York SAFE Act (May 31, 2013), www.nyspsych.org.

44. Health Insurance Portability and Accountability Act of 1996, Pub. L. No. 104-191, 110 Stat. 1936 (1996).

45. 45 C.F.R. § 164.508.

46. *Id.* at § 164.512(a).

47. US Department of Health & Human Services, *Guidance Regarding Methods for De-identification of Protected Health Information in Accordance with the Health Insurance Portability and Accountability Act (HIPAA) Privacy Rule* (2012), www.hhs.gov.

48. Office of NICS Appeals & SAFE Act, *NY SAFE Act FAQ's*, http://nics.ny.gov (last visited December 24, 2018).

49. Testimony of Glenn Martin; N.Y. Mental Hyg. Law § 9.46(c).

50. 45 C.F.R. § 164.512(j).

51. HIPAA Privacy Rule and the National Instant Criminal Background Check System (NICS), 78 Fed. Reg. 78 (proposed April 23, 2013) (to be codified at 45 C.F.R. pts. 160 & 164).

52. N.Y. State Psychiatric Ass'n, *The SAFE Act: Guidelines for Complying with the New Mental Health Reporting Requirement*, www.nyspsych.org (last visited December 24, 2018).

53. Medical Society of the State of New York, *MSSNY'S 2014 Legislative Program*, www.mssny.org (last visited December 24, 2018).

54. § 33.13(6) of the New York Mental Hygiene Law authorizes but does not mandate disclosure in such circumstances. *See* N.Y. Mental Hyg. Law § 33.13(c)(6); *Id.*

55. Medical Society of the State of New York, *MSSNY'S 2014 Legislative Program.*

56. N.Y. State Office of NICS Appeals & SAFE Act, *NY SAFE Act Introduction for Mental Health Providers* (March 12, 2013), www.nics.ny.gov.

57. Curtis Skinner, *SAFE Act Registry of Mentally Ill Nets Few Gun Permit Holders*, New York World (June 3, 2013), www.thenewyorkworld.com.

58. *District of Columbia v. Heller*, 554 U.S. 570 (2008); *McDonald v. City of Chicago*, 561 U.S. 742 (2010); *Heller*, 554 U.S. at 626.

59. The SAFE Act's reporting requirements for health care professionals have not been as vigorously challenged in court as compared to assault weapon provisions. *See* James B. Jacobs, *Why Ban "Assault Weapons"?*, 37 Cardozo L. Rev. 681 (2015). However, the topic of gun violence and mental illness has attracted a great deal of professional and academic attention. *See* Lindsay Bramble, *Putting a Band-Aid on a Bullet Wound: Why Gun Legislation Targeting Individuals with Mental Illness Isn't Working*, 17 J. Health Care L. & Pol'y 303 (2014); Clayton E. Cramer, *Mental Illness and the Second Amendment*, 46 Conn. L. Rev. 1301 (2014); M. Roxana Nahhas Rudolph, *Balancing Public Safety with the Rights of the Mentally Ill: The Benefit of a Behavioral Approach in Reducing Gun Violence in Tennessee*, 45 U. Mem. L. Rev. 671 (2015); Joseph R. Simpson, *Bad Risk? An Overview of Laws Prohibiting Possession of Firearms by Individuals with a History of Treatment for Mental Illness*, 35 J. Am. Acad. Psychiatry & L. 330 (2007); Tom Wiehl, *The Presumption of Dangerousness: How New York's SAFE Act Reflects Our Irrational Fear of Mental Illness*, 38 Seton Hall Legis. J. 35 (2014). For academic commentary on the SAFE Act's mental health reporting requirements, see Matthew Gamsin, *The New York SAFE Act: A Thoughtful Approach to Gun Control, or a Politically Expedient Response to the Public's Fear of the Mentally Ill?*, 88 S. Cal. L. Rev. 16 (2015); Shaundra K. Lewis, *Firearm Laws Redux—Legislative Proposals for Disarming the Mentally Ill Post-Heller and Newtown*, 3 Mental Health L. & Pol'y J. 320 (2013–2014).

60. *United States v. Nathan Rehlander*, 666 F.3d 45 (1st Cir. 2012).

61. *Id.* at 47. Me. Rev. Stat. tit. 34-B, § 3863(1)–(3).

62. *Rehlander*, 666 F.3d at 47.

63. *Id.* at 50.

64. *Id.* at 48.

65. *Tyler v. Hillsdale Cnty. Sheriff's Dep't.*, 775 F.3d 308, 316, 342 (6th Cir. 2014).

66. N.Y Mental Hyg. Law §§ 9.31, 7.09(j), 13.09(g).

67. *Id.* at § 7.09(j)(2).

68. Cal. Welf. & Inst. §§ 8100, 8103.

69. *Id.* at § 8100(b)(3)(B).
70. Nathalie Baptiste, *What You Need to Know about Red Flag Gun Laws*, Mother Jones (March 7, 2018), www.motherjones.com. See also Alex Yablon, *Use of Red Flag Laws Varies Widely Among Local Police*, The Trace (April 23, 2019), www.thetrace.org.
71. Governor's Press Office, *Governor Kicks Off Bus Tour to Pass Red Flag Gun Protection Bill* (June 11, 2018), www.governor.ny.gov.
72. New York State Office of Mental Health, *New York State Assisted Outpatient Treatment Program Evaluation, Appendix A Kendra's Law Overview and Statute* (June 30, 2009), www.omh.ny.gov.
73. *Id.*
74. *Id.*
75. *Id.*
76. N.Y. Mental Hyg. Law § 9.60.
77. New York Association of Psychiatric Rehabilitation Services, *MHW: NYS Gun Law Prompt MH Community to Address Access, Stigma Issues* (February 11, 2013), www.nyaprs.org.
78. New York Civil Liberties Union, *Statement on Kendra's Law*, www.nyclu.org (last visited December 24, 2018).

CHAPTER 7. DISARMING PERSONS SUBJECT TO DOMESTIC VIOLENCE PROTECTION ORDERS

1. Press Release, New York State, *Governor Cuomo Signs Domestic Violence Firearm Protection Legislation* (August 1, 2011), www.governor.ny.gov.
2. Press Release, New York Courts, *Chief Judge Announces Pioneering New Program to Promote Access to Justice for Victims of Domestic Violence* (November 4, 2016), www.nycourts.gov.
3. New York State Office for the Prevention of Domestic Violence, *New York State Domestic Violence Dashboard 2015* (October, 2016), www.opdv.ny.gov.
4. 18 U.S.C § 922(d)(8)(B).
5. *Id.* at §§ 922(d)(8)(A), 922(d)(8)(C).
6. Michael Luo, *In Some States, Gun Rights Trump Orders of Protections*, New York Times (March 17, 2013), www.nytimes.com.
7. See Patrick, McGreevey, *10,000 Californians Barred from Owning Guns Are Still Armed: This Law Aims to Change That*, L.A. Times (January 18, 2018), www.latimes.com.
8. See Prosecutors Against Gun Violence & Consortium for Risk-Based Firearm Policy, *Firearms Removal/Retrieval in Cases of Domestic Violence* (February 2016), http://efsgv.org.
9. See *Weinstein v Krumpter*, 120 F. Supp. 3d 239, 242 (E.D.N.Y. 2015).
10. 38 RCNY §§ 5-22(c)(1), 5-30(c)(1), 5-30(d), and 5-30(g).
11. N.Y. Crim. Pro. Law § 530.12(1).
12. N.Y. Family Court Act § 812 (1)(a)–(e).
13. The VAWA requires that states provide victims with this service at no cost.

14. N.Y. Family Court Act § 842-a(7).
15. *Id.* at § 154-d(1).
16. N.Y. Pen. Law § 70.02 defines "violent felony offense" as "a class B violent felony offense, a class C violent felony offense, a class D violent felony offense, or a class E violent felony offense" as are then particularized in that provision.
17. Other jurisdictions have also experienced difficulty implementing laws authorizing or requiring surrender of protection-order respondents' guns. See, e.g., Tasha Tsiaporas, *Dallas County Plan to Disarm Domestic Abusers Seizes Just 60 Guns in 2 Years—a Fraction of Goal*, Dallas Morning News (May, 2017), www.dallasnews.com (county officials had anticipated surrender of seven to eight hundred guns per year). See also Anne Sweeney, *More than 34,000 Illinoisans have lost their right to own a gun. Nearly 80% may still be armed*, The Chicago Tribune (May 23, 2019), www.chicagotribune.com.
18. "Physical injury" is defined in N.Y. Pen. Law § 10.00(9).
19. For example, see New York's Office of the State Comptroller's report on inadequate recordkeeping and disposal practices of the firearms inventory held by the Herkimer County Sheriff's Office (February 17, 2015), www.osc.state.ny.us.
20. *Pearson v County of Cattaraugus*, 6 Misc. 3d 1034(A), 800 N.Y.S. 2d 352 (March 7, 2005).
21. Mrs. Pearson sued Cattaraugus County, alleging that its employees' failure to confiscate her husband's guns caused her son's wrongful death. The court dismissed the lawsuit, on the ground that municipalities are not liable for injuries resulting from failure to provide police protection. The court held that Mrs. Pearson's knowledge that her husband still possessed firearms (and that her son fired those guns on visits to his father) broke the causal link between the sheriff's alleged inaction and her son's death. The court rejected her argument that the deputy should have arrested Mr. Pearson when he refused to disclose to whom he had transferred his guns.
22. *Voisine v. United States*, 579 U.S. ___ (2016), 136 S. Ct. 2272.
23. *Voisine et al. v. United States*, No. 14-10154, slip op. at 18 (U.S. June 27, 2016).
24. Second Amendment: *United States v. Bayles*, 310 F.3d 1302 (10th Cir., 2002), *United States v. Lippmann*, 369 F.3d 1039 (8th Cir., 2004), *United States v. Mahin*, 668 F.3d 119 (4th Cir., 2012). Fifth and Fourteenth Amendments: *United States v. Baker*, 197 F.3d 211 (6th Cir., 1999); *United States v. Napier*, 233 F.3d 394 (6th Cir., 2000).
25. *United States v. Chapman*, 666 F.3d 220 (4th Cir. 2012).
26. Attempts to amend the federal law so that persons subject to temporary restraining orders are also required to surrender their firearms for the duration of the order have raised due process concerns. *See* AirTalk, *Should Temporary Restraining Orders Trigger Gun Surrenders across the Country?*, 89.3 KPCC—Southern California Public Radio (June 28, 2016), www.scpr.org.
27. *See* Linda Mills, *Violent Partners: A Breakthrough Plan for Breaking the Cycle of Abuse* (2009); Jeannie Suk, *At Home in the Law: How the Domestic Violence Revolution Is Transforming Privacy* (2011).
28. National Center on Domestic and Sexual Violence, *The Practitioner's Guide to Litigating Family Offense Proceedings*, www.ncdsv.org (last visited December 24, 2018).

29. Meaghan Kenneally, *New York Passes Law to Take More Guns Away from Domestic Violence Offenders*, ABC News (May 2, 2018), https://abcnews.go.com.

30. Evaluators of Maryland's effort to disarm domestic violence protection-order respondents report that "if implementation goes awry, an evaluation of the law may conclude that the law is ineffective, when the law has been well designed, but was underfunded, mismanaged, or not enforced." Shannon Frattaroli & Stephen P. Teret, *Understanding and Informing Policy Implementation: A Case Study of the Domestic Violence Provisions of the Maryland Gun Violence Act*, 30 Evaluation Review 347, 358 (2006).

CHAPTER 8. RECERTIFYING HANDGUN LICENSEES

1. Press Release, Diane J. Savino, N.Y. State Senate, *Senator Savino Supports Bill Requiring Handgun License Renewals Every Five Years* (April 23, 2009), www .nysenate.gov.

2. Mary Lou Lang, *Defiance against NY's Gun Control Law Continues Two Years Later*, Washington Free Beacon (January 21, 2015), http://freebeacon.com.

3. N.Y. Pen. Law § 400.00(10)(b).

4. *Id*. at § 400.00.

5. *Id*. at § 400.00(11); New York State law's categories of license ineligibility mirror the federal categories. Until 2018, New York law did not disqualify persons convicted of misdemeanor crimes of domestic violence.

6. *Id*. at § 265.01-b(1)

7. *Id*. at § 400.00(10)(b).

8. Michael Virtanen, *NY Lawmakers Want 5-Year Handgun Licenses*, New York State Senator Eric Schneiderman's website (April 22, 2009), www.ptpllc.com.

9. *See* Manny Fernandez & Nate Schweber, *Binghamton Killer Kept His Fury Private*, New York Times (April 11, 2009), www.nytimes.com.

10. *Id*. at § 400.02.

11. Joseph Spector, *SAFE Act: State Police Won't Charge Gun Owners Who Unknowingly Fail to Recertify Permits*, Democrat & Chronicle (January 17, 2017) http://democratandchronicle.com.

12. Jim Kenyon, *Who's Packing Heat: New York Gun Data Goes Public*, CNYCentral. com (August 10, 2010).

13. States are divided with respect to treating gun licensees' information as public or confidential. *See* Aaron Mackey, Reporters Committee for Freedom of the Press, *Chart: Gun Permit Data Accessibility in All 50 States* (2013), www.rcfp.org.

14. S2360 and A1811 (similar versions were introduced in the 2009–2010 legislative session: S7911 and A820).

15. Dwight R. Worley, *The Gun Owner Next Door: What You Don't Know about the Weapons in Your Neighborhood*, Lohud.com (January 20, 2013), http://people.sju.edu.

16. *See In re Gannett Satellite Info. Network, Inc. v. County of Putnam*, No.003564/13 (March 5, 2014), affirmed on appeal by the New York Supreme Court, Appellate Division, 2016 N.Y. Slip Op. 05999 (N.Y. App. Div. 2016) (September 14, 2016).

17. Erik Wemple, *Gawker Publishes N.Y.C. Gun-Permit Holders*, Washington Post (January 8, 2013), www.washingtonpost.com.

18. KC Maas & Josh Levs, *Newspaper Sparks Outrage for Publishing Names, Addresses of Gun Permit Holders*, CNN.com (December 27, 2012), www.cnn.com.

19. NRA-ILA, *New York: Newspaper Publishes List of Firearm Permit Holders* (December 28, 2012), www.nraila.org.

20. Nick Carbone, *Outrage after New York Paper Posts Map of Gun Owners' Names and Addresses*, Time.com (December 26, 2012), www.newsfeed.time.com.

21. Richard Liebson et al., *593 Burglaries between Dec. 23 and May 1*, Journal News (June 16, 2013).

22. Form available at New York State Police, *Firearms/Public Record Exemption*, https://troopers.ny.gov (last visited December 26, 2018).

23. N.Y. Pen. Law § 400.00(5)(b).

24. Mary Ellen Odell, *NY SAFE Gun Law Exonerates Putnam Clerk, Executive on Privacy and Public Safety Stance: State Officials Speak Out on Passage of New Gun Law*, Putnam County Online (January 22, 2013), www.putnamcountyny.com.

25. *Id.*

26. *Id.*

27. Joseph Phelan, *Rollout of Handgun Recertification Draws Fire from Sheriffs, County Officials*, Troy Record (January 7, 2017), www.troyrecord.com.

28. New York State Association of County Clerks, *2013 Position Statement* (2013), www.nyscc.com.

29. NY SAFE Resolutions, *Cayuga County Resolution Denying NYS Permission to Use Name, Seal, Letter Head, or Address for SAFE Act Correspondence* (January 28, 2014), www.nysaferesolutions.com.

30. New York State Police, *Pistol/Revolver License Recertification*, https://troopers.ny .gov (last visited December 26, 2018).

31. Tina Russel, *Pistol Recertification Could Trigger Problems*, Utica Observer-Dispatch (January 7, 2017), www.uticaod.com.

32. Thomas Dimopoulos, *Saratoga County Sheriff Pushes Back on SAFE Act Provision*, Saratoga Today (January13, 2017), http://saratogatodaynewspaper.com.

CHAPTER 9. REGULATING AMMUNITION SALES AND PURCHASERS

1. Fred Schulte, Center for Public Integrity, *Internet Ammunition Sales Draw Scrutiny* (January 15, 2013), www.publicintegrity.org.

2. NRA-ILA, *Anti-Gun Lawmakers Push Ammunition Sales Ban* (August 3, 2012), www.nraila.org.

3. Press Release, Office of the Governor, *Governor Cuomo Signs New York SAFE Act in Rochester* (January 16, 2013), www.governor.ny.gov.

4. Giffords Law Center to Prevent Gun Violence, *Ammunition Regulation*, http:// smartgunlaws.org (last visited on December 26, 2018).

5. Gun Control Act of 1968, Pub. L. No. 90-618, sec. 102, § 923(a), (g), 82 Stat. 1213 (1968) (codified as amended at 18 U.S.C. §§ 921–928 (1986)).

6. 18 U.S.C. § 922(a)(2).

7. *Investigation of Juvenile Delinquency in the United States, Oversight of the 1968 Gun Control Act—The Escalating Rate of Handgun Violence: Hearing before the Subcommittee to Investigate Juvenile Delinquency, Senate Committee of the Judiciary*, 94th Cong. (1975) (statement of Rex D. Davis, Director, Bureau of Alcohol, Tobacco, and Firearms, US Dep't of the Treasury).

8. Stephen Higgins, Bureau of Alcohol, Tobacco, and Firearms, US Dep't of the Treasury, *Memorandum to Assistant Secretary, Enforcement and Operations*, CC-34,270 (February 10, 1986) at 1.

9. Firearms Owners' Protection Act, Pub. L. No. 99-308, sec. 102(1), § 922(a)(2), sec. 103(7), § 923(g), 100 Stat. 449 (1986). FOPA also prohibited the manufacture, sale, and possession of "armor piercing ammunition" in order to protect police officers from being shot with ammunition capable of penetrating their ballistic vests.

10. 18 U.S.C. § 922(d).

11. Youth Handgun Safety Act of 1993, S.1087, 103rd Cong. (1993).

12. Joseph von Benedikt, *Dual Wielding: The Best Same Caliber Rifle-Handgun Combos*, Shooting Times (February 4, 2014), www.shootingtimes.com.

13. Real Cost of Ammunition Act, S.179, 103rd Cong (1993).

14. A "hollow-point" bullet has a pit or hollowed-out shape at its point that causes the bullet to expand when it strikes a target, thereby disrupting more tissue. This is the opposite of ammunition designed to pierce armor.

15. Real Cost of Destructive Ammunition Act, S.124, 104th Cong. § 2 (1995).

16. Gun Violence Prevention Act of 1994, H.R.3932, 103rd Cong. sec. 204(a), § 922(x) (1994).

17. "Non-sporting ammunition" includes Dragon's Breath (an incendiary shotgun shell), fifty-caliber BMG (designed for the Browning machine gun and used in long-range target and sniper rifles), any ammunition containing an incendiary or explosive charge, handgun ammunition measuring more than .45 inches in diameter, and any handgun ammunition that produces a force at the muzzle in excess of twelve hundred foot pounds.

18. Handgun Control and Violence Prevention Act of 1995, H.R.1321, 104th Cong., sec. 101(a), 701, 702 (1995).

19. Jack Healy, *Suspect Bought Large Stockpile of Rounds Online*, N.Y. Times (July 23, 2012), at A1.

20. Stop Online Ammunition Sales Act of 2013, S.35, 113th Cong. sec. 2(a), (b), (d) (2013).

21. Ammunition Background Check Act of 2013, S.174, 113th Cong. (2013).

22. Stop Online Ammunition Sales Act of 2015, H.R.2283, 114th Cong. (2015).

23. *Parker v. State of California*, F062490 (Cal. Ct. App. 5th 2013).

24. N.Y. L. 1969, c. 709 (codified at N.Y. Pen. Law § 270.00(5)).

25. N.Y. Pen. Law § 265.01(7), (8).

26. *Id.* at § 265.00(24); NY SAFE Act of 2013, S.2230, sec. 50, § 400.3, Reg. Sess. 2013–2014 (N.Y 2013).

27. N.Y. Pen. Law § 400.03(8).
28. *Id.*
29. *Id.* at § 400.03(7).
30. Open letter from Joseph A. D'Amico, N.Y. State Police Superintendent (January 2014), www.governor.ny.gov.
31. All government units that employ police or peace officers (as listed in NYS Crim. Proc. Law §§ 1.20, 2.10) are automatically deemed keepers of ammunition. They can purchase and receive ammunition directly from manufacturers for official police use.
32. New York State Police, Ammunition Unit, *The Keeper of Ammunition Registration Form* (PPB-7A), https://safeact.ny.gov (last visited December 27, 2018).
33. NY SAFE Act, sec. 50(6).
34. *Id.* at sec. 50(4), N.Y. Pen. Law § 400.03 (2), (5).
35. N.Y. Pen. Law § 400.03(2), (5). In the absence of a serial number, the seller must record "any other distinguishing number or identification mark on such ammunition."
36. *Id.* at § 400.03(5).
37. *Id.* at § 400.03(8).
38. SST Inc.'s 2014 National Gunfire Index indicates that on average three and a half shots were fired per incident that year, on the basis of recordings from microphones that monitor and report gunfire (the organization did not track this statistic in subsequent years). *See* SST Inc., *2014 National Gunfire Index* (2014), www.shotspotter.com.
39. *Colorado Theater Shooting Fast Facts*, CNN.com (last updated July 4, 2016), www.cnn.com.
40. WFTV-Orlando, *Law Enforcement Source: 202 Rounds Fired during Pulse Nightclub Shooting in Orlando*, WSOCTV.com (Jun.13, 2016), www.wsoctv.com.
41. Francis Clines, *Death on the L.I.R.R.*, N.Y. Times (December 9, 1993), at B10.
42. Robert McFadden, *Upstate Gunman Kills 13 at Citizenship Class*, N.Y. Times (April 3, 2009), at A1.
43. *New York State Rifle and Pistol Ass'n, Inc. v. Cuomo*, 990 F. Supp. 2d 349 (W.D.N.Y. 2013), *aff'd in part, rev'd in part*, 804 F.3d 242 (2d Cir. 2015).
44. *New York State Rifle and Pistol Ass'n, Inc.*, 990 F. Supp. 2d at 379–380.
45. *New York State Rifle and Pistol Ass'n, Inc.*, 804 F.3d at 251, fn. 20.
46. Lucky Gunner, *Buying Ammo in New York* (last visited April 5, 2017), www.luckygunner.com (explaining New York's ammunition-purchase laws in layman's terms and listing New York retailers willing to act as intermediaries and their fees).
47. *Id.*
48. The governor's 2013–2014 budget requested $32.7 million for creating and maintaining an ammunition database. New York State, *2013 New York State Executive Budget* 61 (January 22, 2013), www.ny.gov. The budget that passed did not include any funding for an ammunition database.

49. Liz Benjamin, *Cuomo Admin Clarifies SAFE Act Changes*, State of Politics (July 12, 2015), www.nystateofpolitics.com.
50. An Act to Amend the Penal Law, S.5837/A.8196 (2015), http://assembly.state .ny.us.
51. *See Memorandum of Understanding Regarding the Statewide License and Record Database Utilization for Eligibility to Purchase Ammunition* (July 10, 2015) (archived at www.nytimes.com).
52. *Id.* Following announcement of the memorandum, Senator Catharine Young's press release said that while Senate Republicans had succeeded in removing from the budget money to create an ammunition-purchaser database, she preferred a legislative solution. *See* Press Release, Sen. Catharine Young (July 10, 2015), www .nysenate.gov. Republican Senator Patrick Gallivan pointed out that the FY2016 Information Technology Budget included "an additional $7 million for creating an Ammunition Sales Database." Press Release, Sen. Patrick M. Gallivan (April 10, 2015), www.nysenate.gov.
53. Benjamin, *Cuomo Admin Clarifies*.
54. Thomas Kaplan, *Plan to Require Background Checks for Ammunition Sales Is Suspended in New York*, N.Y. Times (July 11, 2015), at A16.
55. *Id.*
56. Robert Farago, *The Truth about the Cost of Reloading*, The Truth About Guns (June 10, 2015), www.thetruthaboutguns.com; Jim Barrett, *Reloading: A Cost Benefit Analysis*, The Truth About Guns (July 9, 2012), www.thetruthaboutguns.com.

CHAPTER 10. NEW AND ENHANCED PUNISHMENTS
1. Press Release, Office of General Eric Schneiderman, Attorney General, State of New York, *A.G. Schneiderman and NYSP Superintendent Beach Announce Charges against Three Men for Illegally Selling More than 100 Assault Weapons in Major SAFE Act Case* (June 21, 2016), www.ag.ny.gov.
2. Jon Campbell, *SAFE Act Charges Are Rising*, Democrat & Chronicle (March 7, 2016), www.democratandchronicle.com.
3. Anthony Braga, *Long-Term Trends in the Sources of Boston Crime Guns*, 3 Russell Sage Foundation Journal of the Social Sciences 76, 88 (December 2017).
4. N.Y. Pen. Law § 265.17(2)–(3).
5. *Chiapperini et al. v. Gander Mountain Company, Inc. et al.*, 48 Misc. 3d 865 (2014).
6. N.Y. Gen. Bus. Law § 898(6).
7. N.Y. Pen. Law § 400.10.
8. *See* Bureau Alcohol, Tobacco, Firearms, and Explosives, *2012 Summary: Firearms Reported Lost and Stolen* 6 (June 17, 2013), www.atf.gov.
9. N.Y. Pen. Law § 400.03(8).
10. *Id.*
11. New York State Governor, *Gun Owners: Frequently Asked Questions*, https://safe act.ny.gov (last visited December 27, 2018).

12. N.Y. Pen. Law § 400.00(16-a). If the police concluded that the assault weapon owner's failure to register was unintentional, they could give the owner thirty days to register. New York State Governor, *Gun Owners: Frequently Asked Questions*.
13. N.Y. Pen. Law § 265.00(22)(h).
14. Eli Rosenberg, *3 New York Men Accused of Selling over 100 Illegal Assault Weapons*, New York Times (June 21, 2016), www.nytimes.com.
15. Max Slowik, *Introducing the AR Mr2 Bullet Button Alternative*, Guns.com (July 19, 2013), www.guns.com.
16. See State of California Department of Justice, *"Bullet Button" Firearms Will Be Considered Assault Weapons Effective January 1, 2017*, https://oag.ca.gov (last visited December 27, 2018).
17. New York's Penal Law defines these felonies as "manufacture, transport, disposition and defacement of weapons and dangerous instruments and appliances." N.Y. Pen. Law § 265.10. Although the SAFE Act created a specific misdemeanor to cover this conduct, the attorney general indicted Jackson under pre–SAFE Act penal-law provisions.
18. Press Release, Office of General Eric Schneiderman, *A.G. Schneiderman and NYSP Superintendent Beach Announce Charges*.
19. Amanda Ciavarri, *Lawyer for Henrietta Gun Shop Owner Says SAFE Act Wasn't Clear*, WHEC.com (June 22, 2017), www.whec.com.
20. Ryan Whalen, *Attorney General: SAFE Act Violators Knew "Exactly What They Were Doing,"* Spectrum News (June 23, 2016), www.twcnews.com.
21. N.Y. Pen. Law § 265.36.
22. *Id.* at § 265.02.
23. See Bradley Hutton & John Furhman, Behavioral Risk Factor Surveillance System, New York State Department of Health, *Firearm Ownership and Safe Storage in New York State* (Winter 1996), www.ibrarian.net.
24. Cassandra K. Crifasi et al., *Storage Practices of US Gun Owners in 2016*, 108 AJPH Research 532 (April 2018).
25. The 2000 omnibus New York gun control law required firearms dealers to include a trigger lock with every new gun sale. N.Y. Pen. Law § 400.00(2). Additionally, New York City, Buffalo, Rochester, and Westchester County ordinances required that a safety-locking device be affixed to a gun when it is "out of the owner's immediate possession or control." New York City's ordinance was upheld against constitutional challenge in *Tessler v. City of New York*, 38 Misc. 3d 215 (2012); 952 N.Y.S.2d. 703. For other New York State municipalities' ordinances, see Jordan Carleo-Evangelist, *Albany Hands Out Gun Locks as New Storage Law Takes Effect*, Times Union (January 14, 2016), www.timesunion.com.
26. The Ninth Circuit rejected a constitutional attack on San Francisco's safe-storage ordinance. Plaintiffs argued that the law "burdens the core of the Second Amendment right" because "having to retrieve handguns from locked containers or removing a trigger lock makes it more difficult "for citizens to use them for the core lawful purpose of self-defense" in the home. This court held that this was not a

"severe burden" justifying strict scrutiny review because "a modern gun safe may be opened quickly." *Jackson v. City and County of San Francisco*, 746 F.3d 953, 964 (2014). The Supreme Court denied certiorari, with Justices Scalia and Thomas dissenting. They argued that the Ninth Circuit's decision was in serious tension with Heller. Justice Thomas wrote, "An elderly woman who lives alone . . . is currently forced to store her handgun in a lock box. . . . If an intruder broke into her home at night, she would need to 'turn on the light, find [her] glasses, find the key to the lockbox, insert the key in the lock and unlock the box (under the stress of the emergency), and then get [her] gun before being in position to defend [herself]." *Jackson v. City of San Francisco*, 135 S. Ct. 2799, 2801 (2015).

27. Press Release, New York State Senate, *Senator Skelos Unveils Tough Plan to Crack Down on Illegal Guns and Criminals Who Use Guns* (January 5, 2013), www .nysenate.gov.

28. N.Y. Pen. Law § 70.00(3)(a)(i); see *People v. Harris*, 67 A.D.2d 665, 412 N.Y.S.2d 31 (2d Dep't 1979) ("The evil sought to be cured by the adoption [of this law] was the then-current spate of assassination attempts against uniformed officers acting in the line of duty, and the aim of the Legislature in passing the amendment was to provide these officers with an extra measure of public support and protection.").

29. N.Y. Pen. Law § 70.00(2)–(3).

30. *Id.* at § 70.00(2)–(3). Other aggravating factors that may elevate a charge to first-degree murder include when the victim is a corrections officer; when the defendant is in custody serving a life sentence at the time of the killing; when the intended victim was a witness to a crime and the death was caused with the purpose of preventing the intended victim's testimony; when the defendant committed the killing in exchange for something of pecuniary value; when the victim was killed while the defendant was in the course of committing a robbery, burglary, kidnapping, rape, or other crime; when the defendant causes the death of another person in the course of a criminal transaction; when the defendant had been convicted of murder prior to the killing; when the defendant acted in an especially cruel and wanton manner; when the defendant caused the killing of two or more persons in separate criminal transactions within a twenty-four-month period; when the intended victim was a judge; or when the victim was killed in furtherance of an act of terrorism. *Id.* at §§ 125.26(1)(a)(ii-a) and 125.27(1)(a).

31. Press Release, Office of the Governor, *Governor Cuomo Signs NY SAFE Act in Rochester* (January 16, 2013), www.governor.ny.gov.

32. *Id.*

33. Cattaraugus County Sheriff's Office, *Sheriffs' Response to NY SAFE Act* (January 24, 2013), www.cattco.org.

34. N.Y. Pen. Law § 265.19 (aggravated criminal possession of a weapon); *id.* at § 265.03 (criminal possession of a weapon).

35. See *People v. Parilla*, 27 N.Y.3d 400, 33 N.Y.S.3d 368 (2016) (prosecutor needs only to prove that the defendant knowingly possessed a firearm; there is no need to prove that the defendant knew that the firearm was operable.)

36. N.Y. Pen. Law § 10.00(21).
37. *Id.* at § 70.02.
38. *Id.* at § 220.77.
39. One such arrest occurred in September 2014, when Eddie Herrera attempted to sell cocaine to an undercover police officer in Westchester County. At the time, he was carrying a loaded 9 mm handgun. Michael Risinit, *Man Tried to Sell Cocaine to Undercover, Police Said,* Journal News (September 27, 2014), www.lohud.com. In April 2015, Bruce Campbell, aka "Animal," was arrested in Schenectady for shooting a man across the street from an elementary school. He was found guilty of aggravated criminal possession of a weapon and other charges in December 2016. Amanda Fries, *Schenectady Man Found Guilty in Shooting near School,* Times Union (December 19, 2016), www.timesunion.com.
40. *2 Teens Arrested in Connection with Staten Island Paintball Gun Attacks,* NBC New York (July 19, 2015), www.nbcnewyork.com.
41. "Drug-trafficking felony" as defined in N.Y. Pen. Law § 10.00(21). The SAFE Act added this definition to the Penal Law. "Violent felony offense" as defined *id.* at § 70.02(1).
42. Shimon Prokupecz & Jonathan Dienst, *I-Team: Gangs' "Community Guns" Make It Harder to Catch Shooters, Police Say,* NBC New York (December 5, 2012), www.nbcnewyork.com.
43. *See* Michael Wilson, *In a Mailbox: A Shared Gun, Just for the Asking,* New York Times (February 10, 2012).
44. Laura Italiano, *"Preppy Gun Moll" Afrika Owes Has Gun-Running Conviction Vacated,* New York Post (June 10, 2013), http://nypost.com.
45. N.Y. Pen. Law § 115.20.
46. There are four basic elements of "criminal facilitation": (1) a person must engage in conduct that provides another person with the "means of opportunity" for the commission of a crime; (2) the facilitator must render that assistance "believing it probable" that he or she is rendering aid to a person who intends to commit the crime; (3) the facilitator's conduct must "in fact" aid the commission of crime; and (4) the principal actor must, in fact, commit the crime. Sentences for criminal facilitation are graded from fourth to first degree depending on the severity of the crime facilitated and the age of the primary offender. Providing aid to younger primary offenders increases the grade of the criminal facilitation offense. *See id.* at §§ 115.00–115.20.
47. *Id.* at § 460.22.
48. *Id.* at § 460.20.
49. *Prosecutor Uses New Law to Upgrade Charges against Gun-Running Suspects,* NBC New York (February 10, 2016), www.nbcnewyork.com.
50. Press Release, Brooklyn District Attorney's Office, *Charges Upgraded in Airplane Gun Trafficking Case: Superseding Indictment Charges Aggravated Enterprise Corruption, Carries Penalty of Up to Life in Prison* (February 10, 2016), www.brooklynda.org.

51. *Id.*
52. N.Y. Pen. Law § 265.00(17).
53. *Id.* at § 400.00(11).
54. *Id.*
55. New York State Department of Health, *Unintentional Firearm Injury Prevention, Children Ages Birth to 19 Years* (February 2018), www.health.ny.gov.
56. N.Y. Pen. Law § 120.00.
57. *Id.* at § 120.05.
58. *Id.* at § 120.20.
59. *Id.* at § 120.05(4-a).
60. In *People v. Wright*, 42 Misc. 3d 428, 975 N.Y.S.2d 644 (Kings Cty. Sup. Ct. 2013), a Kings County (Brooklyn) court held that the definition of school grounds found in N.Y. Pen. Law § 220.00(14), which deals with controlled substances ("school grounds" includes any area within one thousand feet of the school's boundary) did not apply to N.Y. Pen. Law § 265.01-(a). Consequently, the court dismissed the charge of possessing a weapon on a public street within one thousand feet of a school.
61. 18 U.S.C. § 922(q)(2)(A) (Federal Gun-Free School Zones Act of 1990).
62. N.Y. Pen. Law § 265.01-(a). "A person is guilty of criminal possession of a weapon on school grounds when he or she knowingly has in his or her possession a rifle, shotgun, or firearm in or upon a building or grounds, used for educational purposes, of any school, college, or university, except the forestry lands, wherever located, owned and maintained by the State University of New York college of environmental science and forestry, or upon a school bus as defined in section one hundred forty-two of the vehicle and traffic law, without the written authorization of such educational institution."

CONCLUSION

1. Associated Press, *NY Safe Act Enables NY to Better Protect NYers, Gov. Cuomo's Spokeswoman Says*, Syracuse.com (December 29, 2013), www.syracuse.com.
2. Shooters Committee on Political Education, *SCOPE Position Paper: Prohibiting the Possession of Ammunition Feeding Devices with a Capacity Exceeding Ten Rounds and Limiting Usage to Seven Rounds*, http://scopeny.org (last visited December 27, 2018).
3. Linda Qiu, *Less than 1% of Noncompliant Gun Dealers Get Their Licensed Revoked. Here's Why*, PolitiFact (October 8, 2015), www.politifact.com.
4. *See, e.g.*, Bureau of Alcohol, Tobacco, Firearms, and Explosives, *Federal Firearms License Revocation Process* (May 2014), www.atf.gov.
5. Americans for Gun Safety Foundation, *The Enforcement Gap—Federal Gun Laws Ignored* (May 2003), http://content.thirdway.org.
6. NYS Attorney General's Office, *Target on Trafficking: NY Crime Gun Analysis* (2016), https://targettrafficking.ag.ny.gov.
7. *Id.*

8. The US Supreme Court upheld the federal straw-purchasing offense in *Abramski v. U.S.*, 134 S. Ct. 2259 (2014). In that case, an FFL in Virginia, after following all legal requirements, sold a gun to a purchaser who passed the NICS background check. However, the purchaser soon thereafter sold the gun to his uncle. The Supreme Court (5–4) rejected Ambraski's argument that his deception was not material because his uncle was legally eligible to purchase and possess a gun.

9. Actually, civilian ownership of automatics is not prohibited. Such firearms can be possessed if one has a permit issued by ATF. Several thousand people, shooting ranges, and clubs hold such permits, which are recorded on ATF's National Firearms and Transfer Record database.

10. Olivia Katrandjian, *New York Probe Finds 62 Percent of Private Gun Sellers Sell to Prohibited Individuals*, ABC News (December 14, 2011), http://abcnews.go.com.

11. A recent *Washington Post* study found that in 85 percent of school shootings, the shooter obtained the guns from home or a friend. See John Woodrow Cox, Steven Rich, Allyson Chiu, John Muyskens, and Monica Ulmanu, *More than 220,000 Students Have Experienced Gun Violence at School since Columbine* (December 19, 2018), www.washingtonpost.com.

12. In 2016, California voters passed Referendum 63 establishing similar background checking for ammunition purchasers.

INDEX

Abramski v. U.S., 246n8
accidents. *See* gun accidents
ACLU. *See* American Civil Liberties
Union
acquisition and distribution records
(A&D), 94
Adams, Eric, 24
aggravated criminal possession of a
weapon, 180–81, 244n39
aggravated enterprise corruption, 183–85
alcohol, 24; gun violence and, 86
Alcohol, Tobacco, Firearms, and Explosives
(ATF), 36, 78, 81; ammunition sales
regulation and, 155–56; FFLs and, 83;
Firearms Owners Protection Act of
1986 and, 103; National Firearms and
Transfer Record database of, 246n9;
responsibility overload of, 194–95; on
straw purchasers, 91
Aldstadt, Stephen, 138
American Civic Association Immigration
Center, 10, 28; handgun license recertifi-
cation after, 141. *See also* Wong, Jiverly
American Civil Liberties Union (ACLU),
105
American Psychiatric Association, 110;
Committee on Judicial Action of, 111
American Psychiatric Nurses Association,
122
American Psychological Association, 122
Americans for Gun Safety, 195
American Tactical Imports (ATI), 41
ammunition-feeding devices. *See* large-
capacity magazines ban

ammunition sales regulation: Aurora, Colorado movie theater and, 161; background
checks for, 2, 6, 157, 208, 246n12; on
black market, 167; database for, 240n48;
Gun Control Act of 1968 and, 154–55;
gun suicides and, 207; for handguns,
156–57, 158; on Internet, 19, 157–58; licensing and, 2; for long guns, 208; mass
shootings and, 154–68, 209; Orlando
nightclub and, 161–62; pre-SAFE Act
regulation of, 158; punishments for,
172–73; in SAFE Act, 158–68, 196–97,
207–9; search warrants for, 209; Second
Amendment and, 166; State Police and,
154, 165, 197, 207, 208–9; in "Stronger
Gun Laws: A Plan to Protect New Yorkers," 11; target shooters and, 162, 209;
universal background checks for, 208
AOT. *See* assisted outpatient treatment
Appelbaum, Paul, 112
AR-15. *See* assault weapons
assault weapons: barrel shrouds on, 45,
47, 58; bayonet mounts on, 45, 46, 60,
201; bequeathment prohibition for,
52; black market for, 49, 61; folding
stocks of, 14, 46, 47, 201; grandfathering of, 48–49; grenade launchers on,
46, 47, 58; limitations on excessive
rate of fire for, 201; manufacturers of,
49, 55; in mass shootings, 200–201;
muzzle brake on, 46, 54; number of
in US, 224n23; pistol grips on, 14, 46,
47, 49, 56, 58; registration of, 45–61,
200–201; at Sandy Hook, 1;

Bureau of Alcohol, Tobacco, Firearms, and Explosives. *See* Alcohol, Tobacco, Firearms, and Explosives
Bush, George W., 215n4

Campbell, Bruce "Animal," 244n39
Canada, assault weapons ban by, 223n9
Can Gun Control Work? (Jacobs), 5
Captains Endowment Association, of NYPD, 72
chief law enforcement officer (CLEO), 82–83, 227n5
child-proofing, 24
Cho, Seung-Hui, 49, 103–4, 227n15
Ciraco, Vittorio, 178
Citizens Committee for the Right to Keep and Bear Arms, 52
The City That Became Safe (Zimring), x
CLEO. *See* chief law enforcement officer
Clinton, Bill, 9–10, 84
Clinton, Hillary, 17
CLMHD. *See* Conference of Local Mental Hygiene Directors
CoBIS. *See* Combined Ballistic Identification System
Coleman, Bonnie Watson, 158
Colorado Outfitters Ass'n v. Hickenlooper, 224n14
Columbine High School, 65, 69, 246n11
Combined Ballistic Identification System (CoBIS), 37–38
Committee on Judicial Action, of American Psychiatric Association, 111
community guns, 181–83
concealed carry licenses, for handguns, 33–35, 138, 139
Conference of Local Mental Hygiene Directors (CLMHD), 116
Consortium for Risk-Based Firearm Policy, 102, 110
controlled substances, 86; in Brady Law, 228n18; at schools, 245n60. *See also* drug addiction; drug-trafficking

Cook, Philip J., 6, 95
Correction Law, 14
county gun controls, 39–40
Court Services and Offenders Supervision Agency (CSOSA), 88
Cox, Chris W., 71
Craigslist, 92
crime. *See* gun crime
criminal facilitation: with community guns, 182–83; elements of, 244n46
Criminal Justice Act of 1968, 102–3
criminal possession at schools, 245n60, 245n62; punishments for, 186
Criminal Procedure Law, 14
Crute, Shanell, 182
Cruz, Nikolas, 105
CSOSA. *See* Court Services and Offenders Supervision Agency
culture wars, 4
Cuomo, Andrew, 2; on ammunition sales regulation, 165–66; CoBIS and, 38; on domestic violence protection orders, 125, 136; on first responder murders, 179; on large-capacity magazines ban, 70–72, 202; on red-flag laws, 119; SAFE Act and, 9–12, 15, 19, 192; on Second Amendment, 9; in 2014 election, 20–23

dark web, 229n41
Davis, Rex D., 155
DCJS. *See* Division of Criminal Justice Services
DCS. *See* director of community services
DEA. *See* Drug Enforcement Administration
Democrats: on ammunition sales regulation, 156–58, 166; on handgun license recertification, 141; on punishments, 178–79; SAFE Act and, 14–15; in 2014 election, 22; on universal background checks, 82
Department of Health and Human Services, US (HHS), 114

FOPA. *See* Firearms Owners Protection Act of 1986
Fourteenth Amendment, 117, 134
Freedom of Information Law (FOIL), NYS: assault weapons registration and, 50; handgun license recertification and, 144–46; mental health and, 115–16; SAFE Act and, 19; State Police and, 41
Friedman, Thomas, 50
Friend, Chris, 17

Gallivan, Patrick, 241n52
gangs, community guns of, 181–83
GAO. *See* Government Accountability Office
GCA. *See* Gun Control Act of 1968
General Business Law, SAFE Act and, 14
Gianris, Michael N., 166
Giffords, Gabrielle, 105
Giffords Law Center to Prevent Gun Violence, 27, 40; assault weapons ban of, 220n4; on large-capacity magazines, 62
Golden, Martin, 72
good cause, handgun licenses and, 33
good moral character, for handgun license, 33, 139
Gottlieb, Alan, 52
Government Accountability Office (GAO), 104
grandfathering: of assault weapons, 48–49; of large-capacity magazines, 69, 70–71, 78, 176, 202
grenade launchers, on assault weapons, 46, 47, 58
gun accidents, 32, 32; with long guns, 197; SAFE Act and, 1
gun borrowing: background checks and, 91; domestic violence protection orders and, 133; mental illness and, 108
Gun Control Act of 1968, 81; ammunition sales regulation, 154–55; on background checks, 82; mental health in, 104

Gun Control Act of 2000, 35–38; assault weapons ban in, 35–36, 45–46; trigger locks in, 38, 242n25
gun crime: assault weapons and, 49; decline of, 1, 13; historical numbers for, 29–30, 29–32; large-capacity magazines ban and, 63, 75, 79; mental illness and, 111; punishment for, 181, 188; straw purchasers and, 203; universal background checks and, 94–99, 97–99
Gun NY2A Grassroots Coalition, 17–18
Gun Rights Across America, 43
Gun Show Accountability Bill, 227n6
gun shows: background checks at, 5, 32, 36–37, 82, 88–89, 100; frequency of, 41
gun suicides, 31, 31; ammunition sales regulation and, 207; with long guns, 197; with mass shootings, 200–201; mental illness and, 111, 204; SAFE Act and, 1; at Sandy Hook, 1; universal background checks and, 94–99, 99
gun-surrender orders, 25; with domestic violence protection orders, 128–32, 206–7, 236n17, 237n30; handgun license and, 140, 185; for mental illness, 205; restraining orders and, 236n26
gun trafficking: FFLs and, 84; NYPD and, 170; punishment for, 25; universal background checks and, 92. *See also* black market
Gun Violence Prevention Act of 1994 (Brady II), 227n6
Gura, Alan, 219n5

Halbrook, Stephen, 23
handgun license: concealed carry, 33–35, 138, 139; domestic violence protection orders and, 127–33, 135–37; good moral character for, 33, 139; gun-surrender orders and, 140, 185; mental health and, 107–8, 205; proper cause for, 33, 139; records computerization for, 141–42; special need for, 33, 138, 139, 219

196–97, 207–9; assault weapons ban in, 2, 15, 16, 18, 19, 29, 45–61, 47, 200–201, 220n4; assault weapons bequeathment prohibition in, 52; assault weapons registration in, 46–61; circumvention of, 5, 49–52; confidential drafting of, 11, 16–17, 192; in courts, 23–24; criticism of, 16–17; Cuomo and, 9–12, 15, 19, 192; decentralized administration of, 197–98; Democrats and, 14–15; design flaws in, 196–97; domestic violence protection orders in, 125–37, 206–7; enactment of, 12–15; execution of, 4; gun accidents and, 1; gun control proposals after, 24–25; gun control regime before, 32–35; gun suicides and, 1; handgun license recertification in, 19, 138–53, 193, 209–10; large-capacity magazines ban in, 2, 15, 19, 62–80, 196, 202–3; leadership lack for, 198–99; long guns and, 197; mental health reporting requirements in, x, 106–24, 204–6, 234n59; necessity of, 27–44; noncompliance with, 199–200; opposition to, 3, 17–23, 19, 193; politics of, 9–26, 192–94; praise for, 15–16; punishments in, 169–89, 187–88; Republicans and, 11, 14–15, 17; resource inadequacies for, 199; safe storage in homes in, 38; Sandy Hook and, 10–11, 25, 191; Second Amendment and, 12, 17–18, 23; sentencing enhancements in, 210–11; 2014 gubernatorial election and, 20–23; universal background checks in, 2, 89–101, 203–4
semiautomatic weapons. See assault weapons
Senate Rules Committee, Republicans on, 14
sentencing: handgun license surrender at, 185; in SAFE Act, 2, 11, 210–11. See also punishment
Seward, James, 166
Sharpe, Gary, 54

Sheppard, James, 16
Shooters Committee on Political Education (SCOPE), 16, 23–24, 43; on gun show background checks, 89; on large-capacity magazines ban, 62, 71, 225n40; on mental health, 115–16; on SAFE Act, 191
shotguns. See long guns
silencers, 58
Silver, Sheldon, 13–14, 218n42
Siragusa, Charles, 89
Skelos, Dean, 11, 13–14, 22, 178; convictions of, 218n42
Skretny, William, 53–54, 58, 59, 74–75, 163–64; on large-capacity magazines ban, 225n40
SLAG. See State Legislators Against Illegal Guns
smart guns (personalized guns), 10
Smith, Malcolm A., 14
Smith & Wesson, lawsuit against, 10, 215n4
Social Security Administration (SSA), 105
special need, for handgun license, 33, 138, 139, 219
Spengler, William, Jr., 171, 179
SSA. See Social Security Administration
State Legislators Against Illegal Guns (SLAG), 11
State Police: ammunition sales regulation and, 154, 165, 197, 207, 208–9; assault weapons and, 220n12; ballistic fingerprinting and, 37; FOIL and, 41; handgun license recertification and, 22, 34, 143, 148–49, 151–52, 209–10; on SAFE Act noncompliance, 199; secrecy of, 4
Stewart-Cousins, Andrew, 166
stigmatization, of mental illness, 109–10
stocks, on assault weapons, 14, 46, 47, 56, 220n6
stolen guns. See lost or stolen guns
Stop Online Ammunition Sales bill, 157–58

ABOUT THE AUTHORS

James B. Jacobs is Chief Justice Warren E. Burger Professor of Law at NYU School of Law. He is the author of fifteen previous books, including *Stateville: The Penitentiary in Mass Society, Drunk Driving: An American Dilemma, Busting the Mob: United States v. Cosa Nostra* (NYU Press, 1994), *Hate Crime: Criminal Law and Identity Politics, Can Gun Control Work?, Breaking the Devil's Pact: The Battle to Free the Teamsters Union from Mob Control* (NYU Press, 2011) with coauthor Kerry Cooperman, and *The Eternal Criminal Record*.

Zoe Fuhr is a New Zealand–based criminal lawyer and a fellow at New York University's Center for Research in Crime & Justice. She is a graduate of New York University (LLM) and the University of Auckland (BA/LLB Hons).